PHILIP
OF
MACEDON

PHILIP OF MACEDON

Edited by
MILTIADES B. HATZOPOULOS
LOUISA D. LOUKOPOULOS

Fellows of the Institute for
Ancient Greek and Roman Studies,
National Hellenic Research Foundation

EKDOTIKE ATHENON S.A.
Athens 1980

Copyright© 1980
by
EKDOTIKE ATHENON S.A.
1, Vissarionos Street
Athens 135, Greece
PRINTED AND BOUND IN GREECE
by
EKDOTIKE HELLADOS S.A.
An affiliated company
8, Philadelphias Street, Athens

Publishers: George A. Christopoulos, John C. Bastias

Editing: Louise Turner

Production Editor: Iris Tzachili-Douskou

Art Director: Angela Simou

Special Photography: Spyros Tsavdaroglou

CONTRIBUTORS

MANOLIS ANDRONICOS
Professor of Classical Archaeology, University of Thessalonike

GEORGE CAWKWELL
Fellow of University College, Oxford

HARRY J. DELL
Professor of History, University of Virginia, U.S.A.

CHARLES F. EDSON
Emeritus Professor of History, University of Wisconsin, U.S.A.

J.R. ELLIS
Senior Lecturer in Classical Studies, Monash University, Australia

G.T. GRIFFITH
Fellow of Gonville and Caius College, Cambridge; Fellow of the British Academy

N.G.L. HAMMOND
Emeritus Professor of Greek, University of Bristol; Honorary
Fellow of Clare College, Cambridge; Fellow of British Academy

GEORGES LE RIDER
Administrateur Général, Bibliothèque Nationale, Ecole Pratique des Hautes Etudes
(IVth division), Paris

PIERRE LEVEQUE
President of the University of Franche-Comté, France

M.B. SAKELLARIOU
Emeritus Professor of Ancient History, University of Thessalonike; Director of the Institute
for Ancient Greek and Roman Studies, National Hellenic Research Foundation, Athens

CONTENTS

PREFACE

In the autumn of 1977, during the course of the excavation of the Great Tumulus at Vergina in Macedonia, the first unplundered "Macedonian" tomb came to light. The marble doors were still in position, unforced, and the unrivalled workmanship and unparalleled richness of the artistic master-pieces they protected left no doubt that this could only be a royal tomb, while the dating of the finds led the excavator ineluctably to the conclusion that the monarch interred therein was none other than Philip, son of Amyntas, king of the Macedonians and the elected leader of all the Greeks. This theory quickly met with almost universal support and naturally caused a sensation both amongst the general public, whose curiosity, excitement and enthusiasm continues unabated, and in scholarly circles, where in recent years a steadily growing interest in the reign of Philip had to some extent prepared the ground for a reappraisal of its historical importance. Even before 1977, there had been an increasing tendency amongst historians to view Philip not simply as the father of his famous son, but, in his own right, as one of the greatest Macedonian monarchs, and perhaps one of the most important historical figures of ancient Greece. His significance for the history of Macedonia is beyond doubt. When he came to power, his country had recently suffered considerable territorial losses, it was politically fragmented, militarily on its knees and culturally retarded; within the space of a quarter of a century he restored and extended its frontiers, welded the state into a political unit, made it the mightiest military power of the period and, as becomes clearer with every new archaeological discovery, raised the cultural level of Macedonia above that of much of the rest of Greece. Not only this, however; Philip is also acknowledged to have been a political figure of Panhellenic standing. He succeeded, by persuasion rather than by force, in achieving unity amongst the Greek city-states, without depriving them of their freedom. Finally — and this is often forgotten — he was one of the most attractive personalities of his time, for all the violence and passion of his nature. "Europe has never known a man the like of Philip, son of Amyntas" wrote his contemporary Theopompos in the preface of his monumental history dedicated to Philip. However this deliberately ambiguous expression is inter-preted, it is undoubtedly the most apposite judgement on the career of the Macedonian king.

The purpose of the present volume is to make a contribution to the reappraisal of the personality and achievement of Philip that has become a matter of urgency in the light of the discovery of the royal tombs at Vergina. Its overall plan is such as to permit the collaboration of as many as possible of those who have devoted themselves to research into the man and his times; a number of interna-tionally distinguished scholars were invited to present the reassessment necessary in the light of the new discoveries, each in his own field. From this point of view the thirteen chapters of the book are independent of each other and each expresses the personal views of its author. Every attempt has been made, however, to guard against the dangers of contradictions and overlap, and to ensure that no significant aspect of the history of Philip has been left untreated. At the same time we have tried to preserve the chronological framework, so that the reader will not lose the feeling of historical continuity. The book begins with the arrival of Philip's ancestors at Aigai and ends with his assassination and burial at the very cradle of the dynasty.

During the course of the writing of the book, however, another personality emerged alongside that of Philip, of equal importance and without which the character and career of the great Temenid ruler cannot be properly understood: the land of Macedonia. Mountains and plains, cities and sanctuaries, the geographical background and the works of man all set their seal on his personality and in turn received the stamp of his achievements. Even the most vivid description of the landscape, however, and the most scholarly analysis of the art will inevitably fail to convey with immediacy the distinctive features of the Macedonian terrain or the inimitable style of Macedonian art. Special efforts have therefore been made to present a photographic documentation of the setting of the historic events narrated in the text, in the hope that the reader will thus get a direct feel for the unparalleled unique character of Macedonia in the 4th century B.C. Almost half the book is devoted to this end, and this is perhaps its most distinctive feature.

The publication of this volume would have been impossible without the generous assistance, in a great many areas, of Professors M. Andronicos and M. Sakellariou. The former has a profound knowledge of Macedonian archaeology and placed at our disposal not only the most valuable of his recent discoveries but also his personal — and therefore invaluable — experience concerning the excavation at Vergina. The book would have been all the poorer, from many points of view, without the unflagging advice of the latter. Special thanks are also due to the Director of the Archaeological Museum of Thessalonike and Ephor of Antiquities, Miss K. Romiopoulou, for her assistance in selecting and supervising the photographing of the artistic treasures of central Macedonia, particularly those items which were assembled in the Museum at Thessalonike for the exhibition of "Treasures of Ancient Macedonia". We also wish to thank the excavator of Dion, Professor D. Pandermalis; the Director of the Numismatic Museum, Mrs M. Oikonomidou and the following Ephors and Epimeletes of Antiquities: Mrs K. Despoini; Mrs K. Koukouli-Chrysanthaki; Mrs M. Siganidou; Mr. J. Touratsoglou; and Mr. D. Triantaphyllos, all of whom offered every assistance and granted permission to photograph archaeological material, most of which was unpublished. Finally, we are grateful to Mr. G.T. Griffith and the Delegates of the Oxford University Press for permission to reproduce the plan of the battle of Chaironeia. Thanks to the assistance of all these, and above all, of course, to the ready response from the authors, we take great pleasure in presenting to the public the latest verdicts of scholarship on the history of Philip, son of Amyntas, king of the Macedonians.

EARLY MACEDONIA

After the end of the Bronze Age another migration of peoples entered the Greek peninsula. These peoples, whom modern scholars call "West Greeks" and of whom the most important single element was the Dorians, came from the rugged Pindos mountains northwest of the Greek peninsula proper. But the Pindos area with little arable land could not support an expanding population and the lands to the south could no longer receive immigrants from the north. Important West Greek elements remained in the Pindos. These are those whom Herodotos calls *"Makednon ethnos"*[1] and there developed a gradual movement towards the northeast across the Pindos range into the region which was to become known as "Upper Macedonia."[2] By around 700 we find "Macednic" tribes occupying the eastern slopes of the Pindos.[3]

Among these tribes were the Orestai in the area of Lake Kastoria. From Orestis — as the region was called — came a clan called the Argeadai, "descendants of Argeas", whose kings claimed descent from the Temenid kings of Argos and thus from Herakles. The validity of this claim was never challenged in antiquity. The Argeadai, in search of fertile land for settlement, moved eastward and occupied the coastal plain along the northwestern shore of the Aegean sea between Mt. Olympus and the Haliakmon river.[4] They expelled the Pieres, who left their name to the region called after them Pieria.[5] In northwest Pieria, close to the Haliakmon, the kings founded their citadel Aigai where the royal tombs were situated. The next step in the expansion of the Argead kingdom was the expulsion of the Bottiaioi from the alluvial plain between the Haliakmon and Axios rivers. The area continued to be known as Bottiaia. These two regions, Pieria and Bottiaia, were to become the heartland of the kingdom. Unlike their "Macednic" relatives in Upper Macedonia the Argead Macedonians were exposed to all the political and economic currents and cultural influences of the Aegean world.[6]

The basic institutions of the kingdom were those

of early Greeks. At the head of the folk was the king who was the war commander and was responsible for the relations of his people with the gods.[7] An assembly of the fighting men chose the new king from the available males of the royal family, usually the oldest son of the former king,[8] and could express the desires and attitudes of the folk. Of high importance were the king's Companions, the *hetairoi*. They were the king's personal retainers. They fought for him in battle and in peace served as he desired. In return they received land grants and other perquisites. In social status and function they recall the Homeric *hetairoi* of the Achaean rulers.[9] This personal relationship of mutual benefit and obligation was to become the specifically Macedonian system of government. It was solemnised by the festival of the *Hetairideia* in honour of Zeus *Hetairides* at which the king presided.[10]

This society had its peculiar customs and practices. There are traces of the blood feud.[11] A Macedonian who had not yet killed an enemy was obliged to wear a halter around his waist.[12] The marriage ceremony was the severing of a loaf of bread by the bride and groom, who then tasted the two portions.[13] Feasting and wassail were the relaxations of the aristocracy and hunting their passionate avocation. In the early spring of each year the formal purification of the army, headed by the king, took place with the fighting men in full panoply.[14] A sham battle ended the purification. Although the basic religion of the Macedonians was Greek, as is shown by the names of the months and by the belief that the folk descended from Makedon, son of Zeus, and the royal family from Herakles, there was strong Thracian influence from the peoples the Macedonians had expelled or subdued. This is the origin of the emotional Sabazios worship among the Macedonians with its local variant of the satyrs, the *Sauadai*, and bacchantes, *Klodones* and *Mimallones*.[15] It is little wonder that to the Greeks of the city-states this society should seem alien, un-hellenic, or, as they would say, "barbarian".

Such is our first view of the Macedonian kingdom. It was a loosely organised society and, after the conquest of Bottiaia, no longer aggressive. The kings did not dispute the presence of two Greek colonies, Pydna and Methone, directly on the Pierian coast of their domain. But the future of the monarchy and people was to be assured by their response to an apparently overwhelming menace from without.

Around 513 the army of the Persian empire entered Europe. The objective of the expedition, the subjugation of the nomads of the Wallachian and south Russian plains, was not achieved, but Persian rule was established over the Thracian tribes and Greek coastal settlements of the eastern Balkans. Persian emissaries visited the court of the Argead king Amyntas I who became a Persian subject. From around 510 to 479 the Argead kingdom was a vassal principality under Persian suzerainty, but not under direct satrapal administration. When a Persian expeditionary force reappeared in 491, the Macedonians made no attempt to oppose it.[16] Eleven years later, when Xerxes arrived with his vast army, Amyntas' able son, Alexandros I, discharged his duties as a subject prince. The Macedonians followed Xerxes southward.[17]

Persian rule could not be challenged by open revolt. Alexandros knew that the one chance for independence was a Greek victory. Before the advent of Xerxes, Alexandros had been honored by Athens for providing material for Athens' fleet and later he secretly informed the Greeks of Persian intentions. And after the final Greek victory at Plataia Alexandros inflicted on the retreating Persians "complete catastrophe".[18]

The retreat of the Persians gave the king the chance to extend his domain. He gained control of

1. The dynasty of the Argeadai had their capital at Aigai near the Haliakmon river, in the foothills of the Pierian mountains. The aerial photograph shows the impressive palace uncovered at Vergina, identified as the site of the ancient Macedonian capital.

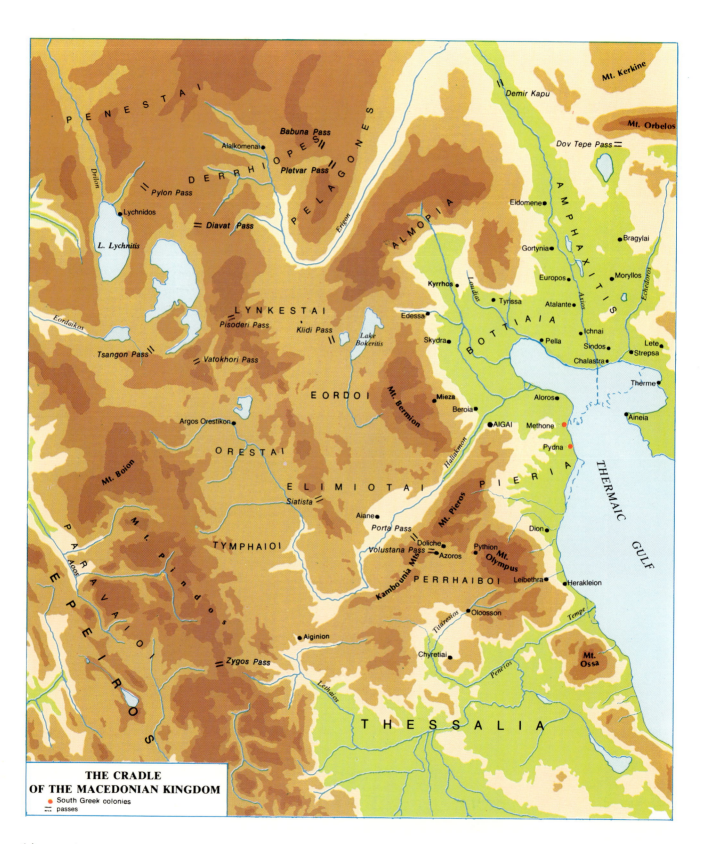

THE CRADLE
OF THE MACEDONIAN KINGDOM
● South Greek colonies
= passes

14

the basin of the lower Axios river and drove the Thracian Edones from the long valley extending from just north of the Thermaic to the Strymonic Gulf.[19] The king then turned west and expelled the Eordoi from the landlocked basin of Lake Bokeritis, west of Bottiaia, and the Almopes from their hollow valley northwest of Bottiaia.[20] With the conquest of the Eordoi the Argead Macedonians came in direct contact with the Makednic tribes of the eastern Pindos and these tribes became, as Thucydides states, "allied and subject"[21] to the Argead king. Alexandros, moreover, gained control over the Thracian Bisaltai along the west bank of the lower Strymon. This tribe was not expelled but remained in its original home and a similar arrangement was made with the Krestones to the west of the Bisaltai.[22] Alexandros also acquired Anthemous, the region due east of the head of the Thermaic Gulf.[23] The whole area of the realm by now had come to be known as "Macedonia".[24] Alexandros had quadrupled the area of his kingdom. He was the first Argead king to strike coins in his own name.[25]

But the conquests themselves created the circumstances which were to confront the Macedonians throughout their existence as an independent state; or rather, even longer, until the emperor Augustus at last established the Danube river as the northern defensive boundary of the classical world. These circumstances were permanently to condition the society and institutions of the country. Beyond the eastern boundary of the kingdom were Thracian peoples, such as the Odomantoi and Edones, and beyond these, in the central valley of the Hebros river, the Odrysian Thracians were soon to found a powerful

empire.[26] To the north, Paionian tribes were difficult neighbors.[27] To the west, beyond the lands of the vassal princes of Upper Macedonia, Illyrian tribes could threaten Argead control over the allied Makednic tribes of the eastern Pindos.[28] Alexandros' conquests required a political method by which the new territories might be more effectively integrated into the kingdom.

Alexandros achieved this by further developing the old institution of the Companions — hetairoi — and extending it to include the yeomanry. From the Companions themselves and the larger landowners the king formed the Companion Cavalry — hetairike hippos. But the basic new departure was the creation of the pezetairoi or Foot Companions. These served as infantry, but the importance of this new institution is that it extended the personal relationship, which had hitherto existed primarily between the king and the aristocratic Companions, to include the ordinary Macedonians. This was the foundation for the specifically Macedonian system of government: the holding of land from the king in return for the obligation to military service.

The purpose of this reform was not so much military as political. By distributing land in the new territories, larger grants to the Companions and Companion Cavalry and smaller allotments to the Foot Companions, Alexandros was able to integrate most of these regions permanently into the realm, and by means of these grants he would increase the prestige of the kingship and the loyalty of the Macedonians to himself and his family. Actually the creation of the Foot Companions did not really bring into being an effective infantry force before the reign of Philip. But from the point of view of the king the Foot Companions could be a counterpoise to the nobility, the Companions proper, and an internal support to maintain the king's position as against the aristocracy.[29]

It is in this context we are to place the developed form of the Macedonian assembly. This folkmoot of the Macedonian people in arms chose the king from

2. The heartland of the Macedonian kingdom of the Argeadai was the region bounded by the eastern slopes of the Pindos range and the coastal plain of Pieria. At about the beginning of the 7th century a branch of the Orestai, a Macedonian tribe, moved eastwards in search of fertile land and settled in Pieria, which thus became the kernel of the Argead Macedonian kingdom.

the members of the royal family and could appoint a regent for a minor king. The king could not legally put to death a Macedonian even on a charge of high treason without a formal trial before the assembly at which the king was plaintiff.[30] The kingship of the Macedonians was not an absolutism but a monarchy based on traditional usage, custom and precedent.

The expansion and reorganisation of the kingdom was accompanied by an urgent menace which was to dominate the history of Macedonia for two generations. This was the new maritime empire of Athens. The north Aegean coast from the head of the Thermaic Gulf eastward to the Hellespont was largely under Athenian control, for the Greek cities and even some barbarian communities on these shores were first members of the Delian League and then subjects of imperial Athens. Macedonia was the nearest and best source of ship-building material, so essential for Athens, and the country was also rich in precious metals. For Athens, access to Macedonia was vital.[31]

The basin of the Strymon river was the prime Athenian objective. In 476 the forces of the Delian League under the command of Kimon had taken Eion, just east of the river's mouth, from its Persian garrison.[32] In 465 the Athenians attempted to colonise the Nine Ways (*Ennea Hodoi*),[33] the strategic point controlling the only crossing over the lower Strymon. But after initial success, the settlers, who had ventured too far inland, were destroyed by the Edones. Alexandros may have played a part behind the scenes in this disaster. But this did not discourage the Athenians from their objective of controlling the lower Strymon basin. Their interest in the area is shown by the charge made against Kimon in 463 by his political enemies that he had failed to seize the opportunity to "cut off a large portion of Macedonia" because he had been bribed by Alexandros.[34] The expression can only refer to Bisaltia, the region along the west bank of the river which was under Argead control. The Tribute Lists of the Athenian empire reveal that the community Berga in Bisaltia, over twenty miles from the coast, paid tribute to Athens

from 452 to 446, although the town is absent from the list for 443-42. At some unknown time before the outbreak of the Peloponnesian War, Perikles sent one thousand Athenian cleruchs to "settle with" the Bisaltai.[35] In 437 Athens finally succeeded in establishing a composite colony at the Nine Ways, now renamed Amphipolis, and thus reasserted her authority in the lower Strymon. This is shown by the reappearance of Berga as a tributary in the years 435 to 431.[36] The rivalry between Athens and Macedonia in the lower Strymon valley during the fifth century is evident.

But direct means of coercion were available to the imperial city. At Strepsa, on the north shore of the Thermaic Gulf, Athens maintained an enclave in Macedonian territory until the outbreak of the Peloponnesian war.[37] The Athenians could at will impose a blockade on the shores of that gulf under Argead rule.[38] It was possible for Athens to exploit, or provoke, dynastic rivalries in the kingdom by supporting pretenders to the throne. So, when Thucydides' narrative opens, we find a state of war existing between Athens and Macedonia because the Athenians had made an alliance with Philip, a younger brother of Perdikkas II, Alexandros' son and successor, and supported this prince's claim to the throne.[39] The rulers of the vassal principalities in Upper Macedonia could be instruments for Athenian policy. The treaty between Athens and Perdikkas II,

3. A grave stele from Aiane (near Kozani) showing a Macedonian family. The dead man is seated; two women and a child stand in front of him and another man behind him. Their dress is of particular interest; though it shares some features in common with the dress of the Southern Greeks, a number of specifically Macedonian elements can be detected, amongst them the broad-brimmed hat (kausia) worn by the deceased, the style of the male chlamys, and the head-dress of one of the women, which resembles the modern "katsouli" worn by the women of this area up to the beginning of the twentieth century. It is the work of a local artist from the middle of the 4th century B.C. Paris, Louvre Museum.

probably negotiated around 413, reveals the imperial city acting on behalf of the king of Lynkos in Upper Macedonia,[40] and the king of Elimeia in the southern portion of the same region had supported the claims of Perdikkas brother Philip, Athens' ally.[41] Barbarian peoples beyond the Macedonian frontiers could be suborned in the Athenian interest. In 429, at Athens' instance, the imposing military forces of the Odrysian empire, accompanied by Athenian representatives,[42] assaulted Macedonia in an attempt to install a pretender, the son of the recently deceased Philip, ravaging and laying waste the central portions of the kingdom.[43] And there is a connection between the honors paid by Athens to the Illyrian chieftain Grabos, surely the king of the Taulantioi in the hinterland of Epidamnos,[44] during the first phase of the Peloponnesian War and the sudden breaking of their alliance by the Illyrians in 423 and their support of Perdikkas' enemy, the king of Lynkos.[45] From the defeat of Xerxes until the destruction of the Athenian expeditionary force at Syracuse in 413, by far the most compelling problem confronting the Macedonian kings was the Athenian incubus.

Alexandros perished by assassination under circumstances unknown to us.[46] There followed an obscure period of confusion and disturbance. This is reflected in the dwindling away of the royal coinage which under Alexandros had been voluminous.[47] Around or shortly after 440, Alexandros' son, Perdikkas II, succeeded in establishing himself as king

4. *The Argead monarchs traced their descent to the Temenid rulers of Argos and through these mythical ancestors to Herakles. This list, which includes both the historical kings and their mythical forebears, is based on a passage in Diodoros (VII, 15-17) in which he has assembled data from various writers of the 4th century B.C.*

5. *Head of Herakles, the mythical forefather of the Argead dynasty. It was part of an earring, or some other piece of jewellery, and was found in grave Z at Derveni. Second half of of the 4th century B.C. Thessalonike, Archaeological Museum.*

THE ARGEAD KINGS AND THEIR MYTHICAL ANCESTORS

Herakles

Hyllos

Kleodaios

Aristomachos

Temenos

Kissios

Thestios

Merops

Aristodamidas

Pheidon

Karanos

Koinos

Tyrimmas

Perdikkas I beginning of 7th century

Argaios

Philip I

Aeropos I

Alketas

Amyntas I c. 540-498

Alexander I the Philhellene c. 498-454

Perdikkas II c. 454-413

Archelaos I 413-399

Orestes 396-393

Amyntas II the Little 393-392

Pausanias 393-392

Amyntas III 393/2-369/8

Alexander II 370/69-369/8

Ptolemaios Alorites 368-365

Perdikkas II 365-360

Philip II 359-336

Alexander III the Great 336-323

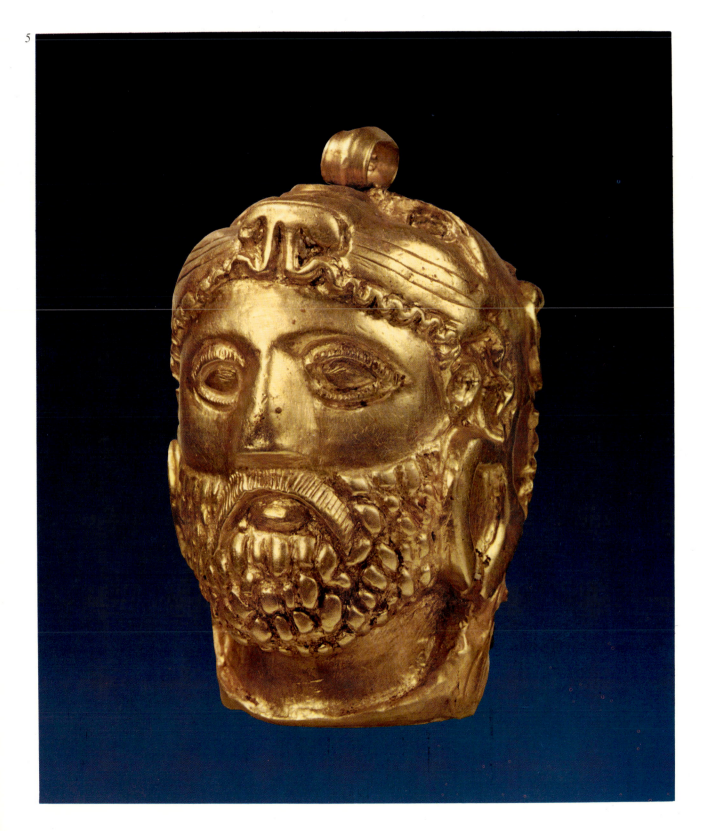

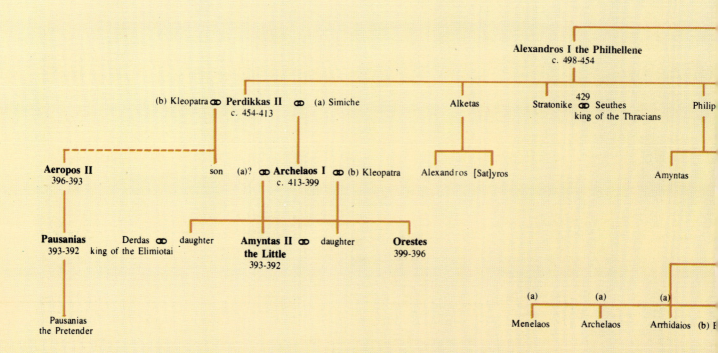

Alexandros I the Philhellene
c. 498-454

(b) Kleopatra ∞ **Perdikkas II** ∞ (a) Simiche
c. 454-413

Alketas

Stratonike ∞ 429 Seuthes
king of the Thracians

Philip

Aeropos II
396-393

son (a)? ∞ **Archelaos I** ∞ (b) Kleopatra
c. 413-399

Alexandros [Sat]yros

Amyntas

Pausanias
393-392

Derdas ∞ daughter
king of the Elimiotai

Amyntas II ∞ daughter
the Little
393-392

Orestes
399-396

Pausanias
the Pretender

(a)
Menelaos

(a)
Archelaos

(a)
Arrhidaios (b) E

Amynt

THE ARGEAD DYNASTY

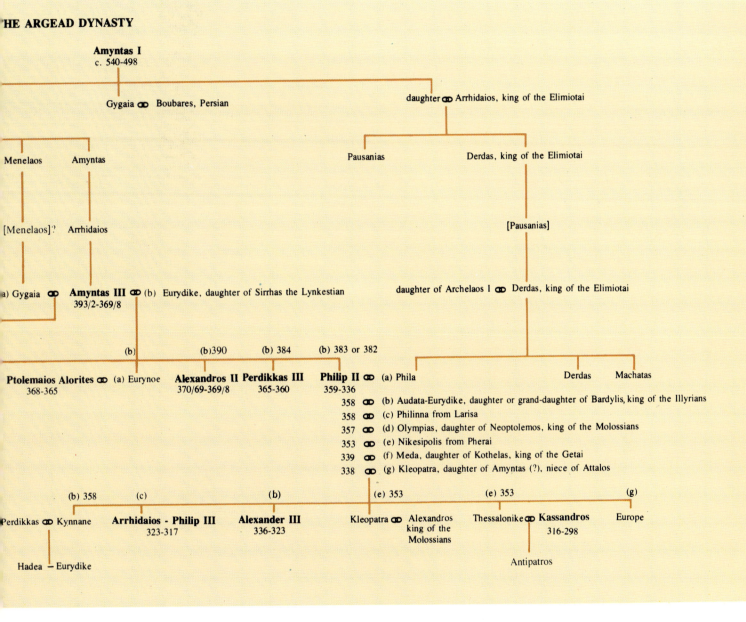

Amyntas I
c. 540-498

Gygaia ∞ Boubares, Persian

daughter ∞ Arrhidaios, king of the Elimiotai

Menelaos   Amyntas

Pausanias   Derdas, king of the Elimiotai

[Menelaos]?   Arrhidaios

[Pausanias]

a) Gygaia ∞ **Amyntas III** ∞ (b) Eurydike, daughter of Sirrhas the Lynkestian
393/2-369/8

daughter of Archelaos I ∞ Derdas, king of the Elimiotai

(b)   (b)390   (b) 384   (b) 383 or 382

Ptolemaios Alorites ∞ (a) Eurynoe   **Alexandros II** **Perdikkas III**   **Philip II** ∞ (a) Phila
368-365   370/69-369/8   365-360   359-336

Derdas   Machatas

358 ∞ (b) Audata-Eurydike, daughter or grand-daughter of Bardylis, king of the Illyrians
358 ∞ (c) Philinna from Larisa
357 ∞ (d) Olympias, daughter of Neoptolemos, king of the Molossians
353 ∞ (e) Nikesipolis from Pherai
339 ∞ (f) Meda, daughter of Kothelas, king of the Getai
338 ∞ (g) Kleopatra, daughter of Amyntas (?), niece of Attalos

(b) 358   (c)   (b)   (e) 353   (e) 353   (g)

Perdikkas ∞ Kynnane   **Arrhidaios - Philip III**   **Alexander III**   Kleopatra ∞ Alexandros   Thessalonike ∞ **Kassandros**   Europe
323-317   336-323   king of the   316-298
Molossians

Hadea — Eurydike   Antipatros

6. *Philip, son of Amyntas and Eurydike, was the descendent of a collateral branch of the famous dynasty of the Argeadai, which came to power at the beginning of the 4th century B.C. with the accession to the Macedonian throne of Amyntas III. Philip assumed power on the battlefield after the death of his brother and predecessor, Perdikkas III. His glorious career as politician and general and his turbulent family life make him one of the most fascinating personalities in the history of the ancient world. He laid the basis for the power and inspired the work of his son and successor, Alexander the Great. The genealogical tree includes all the members of the dynasty, from Amyntas I to Alexander the Great.*

THE MACEDONIAN CALENDAR

MACEDONIAN	ATTIC	MODERN
Dios	Pyanopsion	October
Apellaios	Maimakterion	November
Audonaios	Poseideon	December
Peritios	Gamelion	January
Dystros	Anthesterion	February
Xandikos	Elaphebolion	March
Artemisios	Mounichion	April
Daisios	Thargelion	May
Panemos	Skirophorion	June
Loos	Hekatombaion	July
Gorpiaios	Metageitnion	August
Hyperberetaios	Boedromion	September

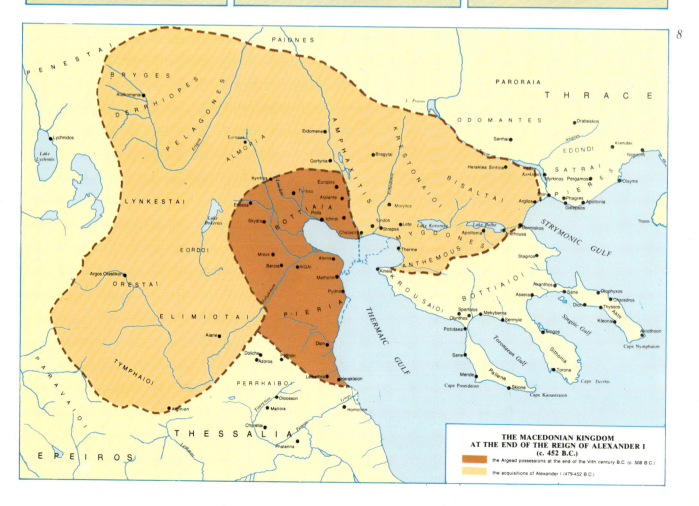

8

THE MACEDONIAN KINGDOM
AT THE END OF THE REIGN OF ALEXANDER I
(c. 452 B.C.)

the Argead possessions at the end of the VIth century B.C. (c. 508 B.C.)

the acquisitions of Alexander I (479-452 B.C.)

in Macedonia, and his position was, for the time being, recognised by Athens in a treaty between the states which created a formal relationship of alliance and friendship.[48] However the basic conflict of interest between the two powers coud not long be concealed, and we have already seen Athens allied with Perdikkas' rebel brother. The founding of Amphipolis in 437 and the consequent reassertion of Athenian power in the lower Strymon was a direct challenge to Macedonian interests. In 434 Athens added to her empire the old Eretrian colony Methone,[49] situated on the west coast of the Thermaic Gulf at the point where the northern extension of the Pierian range touches the sea. The possession of this site made it possible for the imperial city directly to intervene in Macedonian affairs, as for example, by introducing Macedonian exiles to harass the king,[50] and also to cut the main route of communication to the south.[51] The treaty of 413 prohibited Perdikkas from exporting ship timber without the explicit permission of Athens.[52] We have already examined other means used by Athens to coerce the Argead ruler. But Perdikkas knew how to exploit the

7. *The Macedonian calendar exhibits especial interest. The unusual names of the Macedonian months, which referred to festivals associated with them, are clearly Greek in origin and constitute one of the strongest arguments in favour of the Greek nationality of the Macedonians. The table shows the corresponding months of the Attic and the modern calendars.*

8. *Until about the end of the 6th century B.C. the kernel of the Macedonian kingdom of the Argeadai consisted of the regions of Pieria and Bottiaia on the western coast and at the head of the Thermaic Gulf. During the third and fourth decades of the 5th century B.C., after the evacuation of the Persian forces from mainland Greece, Alexandros I succeeded in quadrupling the territory of his state and extended his authority to the regions bordering on it at the expense of the neighouring tribes — the Edonoi, the Eordoi, the Almopes and the Bisaltai. He also brought into alliance or under his domination the inter-related tribes of upper Macedonia.*

crisis of the Peloponnesian War for his own ends and by a policy of tergiversation between the two combatants brought about the ruin of the Athenian empire on the Macedonian coasts.

Perdikkas died in 413 or 412. His son and successor Archelaos reaped the fruits of his father's policy.[53] The disaster at Syracuse made it impossible for Athens to continue the methods she had hitherto employed to impose her will on Macedonia. Of necessity, her new role was that of petitioner. So in the Athenian year 407/6 we find Athens honoring Archelaos as "*proxenos* and benefactor" in recognition of naval material provided by the king. The Athenian politician Andokides, who had been exiled by the *demos* for his alleged participation in the mutilation of the Herms, recounted that among the services he had rendered to his native city even as an exile was the procuring of ship timber from Archelaos.[54] The new freedom from Athens enabled the king to strengthen the administrative and military organisation of the realm. Forts were built throughout the country, roads constructed and the armed forces supplied with weapons, horses and other equipment. In these respects it was Thucydides' considered judgement that the king accomplished more than all Argead rulers before him.[55] It was probably Archelaos who moved the administrative center of the kingdom from Aigai to Pella,[56] a location with access to the sea through the channel of the Loudias river.[57] The freedom from Athenian interference and the increased resources of the kingdom made it possible for Archelaos to discipline the vassal princes of Upper Macedonia,[58] and successfully intervene in the disturbed politics of Thessaly to the south.

There is, however, another aspect altogether to the impact of Athenian imperialism on Macedonia throughout the fifth century. Greek culture was introduced into Macedonia by Athens in the days of her greatest power and creativeness and essentially in an Athenian form. The continuous military, diplomatic and commercial contacts between Athens and the Argead kingdom produced cultural consequences decisive for Macedonia and for the world. Relations of guestfriendship — *xenia* — were established between prominent Athenians and the kings, and the latter supported Greek writers and artists.[59]

The court and the aristocracy became increasingly familiar with Greek art, literature and thought, and Attic Greek was to become the administrative language or the preferred speech of at least a significant portion of the nobility. The native Macedonian speech declined to the status of a rustic patois which has left behind no literary monument, no administrative document, not a single inscription.[60] If, as Perikles said, Athens had become the "school of Hellas", Macedonians of the ruling class were among her earliest and most receptive, if hardly her most talented, pupils. The Greek culture which the conquests of the Argead king Alexander III were to introduce into western Asia, Egypt and Iran was, basically, that of Athens.[61]

As a youth Alexandros I had sought to compete in the Olympic games. His participation was challenged on the grounds that he was not a Greek, but the *hellanodikai* judged that the Argead house took its origin from the Temenids, the old royal family of Peloponnesian Argos, and Alexandros was allowed to enter the stadion race: he tied for first.[62] This claim of the Argead kings to be of Hellenic stock and to trace their origin to Argos illuminates the significance of the names given to the first two Macedonian towns situated on the main route running into Pieria from the south through the Vale of Tempe, Herakleion and Dion.[63] The first takes its name from the Argive hero Herakles, who was regarded as the progenitor of the royal clan, and the second from Zeus, the chief of the Greek gods, who was not only believed to be the divine father of Herakles,[64] but also, according to the old Hesiodic genealogy,[65] the father of Makedon, the eponymous ancestor of the Macedonians themselves by the nymph Thyia. The names of these two towns, whose existence is attested by the time of the outbreak of the Peloponnesian War, is clear evidence of an attempt to emphasize,

the Hellenic origin, not only of the dynasty, but also of the nation and there can be little doubt that both were foundations of Alexandros.[66]

The king encouraged Greek settlement in his kingdom. At the time of the destruction of Mycenae by Argos soon after 478 he received over half the common people, the *demos* of Mycenae, into Macedonia.[67] When the Athenians under Perikles' personal command in 446 took the city Histiaia on the north coast of Euboia by assault, the inhabitants migrated to Macedonia.[68] And a generation later, in 423, we find a hoplite force of three thousand "Greeks resident in the kingdom" serving in the army of Perdikkas II.[69] Alexandros patronised the famous poets Pindar[70] and Bakchylides.[71] The latter composed for the king, appropriately, a drinking song.

Under Perdikkas II, the head of Herakles, the heroic ancestor of the dynasty, for the first time appears on the royal coinage,[72] and this type was continued with greater frequency by Archelaos.[73] The manifold political and military problems which confronted Perdikkas throughout his reign seem to have given the king little opportunity to encourage the reception of Greek culture.[74] But his son, an educated ruler and one with a marked taste for Greek artists and intellectuals,[75] enthusiastically invited all that was best in Greek art and thought. The royal residence was decorated by the famous painter Zeuxis of Herakleia.[76] The epic poet Choirilos,[77] the choral poet Timotheos,[78] and the Athenian dramatist Agathon[79] were the king's guests. Socrates himself is said to have received an invitation from the king which the philosopher refused.[80] At Dion in Pieria, just below the northern face of Mt. Olympus, Archelaos founded a religious festival called the *Olympia*,

9. Aerial photograph of ancient Pella, to which the ancient Macedonian capital was moved, probably by Archelaos. In ancient times Pella was linked to the sea by the river Loudias. The excavations have revealed an extensive city with large, luxurious buildings.

sacred to the Olympian Zeus and the Muses. The festival consisted of athletic and, in the Greek sense, musical contests and lasted for nine days, one day for each of the nine Muses.[81]

But the reception of Greek culture in its Athenian form is most strikingly symbolized by the arrival of Euripides at Archelaos' court. The poet, depressed by the hysterical atmosphere in his native city during the final somber years of the great war, sought refuge in Macedonia. The king honoured him with the rank of Companion, [82] and the poet in return composed the "Archelaos", a play named for his royal patron in which he gave definitive literary form to the foundation legend of the Argead monarchy.[83] The qualities of noble descent, bravery and endurance[84] were strongly emphasized in the drama. For us, the most moving evidence of Euripides' sojourn in Macedonia is the most extraordinary of his plays, the "Bacchae". The ideas with which the tragedy deals seem to owe nothing to the poet's new environment, but the untouched freshness of the Macedonian landscape and the sight of women in the throes of Dionysiac frenzy cannot but have had their effect on the poet. Euripides died in Macedonia and was buried at Arethousa near the eastern end of Lake Bolbe where his grave was to be pointed out for centuries.[85] The Athenians asked the return of the poet's remains. The Macedonian assembly by unanimous vote refused the request.[86]

During Archelaos' reign Macedonia seemed to have become one of the important powers of the Aegean world. But the aristocracy, and members of the royal family as well, were not sufficiently disciplined to support and further the cohesion of the realm. Archelaos, an overconfident type,[87] was assassinated by a disgruntled noble.[88] His heir was a child. There followed a period of four decades during which the Macedonian state all but went down.[89] The break in the direct line of succession provoked a series of pretenders whose ambitions and intrigues plagued the kingdom. The weakness of the monarchy enabled the Chalkidic League to expand inland into

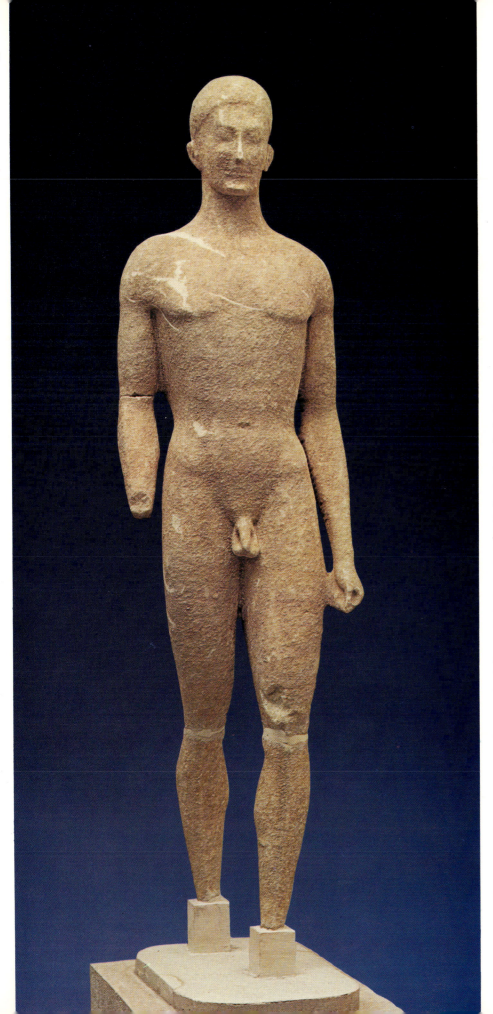

10. The areas of central and eastern Macedonia embraced by the state of Alexandros I had in earlier times been settled with colonies from southern Greece, which exercised a strong cultural influence on the regions surrounding them. The foundations of a large Ionic temple, dating from the end of the 6th century, were found in the centre of modern Thessalonike. All that survives from it are a few architectural members and the small head illustrated here, which was perhaps part of the decorative sculpture. Thessalonike, Archaeological Museum.

11. Representation of a young girl, from a grave stele found at Dion. About the middle of the 5th century B.C. Thessalonike, Archaeological Museum.

12. The Kilkis Kouros is the only archaic Kouros from northern Greece. It was found in the area of ancient Europos, to the west of the Axios. The photograph was taken before the statue was mutilated by antique smugglers. Kilkis, Archaeological Museum.

13. *Stater of Archelaos. On the obverse, the usual device of Macedonian coins (a man on horse-back wearing a broad-brimmed hat and chlamys and carrying two spears); the reverse shows the front part of a goat. London, British Museum.*

14-15. *Staters of Amyntas III and Perdikkas III. On the obverse, the head of Herakles, the mythical forefather of the Macedonian dynasty; on the reverse, the name of the king and a horse. On the reverse of the stater of Perdikkas the club of Herakles, another symbol of the Macedonian dynasty, can be seen between the legs of the horse. London, British Museum.*

16. *Silver octadrachm of Alexandros I. The Macedonian monarch was surnamed "Philhellene" because of the keen interest he displayed in matters of common Greek concern. He was the first ruler to strike coins bearing his name. Paris, Bibliothèque Nationale.*

16

17. Dion was one of the most important Macedonian cities. Its name was connected with Zeus (gen. Dios), father of Makedon, the eponymous hero of the Macedonians. The most important festival of the god at Dion (which was close to Mount Olympus) was the Olympia, which consisted of athletic and musical contests and lasted for 9 days. Each day was devoted to one of the Muses, and was named after her. The aerial photograph shows the ruins of ancient Dion. In recent years, archaeological excavations conducted by the University of Thessalonike have uncovered the defensive walls, several roads, buildings and Sanctuaries.

19

18-19. *The worship of Dionysos was widespread in Macedonia, where it had its own particular character. It is no coincidence that Euripides first presented his "Bacchae" at the court of Archelaos. The plates show details from the Derveni krater (c. 330 B.C.) showing a Satyr and Mainads. Thessalonike, Archaeological Museum.*

Macedonian territory as far as Pella and this threat could only be met at the price of an appeal to Sparta, for the time being the dominant power in the Aegean world. Later Thebes and Athens were to exploit the frequent occasions of Macedonian weakness. For most of this troubled period, only the energy and diplomacy of king Amyntas III, a scion of a collateral branch of the royal family, maintained any semblance of order and continuity.

Intensive and repeated barbarian attacks harassed the kingdom. Even the savage Triballoi of the northern Balkans raided south to the Aegean coast, and the Argead realm was not spared their assaults.[90] North of Macedonia in the basin of the Axios river the Paionians had become united under their own kings.[91] Far away in central Europe a great movement of peoples was under way. Important elements among the Celts were advancing eastward along the Danube. Their advent disturbed Illyrian tribes of the northwest Balkans and forced them south on Macedonia. Amyntas III was expelled from his kingdom at least once by the Illyrians, and Macedonia had to pay them tribute.

During the short reign of Amyntas' second son, Perdikkas III, a degree of recovery and stability seemed to have been attained. But in the spring of 359 Perdikkas and four thousand of his Macedonians perished in a great battle on the northwest frontier. Macedonia lay open to invasion on the west, north and east. No less than three pretenders appeared, one supported by the Athenian fleet and a force of the Thracians. It was this moment of crisis and desperation which forged a nation out of the Macedonian people. All elements of society could now apprehend that mere survival depended upon willing obedience to the royal authority. The princes of Upper Macedonia were soon to face the choice of remaining exposed to Illyrian assault or accepting integration into the Argead kingdom. The meteoric rise of Macedonia to the position of a great power under the genial rule of Perdikkas' younger brother, the famous Philip II, remains a classic instance of courageous and successful response to seemingly insurmountable external pressures.

20. Dionysos, from a mosaic at Pella. The god is depicted naked, holding the thyrsos in one hand and the neck of the panther on which he is riding with the other. Dionysiac subjects were particularly popular in Macedonia and the rest of Greece. End of the 4th century B.C. Pella, Archaeological Museum.

THE UNIFICATION OF MACEDONIA

It would be difficult to exaggerate the importance of the external threats facing Macedonia during Philip's reign, those threatening to dismember the state at his accession and those that developed as, under his rule, new fears were provoked among those who had rarely before had to take a Macedonian seriously. Nevertheless, substantial as such challenges were to Macedonian security, the most fundamental and debilitating problem with which the new king had to deal — the one which unresolved had long weakened the kingdom — was that of disunity. And it is arguably in his nurturing, for the first time, of an effective national unity that Philip's greatest contribution to the history of Macedonia lay.

Predominantly this disunity was the manifestation of the divisiveness of west from east, uplands from lowlands, and it stemmed from several sources. Seventy years before Philip's accession the historian Thucydides distinguished Lower Macedonia, which Perdikkas ruled, from the Macedonians of the uplands, who included "the Lynkestai, the Elimiotai and the other upland tribes, who, though allies of the lower Macedonians and subject to them, have their own kings".[1] Although linguistic criteria confirm the Macedonian culture of at least their ruling classes, the geographical isolation of the Upper Macedonians, barricaded away on the rugged mountain-slopes and in the small valleys of the western highlands hard over against the Molossian kingdom of Epeiros and the Illyrian peoples to the west and northwest, tended to separate them from their kinsmen of the lowlands. Although it had its own mountains, Lower Macedonia contained, with Thessaly, the largest plains of the Hellenic peninsula, and it was probably upon them that the bulk of the population of central and eastern Macedonia was concentrated. The economy was largely agrarian, supported by the rich alluvial soil. Upper Macedonia, however, had few cities and the area of its plains was small. Its economy, to judge from the terrain and from the practices of its inhabitants in more recent times, was largely pastoral. Like most mountain pastoralists, in

particular in regions in which climatic severity made the seasonal transfer of livestock unavoidable and thus discouraged permanent settlement of the population, the uplanders were extremely tough, intensely insular and fiercely resentful of any semblance of outside control.

This independence and the friction it created with the central, Argead government — which will have required of these men at least allegiance and perhaps military service and taxes — had a long and powerful tradition in Macedonian history.

We are not yet able to explain fully why and how the Upper Macedonian people (who evidently had remained behind when in the later seventh century the Argeads and their followers moved down from the southwestern mountains and occupied the plain-lands below) became subject to their more adventurous kinfolk.[2] But it is likely that the first beginnings of political domination occurred during the reign of Alexandros I (c. 498-454). The evidence is slight enough, but it seems that one of the consequences of the Persian invasion of mainland Greece was the growth of Argead contacts with at least some, and perhaps all, of the upland principalities.[3] And from about that time we begin to learn too of the tensions that will appear more or less constant in succeeding decades. The details may be disputed, but there are clear signs of close connections between the sons of Alexandros and the ruler of Elimeia.[4] Intermittently, similar glimpses are caught during the following century, down to the marriage by Philip II of an Elimiote princess.[5] But the contacts are often overshadowed by antagonism. During the Peloponnesian War (431-404) the Elimiotai fought at least once against the Macedonian king.[6] Later, during Philip's reign, we find the brother of his Elimiote wife among those who fought against him at Olynthos in 349/8.[7]

Such divisiveness is typical — considerably more typical, it seems, than co-operation — of the relationship between the upland cantons and the Argead rulers; on this, for all their scarcity, our fragments of evidence are quite consistent. Particularly antipathe-tic to the central kingdom were the rulers of Lynkos and Pelagonia, in the northwest. The claim of the Lynkestian dynasty to descent from the Bakchiadai of Corinth[8] may or may not have been valid, but it was at least symptomatic of the independent and anti-centralist ideals of the mountain ruling-group. Arrhabaios, son of Bromeros, whose name had appeared in a treaty between Macedonia and Athens in 423/2 as a friend and ally of King Perdikkas,[9] was nevertheless at war with him by 418 and fought against King Archelaos a few years later.[10] One Menelaos, a Pelagonian, who may have been from the ruling dynasty of Lynkos, left his native princedom during the 360s and devotedly and effectively served the Athenians as an opponent of Macedonia.[11] Such incidents, though not often documented, seem to be characteristic. The especially remarkable insularity of this group may well have arisen from its close connections with the Illyrian tribes to the west of Lynkos; for some observers, at times, it was difficult to distinguish between Lynkestians and Illyrians. Eurydike, for example, the wife of Amyntas III and mother of Philip II, seems to have been brought up at the court of her Lynkestian grandfather, Arrhabaios, but she is often referred to as Illyrian.[12] And perhaps this was more than a simple geographical confusion, for her marriage to Amyntas c. 392 appears to have been forced upon him as the price of Illyrian withdrawal from Macedonia,[13] just as Philip's marriage to the Illyrian Audata was probably a diplomatic necessity at a time (early 359) when he was unable to fight her fellow tribesmen.[14] Such occurrences suggest an affinity of convenience between the Lynkestians and some of the Illyrian tribes — perhaps because such co-operation did not as a rule lead to political controls — that rarely existed between Lynkos and the Argeadai of the central plain.

Such affinities and antagonisms may have been fairly general. Although the Elimiote dynasty was comparatively favourable to the Argeadai (they may have been connected by intermarriage at some points in their past) most of Upper Macedonia was sufficiently difficult of access to all but the best trained light infantry to preserve a relative isolation. Its loyalties, by way of additional insurance, may have tended to gravitate towards the north and west.

It is against such a background that the difficulties facing Philip at the time of his accession in the winter of 360/59 take on their full significance. In the aftermath of the great battle against the Illyrian Bardylis, king of the powerful Dardanian tribe, Perdikkas and four thousand Macedonians lay dead, the Illyrians — already controlling probably much of Upper Macedonia — prepared to push deep into the heart of the kingdom, the Paionian king Agis began pressing southwards down the Axios valley in search of plunder. The Athenians and the Thracian king Kotys each supported contenders for the vacant throne. Macedonia was weighed down with fear and despondency.[15] But it was not only these external problems themselves that were so destructive; it was also that they fed upon, and in turn were bound to exacerbate, this fundamental internal weakness that already existed. In particular, Upper Macedonia must have seemed virtually lost to Bardylis, beyond hope of recovery.

And yet — to look forward, for a moment, to the situation later in Philip's reign and in that of Alexander — within a relatively short time the internal dissensions seem to have been practically healed. There is no suggestion in our much fuller sources for the period from about 350 onwards (at least, except possibly in the desperate circumstances that followed the assassination of Philip in 336) that Macedonia was any longer a country divided against itself. What had Philip done?

To that question there are probably two main answers. The unification of the disparate elements of the state was a process that must have taken some time, but in the first place Philip had to find urgent solutions to difficulties that would allow no delay. And in his initial actions as king we see exemplified much of the genius that characterised this reign, that dazzling combination of military inventiveness and skill with diplomacy that continued to serve Macedo-

nian interests so efficiently and effectively.

The Illyrian designs he delayed, apparently by offering some form of alliance cemented by royal marriage. Philip took Audata, probably Bardylis' daughter, as his wife.[16] The payment of tribute, a feature of past dealings with the Illyrians, no doubt resumed. (At most times, in fact, Illyrian desires were measured more in plunder than in territorial acquisition.)[17] Gifts and promises were sufficient to give check for the time being to Agis' Paionians. Simultaneously, the Macedonian troops lent to Amphipolis by Perdikkas III in support of the resistance there to Athenian ambitions were withdrawn. The Athenians promptly abandoned their support for Argaios, one of the pretenders to the throne, and his attempt came to nothing before Philip's prompt military action. By some form of persuasion he induced the Thracian king Kotys, to kill his nominee, the second pretender, Pausanias.[18] With at least some temporary respite from the most pressing problems, the Macedonian king was now able to give time and energy to finding more lasting solutions; he turned to recruiting and training an effective army and to raising the morale of his disconsolate subjects.[19]

Within a year of his accession he was able to do battle with the Paionians and to drive them back to the northern valleys whence they had come. Early in 358 he turned and, with an army of 10,000 foot and 600 horse, devastated the forces of the Dardanian Illyrians.[20]

But such military ventures and military victories were only the more visible part of Philip's solution to Macedonia's problems. They were indeed important; most of all they established the beginnings of that wave of success that bore the kingdom on its

21. *The star, emblem of the Macedonian Argead dynasty, decorates here a miniature "Shield". These small discs of silver, gold or gilded metal, in the form of a Macedonian shield, were affixed as decorative elements to a variety of objects. From the "Macedonian" tomb at Katerini. 400-350 B.C. Thessalonike, Archaeological Museum.*

triumphant crest through danger after danger. But neither the military reforms that set the fighting forces on a proper basis nor the social changes needed to create a more unified, more national outlook could be effected quickly or easily. And, although our few surviving references to such matters tend to concentrate them within short sections of the reign, we have to understand that Philip's creation of a genuine national state, however consciously or unconsciously effected, must have been something to which considerable efforts were directed over a good number of years.

In surveying these achievements we may briefly note the expansion, under Philip, in the size of the armed forces. Of the growth in numbers of the heavy Macedonian horse — the so-called Companion Cavalry — and the main body of the infantry — the phalanx — we know a little. We are given battle figures only four times for the reign — or, rather, five if we include those for Alexander's army in 334, which cannot have altered much in the two years or less since Philip's death. In the battle of 358 against Bardylis there were 10,000 Macedonian infantry and 600 cavalry.[21] In 352, we are told, 20,000 foot and 3,000 horse could be deployed[22] and, by 340, a total of 30,000 men.[23] In 338, at the battle of Chaironeia, 30,000 foot and 2,000 horse were used,[24] which accords well with figures of some 24,000 plus 3,300 four years later at the launching of Alexander's eastern campaign.[25] These may in some cases be misleading; those for 352 and 340 may contain substantial allied elements, for it seems to have been characteristic of Philip to make no more use of actual Macedonians than was essential. Nor do we know, even with the most certainly Macedonian figures, those for 358 and 334, the proportion of the total potential levy represented by those soldiers known to be in the field. But, while precision is therefore impossible, we are nevertheless aware of what seems to be a very considerable expansion in military numbers. The combined total of available horsemen and infantrymen must have at least doubled during Philip's reign, and the increase may have been much higher. Some of this, showing up in the latest figures, is undoubtedly due to natural population increase such as often accompanies a period of relative stability; some of it is the result of territorial expansion into the Chalkidian peninsula, western Thrace and elsewhere. But to some extent, possibly a large one, it must have been produced by a heavier levy on the Macedonian citizenry.

In part, too, the expansion seems to follow from military innovation.[26] Although the details may be disputed, it is clear that Philip may be credited with the virtual (if not the actual) creation of the phalanx, which was the name given to the massed body of infantry known as the *pezetairoi* ("Foot-companions"). If it is correct, as recently suggested,[27] that the *asthetairoi* represented the Upper Macedonian element in the phalanx, then their addition to the army probably follows upon Philip's settlement of that area in the second year of his reign. The other branch of the infantry, the so-called *hypaspistai* (literally "Shieldbearers"), seems to have expanded greatly under Philip. Originally, as the name suggests, an élite corps serving as the Bodyguard of the King (a title by which they were sometimes called), the Hypaspists grew from small numbers, perhaps one thousand, or less, to three thousand by the end of the reign.

Large numbers, of course, do not by themselves create unity. But devices through which an overriding loyalty to the military organisation is fostered may be important, and a striking feature of Philip's arrangements is the system of incentives and rewards open to all soldiers. Promotion through the ranks was of course possible. But even before promotion to the lowest grade of "non-commissioned officer", the *dekadarchia*, there were bonus pay-rates available for outstanding service; we hear of "ten-stater" and "double-rate" soldiers.[28] The twin pinnacles were occupied by the Companion Cavalry and the Hypaspists, the two élite bodies. Both could be referred to peculiarly as "royal". The Hypaspists were evidently not levied but specially recruited from the bulk of the Pezetairoi — and recruited, it can hardly be doubted, on the basis of excellence, which is to say that the existence and the expansion of this body was an incentive to devoted and noteworthy service on the part of the infantryman and a reward for his achievement of it. Most probably, though not certainly, the Hypaspist received a higher rate of pay than the ordinary Pezetairos. (The rate for the former at the end of Philip's reign was thirty drachmai per month; "ten-stater men" received forty and "double-raters" perhaps fifty, which may have been twice the rate for Pezetairoi.)

Similarly, perhaps, with the cavalry. The term *hetairoi* ("Companions"), in the broadest sense, referred to the nobility of Macedonia, but it also meant, in a narrower sense, the younger members of this order serving as heavy cavalrymen, the main striking arm of Philip's and Alexander's army, distinct, in this function and in their higher status, from the light-armed cavalry, or *prodromoi* ("Scouts"). Since the Companion Cavalry were in some sense noble, we might expect the basic difference between them and the other elements of the army to have been the unbridgeable one of birth — and conceivably before Philip's time this had been so. But there is no doubt that Philip created *hetairoi*, and from among

22-23. *The question of the unification of Macedonia was one of the most serious problems faced by Philip after his rise to power. The remote Macedonian tribes continuously displayed tendencies towards independence and resisted all attempts to impose central authority. It was only by repeated and determined effort that Philip was able to assert control in the northwest, over the tribes of Upper Macedonia, and in the east where he succeeded in extending the boundaries of his kingdom as far as the region of Mount Pangaion, beyond the river Strymon. The rich metal deposits of eastern Macedonia had been exploited from early times by the Bisaltai and the Edonoi, who were striking beautiful silver coins of high denominations as early as the 5th century. Illustrated here are octadrachms of the Edonoi (22) and of the Bisaltai (23). London, British Museum, Paris Bibliothèque Nationale.*

22

23

Thessalians and other Greeks, not just Macedonians. These promotions too — though our contemporary source for them, for his own purposes, chooses to say otherwise — will doubtless have been made on the basis of excellence.[29] In primarily agrarian societies it is generally true that the most visible symptom of nobility is the possession of substantial estates, and we observe that grants of land were certainly made to the new appointees. (Around 340 B.C., no more than 800 *hetairoi* are said, and perhaps this is exaggerated for effect, to have owned more land than the "ten thousand richest men among the Greeks"[30] — a sign not only of the different scale of land-ownership operating in spacious Macedonia, but also of the importance of the nobility within the society. There is also some reason for supposing that similar grants, presumably on a significantly smaller scale, were made to ordinary infantrymen.)[31] So far as we can see then, on a basis similar to that applying to the Hypaspists, the Companion Cavalry could be seen by some as a supreme goal, even carrying with it, apparently, elevation into the nobility.

What emerges is that inducements to outstanding service and to loyalty to the military system and its commander, the king, were very considerable and must have justified in the mind of the Macedonian soldier the firm discipline required of him and the physical rigours involved in his service. It must have eased too the strains of subordinating his local loyalties to the national organisation. The inducements, along with the common training, the discipline and the service, served to bind the army together as a unit with its allegiance to the king-commander, a tie that can only have been further strengthened by the lengthening string of victories won by it. The Macedonian state was historically heterogeneous; but the creation of a national army imbued with national goals and ideals provided a powerful impulse towards unity.

In the aftermath of his victory over Bardylis in 358 Philip must have given time and energy to the problem of Upper Macedonia. Always fractious, it must have been in chaos following the withdrawal of

the defeated Illyrians. Perhaps local feelings were mixed: to some, a year or so of Illyrian occupation may have been a less than welcome imposition, while to others it may have been preferable to Argead dominion. At all events, the situation was appropriate for Philip's intervention. The frontiers, such as they were, must now have been almost obliterated, local loyalties even more mixed than usual and the possibility of effective local opposition remote. It may be in this context that the marriage of the king to the Elimiote princess Phila belongs.[32] What is also probable is that he engineered re-arrangements of the population in this area — as he was to do later in other border-areas — partly to define and consolidate the frontiers, differentiating between Macedonian and non-Macedonian elements, but, also, probably, to divide up and dilute the traditional local groups over which the Upper Macedonian princely families exercised their authority.[33]

We hear, for example, of the transplanting of an entire town, Illyrian and close to the Macedonian frontier. Capturing the inhabitants, the Sarmisioi, Philip and his soldiers "led them off to Macedonia,[34] 10,000 of them". On the frontier they were a danger, but they could be accommodated safely elsewhere, surrounded by reliable population-groups which could absorb and employ their energies. (Such additions to the population — on a very large scale, when, in particular, the Chalkidian peninsula and western Thrace were annexed — must have added greatly to a serf-like labouring class similar to the *penestai* of Thessaly or the *heilotes* of Lakonia, making it possible for large numbers of citizen-soldiers, especially during Alexander's extended campaigns, to be removed from the kingdom without apparent detriment to the food-supply and the eco-

24. After Philip's successive victories, the rulers of the tribes of Upper Macedonia recognised the authority of the Argead monarchs and became their subjects. This bronze cheek piece from a helmet found at Tymphaia, near modern Grevena, shows a winged Nike, holding shield and spear. 4th century B.C. Thessalonike, Archaeological Museum.

nomy). It is on the principle underlying this Illyrian incident that one of Philip's unifying devices seems based. Writing much later, Justin refers to his transplanting of people and populations from one place to another "as shepherds drive their flocks, sometimes into winter, sometimes into summer pastures":

"some people he planted on the frontiers of his kingdom to oppose his enemies; others he settled at the extremities of it. Some, whom he had taken prisoner in war, he distributed among certain cities to fill up the number of inhabitants; and thus out of various tribes and nations he formed one people."[35]

Most of the contemporary evidence on which such an account may have been based is now lost to us. But it is interesting that Alexander himself is made to refer, in a speech attributed to him, to Philip's activities in similar terms:

"for Philip found you vagabonds and helpless, most of you clothed with sheepskins, pasturing a few sheep on the mountainsides and fighting for these with ill success against the Illyrians and Triballians and Thracians on your borders... He brought you down from the hills to the plains."[36]

The allusions here are to the western and northwestern frontier (against the Illyrians), the northern and the eastern (against the Triballoi and the Thracians, respectively), all of them regions susceptible to border-raids and interference; and there is no doubt that Philip must have amalgamated the scattered pockets of population in the border-regions into defensible settlements on the more level ground,

25. Stater of Lete. A satyr carrying off a nymph, who is struggling to escape, 500-480 B.C. The subjects depicted on Macedonian coins are frequently connected with the worship of Dionysos. Athens, Numismatic Museum.

26. Stater of Aigai, 500-480 B.C. The goat is associated with the legendary founding of the Macedonian kingdom. Paris, Bibliothèque Nationale.

partly for defence and partly in order to differentiate Macedonian from foreign elements. But, as Alexander's words show, there was more to it than that. For example, in Thrace during the campaign of 342-341, Philip established a number of Macedonian colonies — like Kabyle and Bine and, further north, in the river Hebros basin, Philippopolis — and settled Macedonians in them (in at least one case, by repute, Macedonian undesirables).[37] In Thessaly, on the slopes of the Pass of Tempe, a similar colony was set up at Gonnoi probably in 352.[38] There was Alexandropolis, founded somewhere near the northern frontier, c. 340, when Alexander was regent.[39] There are, no doubt, others of which we know nothing.[40] In all of these cases there were, it is very likely, other motives for such manipulation; but, equally, many of these cases provided opportunities for Philip to work towards the easing of parochial strains within the kingdom (though one could hardly doubt that discontents could also be *created* in the process), and, in view of his other activities directed towards the same ends, it is difficult to deny that this was consciously and deliberately done.

Referring to Philip's activities of this sort, Machiavelli, more than eighteen centuries later, advises the would-be ruler of a state to leave "nothing of that province intact and nothing in it, neither rank, nor institution, nor form of government, nor wealth, except it be held by such as recognise that it comes from him".[41]

Scattered references suggest that this was indeed true of Philip's approach to such subject-areas as Thrace and perhaps Paionia and the nearer provinces of Thessaly. But it is true too of some of his attested actions within Macedonia. We have already noticed, for example, that this king was responsible for a marked increase in the size of the Macedonian *hetairos*-class, the nobility, with many of those added coming from Thessaly and elsewhere outside the kingdom. The estates he granted them from captured territory made it possible for the army to levy squadrons of the Companion Cavalry from such new areas as Anthemous and Amphipolis.[42] But additions of that sort to the class served the additional purpose, among others, of diluting the power of the traditional nobility and of creating a large number of comparatively powerful men of the "officer" class whose elevation had come about through the personal patronage of the king.

A related device may be added. The taking of hostages may serve to keep dissident elements in a society under control, and, to Philip, who had himself been a hostage during his youth,[43] there can have been little to learn in this regard.[44] According to one account:

"it was a practice going back to Philip's time that the sons of Macedonian notables who had reached adolescence should be enlisted in the service of the king; and besides general attendance of his person, the duty of guarding him when asleep had been entrusted to them. Again, whenever the king rode out, they received the horses from the grooms and led them up and they mounted the king in Persian fashion and were his companions in the rivalry of the chase."

Now these boys, the "Royal Pages", occupied a privileged position at the court and in society. They associated closely with the king and his family, some (perhaps all) being educated in company with the king's sons,[45] and they could expect with confidence to move into positions of responsibility and status in the army and state as they grew older.[46] In them the king, on his part, gave himself the opportunity to foster and encourage loyalty to the throne in the officer class of the future. But, of course, quite apart from all the privileges, the honour and the convenience, these boys in the last resort stood hostage for the co-operation of their families, whether or not this ever had to be acknowledged openly.

Our sources for Macedonian internal history are pitifully sparse and it is no surprise that on this subject little remains; however important, it has none of the attraction of the eyecatching military exploits.

But there is just enough, perhaps, to indicate, as we have seen, that Philip both recognised and worked to overcome Macedonia's disunity. It is worth noting finally, however, that all the brilliant devices and all the clever safeguards in the world will not unify a nation. In all probability the major credit for the remarkable change in Macedonia during Philip's reign ought to be given to the general success achieved by him as its king and as commander-in-chief of its army. If loyalty to the head was necessary, then the head crowned with victory and prosperity might attract it where that bowed in failure could not. The old particularism was admittedly not finally and utterly dead. On two occasions in later centuries it may have reached significant proportions, first in the defection in 288 of what appear to have been largely Upper Macedonians to the army of Pyrrhos, and again in 198 or 197 in the defection of Orestis to the Roman side. (Flamininus' subsequent proclamation of the independence of Orestis from Macedonia, while no doubt payment for services rendered, was also an expression of the recognition of the local separatist feeling).[47] In both of these cases, matters were complicated by the traditional closeness between Orestis and Epeiros, but it is possible that some of the old factiousness still existed — though at that remove from Philip's time one could scarcely be confident, even so, that it was not a new phenomenon altogether. Apart from a few possible signs of it in the chaotic situation that followed immediately upon Philip's assassination (when a Lynkestian family was thought to be planning treason),[48] for all practical purposes, it seems, Philip had succeeded in ridding the Macedonian kingdom of its most serious problem.

27. *Under Archelaos the administrative centre of the Macedonian Kingdom was transferred from Aigai to Pella. The new capital was consequently the centre of Philip's power and authority. The imposing buildings that have so far been excavated are considered by some scholars to be private residences, while others claim they are public buildings. Late 4th century B.C.*

THE COINAGE OF PHILIP AND THE PANGAION MINES

When Philip succeeded his brother Perdikkas III in 359,[1] one of his first acts, dictated as much by necessity as by prudence,[2] was to relieve Amphipolis of its Macedonian garrison. His kingdom thus found itself reduced to the plain of Pella and the slopes of the surrounding mountains. Although Philip had access to the northern coast of the Thermaic Gulf, navigation on the gulf itself was controlled by the independent Greek cities of Methone, Pydna and Olynthos. Macedonia, shortly after the accession of Philip, thus had the appearance of a kingdom limited in both size and means of action.

It is difficult to say whether at this period gold and silver mines were already being exploited in the territory under Philip's control.[3] In any case a state did not need mines in order to be able to mint coins,[4] since it had a perfect right to buy metal from the states that produced it, and it could also use the silver brought in by commercial exchange in the form of ingots, articles or coins; the coins thus acquired were melted down or sometimes directly overstamped.[5] Also, a state had no hesitation in melting down or overstamping its own coins when they became obsolete.

I have set out elsewhere the reasons which suggest that Philip was striking silver coins at Pella from 359 on.[6] In this he was following the example of his predecessors, and stamping his name and equestrian image on the coins was for him a way of declaring clearly and firmly his sovereignty.

It should be noted that he did not issue gold coins at the beginning of his reign.[7] I will return to this point later, but it may be observed here that, even if in 359 he had had the means of striking gold pieces, he would probably not have done so; none of the Macedonian kings who preceded him had minted coins in this metal, the use of which for coins was in any case not usual among the Greeks.

As soon as Philip had rid himself of his rivals, reorganized his army and sent his troops against the Illyrians, he prepared for the conquest of Amphipolis and the Pangaion region. The town was taken in 357

at the end of summer or beginning of autumn. Shortly afterwards, during the year 357/6, Philip gained possession of Mt. Pangaion and extended his dominion as far as the Nestos river.

This conquest constituted a remarkable success: on the one hand Philip gained control of a powerful city, commanding the Strymonic Gulf, and on the other, he became master of the Pangaion region, which provided him with useful resources.

The riches of this territory have been described by Paul Collart:[8] "there were magnificent forests, which furnished wood for the shipyards, and above all the mines... of gold and silver. The mines of Pangaion were famous from remotest antiquity; it was at Pangaion, according to a tradition related by Pliny, that gold was first discovered and melted by the Phoenician Kadmos, and it was to Pangaion, according to him, that Peisistratos and Histiaios of Miletos came in order to make their fortune. The wealth of the Pangaion gold and silver, which is also mentioned briefly by Herodotos, Theophrastos and Strabo, had been used since the Archaic period for the production of abundant coinage."[9]

Even though, as seems probable and as Collart emphasizes, the silver mines of Pangaion were more numerous and productive than the gold mines, the latter held a real fascination for the Ancients. Diodoros' account of the city of Philippi is significant:[10]

"After this he (Philip) went to the city of Krenides, and having increased its size with a large number of inhabitants, changed its name to Philippi, giving it his own name, and then, turning to the gold mines in its territory, which were very scanty and insignificant, he increased their output so much by his improvements that they could bring him a revenue of more than a thousand talents. And because from these mines he had soon amassed a fortune, with the abundance of money he raised the Macedonian kingdom higher and higher to a greatly superior position, for with the gold

coins which he struck, which came to be known from his name as Philippeioi, he organized a large force of mercenaries, and by using these coins for bribes induced many Greeks to become betrayers of their native lands."

This famous passage of Diodoros has often given rise to the belief that it was soon after the capture of Krenides that Philip began to issue gold coins; a number of historians and numismatists have placed the start of this coinage at around 356.[11] I have tried to show that this was not the case and that Philip only began striking gold coins in the second part of his reign, perhaps around 345 or even as late as 342-340,[12] and that under these circumstances the quantity of gold coins issued during his lifetime was relatively small.[13]

The city of Philippi itself struck some gold (and silver) coins from 357/6 onwards, with the inscription ΦΙΛΙΠΠΩΝ. These coins follow immediately after the gold staters issued in the name of the "mainland Thasians"[14] shortly before the king of Macedonia conquered Krenides. It has also been thought that for several years Philip entrusted the Philippians with the production of the gold staters that he needed.[15] If, however, one examines carefully the coinage of Philippi, it is clear that its gold (and silver) coins fall stylistically into two very distinct groups, and that the second group was perhaps struck under Alexander, while the first, which certainly dates from the years following the capture of the city by Philip, contains only two issues of gold staters (and six of silver coins).[16] Thus we have to do with a very limited coinage bearing little relationship to the wealth claimed by Diodoros for the mines of Philippi, and not very likely to have brought the Macedonian king substantial means.

It should also be noted that Philippi was not reduced after its conquest to the rank of a royal Macedonian city, but preserved its status as a Greek πόλις enjoying considerable internal autonomy.[17] It might, indeed, be supposed that she would under

28. Following the example set by his predecessors, Philip's silver coins were minted at Pella from the first year of his rule. Shortly afterwards, in 375/6 when Philip had extended his authority to the Pangaion area, a second royal mint was established at Amphipolis. The illustration shows one of Philip's silver tetradrachms. The obverse has the head of Olympian Zeus, and the reverse shows a mounted youth holding a victor's palm, a reference to Philip's equestrian victory in the Olympic games of 356. The Macedonian monarch used the occasion to promote his panhellenic policy. Athens, Numismatic Museum.

29. After the acquisition of Amphipolis, 357, and Krenides, 356, renamed Philippi, Philip became master of the gold and silver mines of Mount Pangaion, famous since remote antiquity. They were intensively worked and are said to have supplied Philip with more than 1000 talents annually. It was only during the second part of his reign, after 345, that the gold of Pangaion was used for striking coins. The gold stater illustrated shows the head of Apollo on one side and a two-horse chariot (biga) on the other. Athens, Numismatic Museum.

some agreement have struck gold staters for Philip; but as we have seen, the modesty of her coin production makes this hypothesis unlikely. It could also be suggested that Philip would have appropriated the greater part of the production of the Philippi gold mines in the form of ingots; but, if this was the case, he did not immediately mint coins in his name, since his coinage in this metal only began around 345, or even later.

However that may be, gaining possession of the Pangaion region brought the king considerable resources. Here I will confine myself to examining how this increase in revenue made itself apparent in the currency, while underlining the fact that this approach is of course very incomplete, because it does not take into consideration the other natural resources of the country. It accounts only for the metal used in minting, but not the ingots and objects of gold or silver which constituted a part of the wealth of the kingdom and which Philip used at times to bribe or tempt persons he had dealings with; as an example may be cited the cups he offered the Theban ambassadors, apparently without success.[18]

From 359 on, as we have said, Philip was striking silver coins in the Pella mint. Soon afterwards, a parallel series of coins in the same metal appeared, clearly produced in a different mint.[19] I have tried to show[20] that the location by Newell of this second mint at Amphipolis is plausible; its beginning may be dated to the year 357/6, soon after the capture of the town and its transformation into a Macedonian city.

The creation of this second royal mint was certainly the consequence of the seizure by Philip of the Pangaion mines. Although Amphipolis was situated close to the mines, the quantity of its issues of silver coins does not appear to have been appreciably more important during Philip's lifetime than that of the Pella issues, either because a part of the Pangaion mineral resources had been transferred to the capital of the kingdom, or because the latter possessed sufficient resources of its own. The activities of these two mints, if my classification is correct, continued

parallel throughout Philip's reign; when around 342 Philip called for an increase in the production of silver coins,[21] the work was shared equally by both mints. Undoubtedly the number of tetradrachms actually known gives precedence to Amphipolis, but the difference is not great.[22] The situation changed entirely under Alexander and his immediate successors; if the number of silver *alexanders* and *philips* struck between 336 and 294 is counted, Amphipolis is well in the lead over Pella.[23]

The situation was not the same, apparently, with the gold coins. Before comparing the production of the two mints, however, it will be useful to go back to the question of the date when Philip decided to mint coins in this metal. As we have already said, our researches lead us to believe that the first staters of the king of Macedonia were issued in 345 at the earliest, and may even be dated as late as 342-340,[24] in other words, during the last years of his reign. If Philip really exploited the abundant gold mines of Pangaion, as tradition states, it must be allowed that for some time, at least, the minting of gold coins did not appear either opportune or necessary; it has

30. The rich gold and silver deposits of Mt. Pangaion were not used exclusively for the minting of coins. They also supplied the raw material for a number of metal workshops that sprang up in the area and produced superb masterpieces of jewellery, vessels and many other objects, all executed with incomparable delicacy. The gold ring illustrated was found at Eleutheres, near Kavala. The hoop, of twisted wire with filigree decoration, terminates in two lions' heads. The bezel is in the shape of a Boiotian shield and has a gorgoneion in the centre flanked by palmettes. Beginning of the 5th century B.C. Athens, National Archaeological Museum, Stathatos Collection.

31-32. Two gold necklaces from grave Z at Derveni. Second half of the 4th century B.C. Thessalonike, Archaeological Museum.

33. Gold necklace from Sedes. The centre piece is a miniature figure of Eros. End of the 4th century B.C. Thessalonike, Archaeological Museum.

34. *Detail of a gold thigh ornament from Sedes, near Thessalonike, in the form of the sacred "Knot of Herakles". Superb craftsmanship from the second half of the 4th century* B.C. *Thessalonike, Archaeological Museum.*

35. *Gold oak-wreath from the area of Amphipolis. 4th century* B.C. *Thessalonike, Archaeological Museum.*

35

been pointed out that none of his predecessors on the Macedonian throne had issued gold coins, and that the Greeks only rarely minted in this metal, unlike the king of Persia, whose *darics* were plentiful and renowned.[25] Philip probably decided to institute a gold currency in the second part of his reign, when he had greater expenses to cope with; the value of the gold coins, which weight for weight were worth about twelve times the silver ones,[26] would have been a strong argument in favour of such a move. If my chronology is accepted, and if the first staters date from the years 345-340, it may be observed that this probably happened just at the time when the production of silver tetradrachms from both mints was increased.[27] Philip seems to have had to meet a growing number of needs at this period, and, finding that increasing the production of silver coins was not sufficient, he may well have decided to mint gold ones.[28]

The chronology proposed here for the gold *philips* requires that most of them be regarded as posthumous.[29] As far as the organization of their minting is concerned, the division of the work between Pella and Amphipolis established by Philip was not greatly modified by his successors. During Philip's lifetime, if my classification is correct, the great majority of the gold coins were struck at Pella;[30] after his death, the production of staters in his name and of his types was twice as abundant at Pella as at Amphipolis, and the fractions of the stater were nearly all issued by the Pella mint.[31] Furthermore, it is probable that the Macedonian gold *alexanders* were struck in greater numbers at Pella than at Amphipolis.[32]

If the gold at the disposal of Philip and his successors came primarily from Pangaion, it might appear surprising that the Pella mint should have been so definitely more active than the one at Amphipolis in

minting in this metal. It could indeed be argued that the greater part of the production of such precious coins was reserved for the capital of the kingdom, but this explanation does not seem entirely convincing. It could be argued with equal probability that the Pangaion gold mines were not as rich as tradition would have us believe, and that the gold of Philip and his successors came, in part at least, from another source.

To sum up, the evidence available at present for the coinage of Philip allows us to make the following suggestions about the Pangaion mines.

The silver extracted from these mines enabled the king of Macedonia to open a second mint at Amphipolis in 357/6. Part of this silver may have been sent to Pella, but on this point we cannot pronounce with certainty. It was owing to these same Pangaion mines that the productions at Amphipolis increased markedly under Alexander,[33] when he had need of large amounts of tetradrachms, and when his campaigns against Darius further gave Amphipolis considerable importance as a liaison centre between Macedonia and the East.

Pangaion gold, on the other hand, was not coined so abundantly. When Philip decided between 345 and 340 to strike gold coins, it was the Pella mint that issued the greater number of pieces, and its predominance was maintained under Philip's successors. Amphipolis appears to have played only a secondary part in the production of these coins, and it might thus be suggested that gold used in the Macedonian mints at this time only partly originated in the Pangaion region.

However, as I emphasized at the beginning of this chapter, these remarks are based purely on a study of the coinage, and apart from the fact that the classification proposed in my book is not definitive, coins can only afford limited evidence for the uses to which precious metals can be put. Pangaion may have provided much more gold and silver than the surviving coinage leads one to suppose. The utilization of this gold and silver could have taken many forms, of which currency was only one.

36. A silver ossuary with supports in the form of four lion's feet. The gold olive-wreath on the lid was found inside the ossuary. 4th century B.C. Kavala, Archaeological Museum.

PHILIP AS A GENERAL AND THE MACEDONIAN ARMY

The title of this chapter suggests a question and also, in part, an answer. How great a general was Philip? Judging by results, few generals ever did more to change the face of his own times and to throw his shadow over the future. By creating the first great Macedonian army he enabled the royal house of Macedonia in forty years to dominate first the Balkan neighbours, next Greece and the Aegean, finally the Near and Middle East to the Indus.

If we seek to know what Philip was like as a general, we have no proper record of his campaigns to tell us. It is a matter of seeing some results and drawing some inferences, supported by a very few glimpses of the king in action. In his boyhood and youth the kingdom was weak: at his death he left it very strong. It was a great military disaster that had brought him to the throne. His earliest plans as a strategist were plans for survival, and his earliest acts as a commander were concerned with the training and equipping of the Macedonians as he found them, defeated and depleted by the Dardanian Illyrians of Bardylis. The landowners of the country had always made up a good cavalry, its nucleus the king's "Companions" (*hetairoi*); but of the famous infantry of "the phalanx", in the wars of the kings before 360 there has been no sign, and the logic of the events themselves point to Philip himself as its principal creator. Alexander his son inherited an army in which the "Companion" cavalry had expanded to over 2,000 strong, and in which the bulk of the infantry phalanx were to win fame under the name of "Foot-Companions" (*pezetairoi*). It was Philip undoubtedly who had increased the cavalry and built up the infantry arm, though the stages of development are mostly hidden from us. We see, however, the name *pezetairoi* in Philip's reign (and probably in the 340s) still as the name of the royal footguards, its natural meaning. (The name *hypaspistai* borne by Alexander's brigade of footguards in Asia is never heard of under Philip.) There is a suggestion here of a change of nomenclature either by Alexander on his accession or by Philip at the very end of his reign.

But names apart, the troops themselves were Philip's without a doubt. It was he who gave Macedonia for the first time a real army and a great one.[1]

From the first Philip had faced the urgent need to improve the army in every way possible: the Illyrian neighbours had struck once with deadly effect, and were sure to strike again. As a boy, too, he had seen Greek interventions taking advantage of Macedonian military weakness, and had even himself spent time as a hostage at Thebes, the strongest Greek city of the time, with a notable force of hoplite infantry, still the final strength of Greek citizen armies.[2] When Philip came suddenly to power on the death of his brother, his first concern was with the army, shattered by recent defeat with heavy losses. With a period of training, and perhaps with some re-arming, he restored its confidence, and within the year, after minor successes in the field, he led it to a great victory over the Illyrians, the first of the three major victories of his career as a general.[3]

This was the beginning of greatness. In the years of his reign Philip built up both the infantry and the cavalry arm from the 10,000 + 600 of this Illyrian campaign to the 24,000 or more + 3,300 of Alexander in the year 334.[4] It was Philip presumably (though we are not told when) who introduced the *sarissa*, the very long pike which became eventually the standard weapon of the Macedonian infantry.[5] Acting in big formations on fairly level and unbroken ground the sarissa-armed infantry was very formidable if the soldiers were well drilled. The same soldiers, when acting in conditions which called for endurance over rougher terrain were armed probably with the conventional hoplite spear and shield and were capable of marching far and fast.[6] Philip believed, too, in hard training and in discipline.[7] The effects can be seen in an occasional glimpse of exemplary discipline of Macedonian infantry in action. A controlled withdrawal in contact with the enemy at an early stage of the battle of Chaironeia is a good example.[8] The Macedonians were numerous enough, no doubt, not to need to serve in every levy of soldiers every year, but were able to take it in turns. Yet few campaigning seasons passed without one campaign or more, and as the years went by, the number of really seasoned and experienced troops became quite large. Except for the guards who were picked men from the whole kingdom, cavalry and infantry were recruited on a territorial basis, each region supplying its quota. Though few details survive, there is some reason to think that by the end of Philip's reign it was from certain regions of Upper Macedonia that the finest fighting units among the infantry (apart from the guards) were drawn.[9]

The Macedonians, cavalry and infantry, were the main strength of Philip's army from first to last. The services which he could command of allies and of mercenaries were always subsidiary but they were not unimportant. The peoples who presently supplied troops for Alexander's invasion of Asia, the Greeks themselves, the Odrysian and other Thracians, the Paionians, the Agrianians, the Illyrians, the Triballians, had all of them (except the last) been reduced to subjection by Philip, and presumably he himself did call on them to supply troops occasionally, though we hear very little of the occasions. His biggest external gain in military strength was by the acquisition of Thessaly, the finest political *coup* of his life; the unprecedented election of a "foreign" king by a Greek federation to their archonship, which Alexander held in succession on his death (πατροπαράδοτον). The good service of the 2,000 Thessalian cavalry in Asia with Alexander is well-known. But for Philip too, the Thessalians are named as principal agents of one of his three decisive victories, over the mercenaries of the Phokian general Onomarchos in the battle of the Crocus Plain.[10] (No details are preserved). The mobility and the versatility of Alexander's army over the vast distances and varying terrains of Asia are foreshadowed on the smaller scale by Philip's endless campaigning in the Balkans "his troops under arms all the time", as Demosthenes described it.[11]

But of all the apparatus of war assembled by

37-38. *The frescoes of the "Macedonian" tomb of Lyson and Kallikles (between Veroia and Edessa) show details of Macedonian weaponry and armour. Left: the Macedonian shield bears the Macedonian star as an emblem; it is flanked by two swords in their scabbards (one of them with the hilt in the form of a bird), suspended by their belts. Below the shield are two helmets and a pair of greaves. Right: a large shield flanked by two trophies consisting of cuirass and helmet. Two swords, similar to the ones in the previous illustration, are hanging on the wall. c. 200 B.C.*

Philip, the most influential, no doubt, was his siege train. Quite early in his reign he besieged and took Amphipolis, Pydna and Potidaia in the space of little more than twelve months (357-6). He followed this up with successful sieges of Methone and of the important Pagasai and Olynthos, besides taking a number of small cities of Chalkidike and elsewhere. This was something new in Greek warfare, in which successful sieges had always been rare and usually very lengthy. Philip's early successes were due to his well-organized use of the equipment then known and available, including the early-type catapults (*gas-traphetai*), the composite laminated bows shooting large arrows or smaller stones, invented for Dionysios I at Syracuse nearly fifty years previously. Philip himself, however, employed an engineer who became famous, the Thessalian Polyeidos, who is thought now to have been the inventor of the much more powerful and effective torsion catapult, early examples of which may have been used at Philip's sieges of Perinthos and Byzantion. The torsion stone-thrower, however, does not appear before Alexander's sieges in Asia.[12] Perhaps, had they been present at Perinthos and Byzantion, they could have brought Philip the quicker results which he needed then, and the two cities would not have survived.

In spite of Perinthos and Byzantion, however, the whole effect of Philip's record as a besieger became undoubtedly one of his greatest assets. So too, perhaps, his whole image as a general dedicated to war and formidable in a way and on a scale that surpassed all his contemporaries and nearly all his predecessors. Yet, for us now, some aspects of his genius are hard, perhaps impossible, to recapture. As a tactician especially, he escapes us almost completely, merely because we have no surviving historian who described him at work. Our record of his battles is a travesty, which does not allow us to see precisely in what ways, for example, the arrival of the *sarissa* changed the tactics of the infantry phalanx.[13] Likewise we learn that for the cavalry it was Philip who introduced a wedge formation for the charge (a Thracian and Scythian style);[14] but we are never given even a few words describing how an attack by his cavalry was actually done. Yet in all three of his "decisive" battles (above) we can infer that it was the cavalry that played a major part in deciding them. For the victory over Bardylis in 358 and for the Crocus Plain victory of 352 this is implied by the quite exceptionally high number of the enemy reported as killed, even allowing for some possible or probable exaggeration (in 358, more than 7,000 out of 10,000 + 500, many of them in a long pursuit: in 352, more than 6,000 out of 20,000 + 500).[15] For Chaironeia the implications are more general and drawn from the whole course of the battle in so far as we can reconstruct it tentatively (below).

In the Bardylis battle Philip was faced by an enemy more or less equal in numbers, who formed themselves into a defensive square. He attacked with a concentration of his best troops on his right, all the cavalry, and his best infantry which he led himself. He ordered the cavalry to outflank the barbarians, we are told — an impossibility so long as the square was intact. Himself he led a frontal infantry attack, presumably in order to break the square at or near one of its angles, so opening to the cavalry the "flank and rear" which they did attack following their orders.[16] The concentration of force at one decisive point recalls Epameinondas with his Theban hoplites, but the co-ordination of the infantry and cavalry arms surpasses him, though there are signs that Epameinondas too had given thought to this.[17]

The victory over Bardylis looks like a rather distinguished and mature performance by a general still very young (24). In the Crocus Plain battle, only the fact of the Thessalian cavalry's distinguishing itself is given to us, but of the manner of it, nothing.[18] At Chaironeia we are told nothing directly of how Philip

39. Detail from a fresco in the tomb of Lyson and Kallikles. The helmet has cheek pieces and is decorated with bands, spirals and three coloured crests — a large one in the centre and two smaller ones above the ears.

40. *Weapons and armour from various parts of Macedonia. Bronze helmet of the 5th century* B.C. *from Lefkadia near Naoussa. The band to which the crest was attached can clearly be seen. The border around the edge is decorated with small circles resembling nails. Thessalonike Museum.*

41. *Neck-piece of a cuirass made of leather with attached bronze scales from grave B at Derveni. Second half of the 4th century* B.C. *Thessalonike, Archaeological Museum.*

42. *Bronze arrow-head, found at Olynthos. The cylindrical socket bears the inscription ΦΙΛΙΠΠΟ, "of Philip". Thessalonike, Archaeological Museum.*

43. *Bronze greaves from a grave at Derveni. 4th century* B.C. *Thessalonike, Archaeological Museum.*

44. *The head and butt of a "sarissa". The "sarissa", a very long spear with an iron point and butt, was the standard weapon of the Macedonian phalanx. Thessalonike, Archaeological Museum.*

45. *Iron sword from Veroia; the hilt is decorated with a miniature golden winged Victory. 370-350* B.C. *Thessalonike, Archaeological Museum.*

41

42

43

44

45

used his 2,000 cavalry. But the common assumption that Alexander's command on the left wing with which he attacked and overpowered the Theban Sacred Band consisted of the Companion cavalry or much of it, is no doubt correct. And Philip's own manoeuvre commanding Macedonian infantry on the right, which drew the Athenians forward from their original station, was clearly designed to make them break formation and lay themselves open to attack, and most effectively of course to attack by cavalry, though we are not told this.[19]

As we see here, Philip did not invariably lead the cavalry charge himself (like Alexander) on the great occasions, a self-denial which may have been for the sake of the closer control which he could keep while at the head of the infantry. Where was he, we wonder, that day in Thessaly when he was outwitted by Onomarchos luring him into a prepared arena overlooked by a semi-circle of hills on which Onomarchos had concealed catapults in position with stores of ammunition?[20] This was an error of over-confidence and, especially, a failure of reconnaissance, for which Philip and the Macedonians paid heavily. After this, the only serious defeat of his life, we find him for the only time having trouble with his men, who showed some reluctance to campaign again.[21] He was obliged to encourage them with talks, and to find a real winner of some kind before next spring and the new campaign. He found two as it happened, one of them no less a personage than Apollo, Apollo of Delphi. This was after all a "sacred" war, Onomarchos and his troops were temple-robbers; the god infallibly must aid those who aided him. The Macedonians, innocent of all knowledge of what this rather disreputable war was about in reality, were glad to be reminded of Apollo, and to accept Philip's issue of laurel-leaves to the army one fine morning next year as they awaited the enemy at the Crocus Plain. Philip's second "winner" for the occasion was his really huge force of cavalry by Greek standards, 3,000 no less, Thessalian and Macedonian combined; a concentration to which really there was no answer except to refuse battle on terrain which gave 'room and scope for 3,000 cavalry to act. But this time it was Onomarchos who was over-confident, to the great glory of the god, and of the Macedonians, and most of all their general.[22]

A soldier's general, then? There seems something of it in this story,[23] and in the story (an isolated one) of the soldiers' pay in arrears, when Philip disarmed their complaints by a piece of buffoonery in the palaistra where they had gathered.[24] (Philip enjoyed telling this anecdote himself, so he must have come out of it well). His great ally here, of course, was his great wealth: the soldiers knew that they would get their money, and this was much more than could be said of most employers of the time. The contemporary historian Theopompos, who resided at Pella for a time and whose History in 58 Books implies inherently some measure of compliment to the great man, once indulged his *culpandi cacoethes* by calling Philip "a soldier" ($\sigma\tau\rho\alpha\tau\iota\acute{\omega}\tau\eta\varsigma$), this for being so grossly extravagant with money and refusing to be bothered with proper accounts:[25] he meant, behaving like a soldier not a general, or a statesman, or a king. Theopompos may have had a point here, but this man of letters did not appreciate that on active service the capacity to behave at times like a soldier can add to the stature of a general. The other soldiers like it. There is also a tale of a terrific fight between Macedonians and Greeks in his army (Philip's life saved by the young Alexander);[26] which suggests that whatever went on among the soldiers Philip was more likely to be on the spot than aloof.

Especially in battle this was so, as his wounds testify: he was badly wounded four times, and perhaps often in a minor way.[27] It was not the practice of Macedonian kings in action to take special care for their own lives, important though these were. And Philip was ubiquitous in war, or nearly.[28] Though his mercenaries on detachment or in garrisons were commanded by a subordinate general or officer according to scale, whenever a Macedonian levy was called out it was most likely to be Philip

46. *Painting of a dead Macedonian warrior from a fresco in the Lefkadia tomb. He is wearing a short chiton, a himation, a cuirass and high-boots, and is holding his scabbard and a spear. End of the 4th century* B.C.

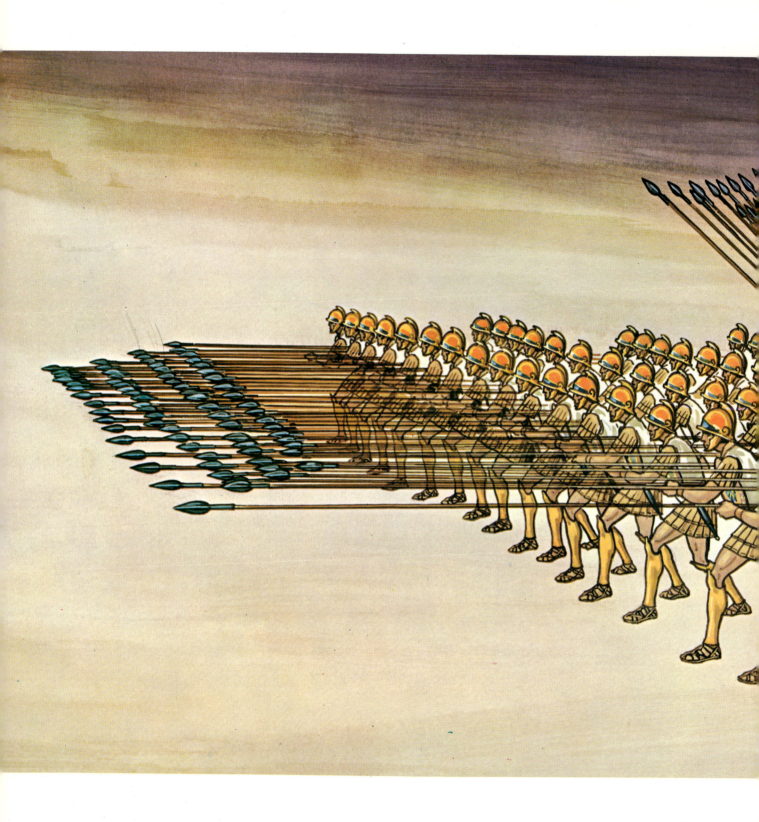

47. *A tentative reconstruction drawing of the Macedonian phalanx, one of the most decisive factors in Philip's military successes. It was a regular infantry formation, drawn up in ranks, each man armed with a "sarissa", the secondary weapon being a short sword. Protective armour consisted of a helmet, greaves and a small shield. During the attack, the hoplites of the first ranks held the "sarissa" with both hands extended horizontally before them, thus presenting the enemy with a dense wall of spear points. The rest held their sarissa upright. The formation looked like a mobile fortress and terrified the enemy.*

himself in command, and it looks as if he delegated very little in the military field unless two or more simultaneous commitments made it unavoidable. He is reported to have said himself that he had only found one general in his life, Parmenion:[29] part of a witticism, this, at the expense of the Athenians, but probably nearer to the truth than we might expect. Alexander inherited no shortage of commanders corresponding to modern brigadiers or major generals, but of full generals ready-made Parmenion was indeed the only one. Antipatros seems no more than a competent "stooge". And except for Antigonos Monophthalmos (as a top-ranking general a late developer) the great names of the Diadochoi are all nearer to Alexander's generation than to Philip's.

For the close-up picture of Philip as soldier and tactician, these few glimpses are all. Philip as a strategist, however, and as a "political general" is another matter. Here we are better placed to see something of the truth. Like Napoleon, but unlike most generals ancient or modern, he did not take the field with instructions from a government: to blockade A, to besiege B, to bring C to battle and destroy them. The political decisions and the grand strategy up to the highest levels, *whether* to do these things or to do certain other things instead, or to do nothing at all, in Macedonia lay with the King alone, taking only such advice as he himself thought fit. His arch-adversary Demosthenes, who spent his life trying to win and keep the ear of a *demos*, remarked on the

enviable contrast of Philip "master of all things public and secret; general, ruler and treasurer all in one": "he executed his own decisions, unpublicized in formal decrees, undiscussed in open council sessions, himself above criticism or impeachment by political enemies, responsible to none, but supreme lord and commander of absolutely everything".[30] The historian Diodoros in his brief obituary summary wrote that Philip owed his success just as much to his diplomacy and geniality as to his bravery in war, and that he himself was prouder of his brains as a general and his diplomatic contrivances than of his valour in battle.[31] Here the strategic and the diplomatic functions are put hand in hand; and included in the diplomatic of course was the use of his great wealth for political bribery and corruption, for which he became notorious.[32] And in reality, on a review of his reign from first to last, it is remarkable how the same conjunction is seen repeatedly, the two functions military and political appearing most often as alternatives.

Thus one of Philip's first acts on his accession (359) was to withdraw the garrison which his brother had thrown into Amphipolis to protect it from being recovered by Athens.[33] For Philip, in the desperate circumstances of his first year, peace with Athens, who supported a rival claimant of the throne, was a first priority. The "war for Amphipolis", as the Athenians learned to call it, started two years later when Philip was ready for it, and not before. Here, his preference for the diplomatic withdrawal, and the delayed timing of the military stroke (retaking Amphipolis), has been universally applauded. Less noticed is the skilful execution of his alliance with the Chalkidian League concluded very soon after (357).[34] The Chalkidians, recently enemies, and "natural" enemies by their position, isolated now when the Athenian alliance which they sought was denied, could be seen as a sitting target for a volatile young king who had won two major victories, as well as two minor ones, in his first two years. Philip, attracted into Thrace by the active mining area of

48. The Macedonian "Companion" cavalry, the "ἑταιρικὴ ἵππος", emerged as a major force in the middle of the 4th century, after Philip's military reforms. The painted grave stele in the illustration has a representation of a mounted warrior and his equipment: spear, cuirass and sword. Alexandria, Greco-Roman Museum.

49. A Macedonian horseman clashes with a foot-soldier. Note the animal skin used as a "saddle". Drawing based on a fresco (now destroyed) from "Kinch's tomb" near Naoussa.

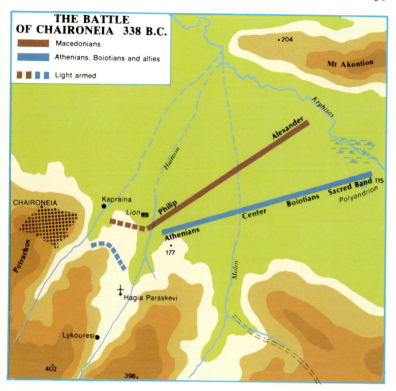

THE BATTLE OF CHAIRONEIA 338 B.C.

Macedonians
Athenians, Boiotians and allies
Light armed

50. The crushing defeat inflicted by Philip on the Athenians and Boiotians at Chaironeia afforded clear proof of his genius as a tactician, as well as the remarkable discipline, mobility and flexibility of the Macedonian army, achieved by continuous training. There is no account of the battle itself, and it is therefore, unfortunately, impossible to reconstruct it. It is generally thought probable, however, that the issue was decided by the tactical retreat of Philip, who was in charge of the right-wing of the Macedonian formation. His opponents fell into the trap and extended their line during the attack, thereby creating gaps which Philip exploited to isolate the more compact companies of the opposition and take them from the side — notably the famous "Sacred Band" of the Thebans.

Pangaion with its new town Krenides, needed to be sure of no trouble from the Chalkidians in his rear, and he could have been tempted to achieve this by intimidating them. Instead, he offered them his alliance, and on terms which made their acceptance really worth while. There were no battles with the Chalkidians for another eight years yet.

The strategy in detail of Philip's forays into Thrace (at times their chronology even) escapes us: they have no historian. But is the repetition itself of the Thracian wars aiming its own criticisms, perhaps, at a general who, in command of the Macedonian army with its newly-emerging superiority, enjoyed something like the advantages of 19th century European powers in their so-called "colonial" wars? The history of those same "colonial" wars supplies part of the answer here, most likely; for the one side their sole preoccupation and a matter of life and death in which they loved, and knew, every inch of the ground; for the other side, most often, a πάρεργον. Coastal Macedonia in the past had been a cockpit subject to incursions or visitations by Thessalians, by Boiotians, by Illyrians, by Paionians, by Athenians, by Chalkidians, by Odrysian and other Thracians, at the times when one or more of these were too strong. Now that the balance of strength had tilted decisively Macedonia's way, the cockpit was transformed into the ideal base for the king and the army with the advantage of interior lines. They could launch their attacks and change their targets easily and at will; but the targets were not enemies to be underrated. Nor should we underrate a constructive side to Philip's approach to these people. By the standards of that time he was not a notably savage or bloodthirsty commander, and it was only in the very last resort that he would elect to "make a solitude and call it peace."[35] Hence repeated Thracian wars. He hoped to live and go on living with these neighbouring kings, once they had recognised his hand and had consented to live yoked lightly but securely in his team. A Kersebleptes might kick against the pricks, once and again and finally once too often; but a Lyppeios in Paionia could settle down sensibly, prepared to wait and to go on waiting indefinitely, for something in Macedonia to go really desperately wrong.[36]

In Thrace, then, σιγά-σιγά, much of the time. And in Thessaly likewise, though naturally not for just the same reasons. These were Greeks, and rather old-fashioned ones, to whom a Herakleid, Temenid monarch with a passion for racehorses still meant something of consequence. In his early years of expansion Philip never entered Thessaly except by invitation, the Thessalian League being split by the defection of the tyrants of Pherai with their satellite cities and *perioikoi*.[37] By his skill in war and the allied arts, by his winning personality which carried him even into a Thessalian marriage (with Philinna of Larisa), and by his parties which were memorable even by Thessalian standards, he made more and more friends in Thessaly year by year, and then when the "crisis" came and his friends needed him in full force, he did not fail them (above, p. 66). True, he "led with his chin", and had to pick himself up and dust himself down; but at least he had "led", and he came back full of fight still, which goes to explain why the Thessalians on their side kept faith too, and supplied their cavalry which, added to the Macedonians, (and Apollo's wreaths of laurel), wiped out Onomarchos and much of his army. The tactics of the Crocus Plain battle were probably exemplary, if only we knew them; but only the diplomacy-cum-strategy-cum-diplomacy again of the previous five years and more could have produced the grand army on the set-piece battlefield to face the general who had defeated him once and thought he could do it again.

This victory — which gave its name Thessalonike to the daughter born of Philip's second Thessalian marriage, who later bestowed it when queen on the second city of modern Greece — led immediately to the most entertaining strategic decision of his life. Thermopylai was held by the Phokians, doubtless with a relatively small force of their mercenaries, and perhaps it was reinforced immediately now by another relatively small force of Athenian hoplites from the fleet, but there is no question that if the victorious army of the Crocus Plain had marched on it without delay, it would have been able to force the pass by a combination of circumvention and frontal assault, as Xerxes had done. But for weeks Philip

never even marched. A clear strategic error, by purely military standards? In political terms, however, he was gathering a prize too valuable to be ignored. By turning now on Pherai and its port of Pagasai, he reunited the Thessalians and received the prize itself, election by them as archon for life of the Thessalian League. For this, with all its far-reaching and permanent advantages, it was certainly right to let Thermopylai wait awhile.[38] And when after midsummer he did march, and found the pass held strongly by the Athenians and other allies of the Phokians, he weighed the risks and the probable casualties of an assault now, and he turned away.[39] One suspects that, as a military operation it was still not impossible to force the pass and following through into Phokis itself, force the Phokians to surrender Delphi. He could then be seen as the vindicator of Apollo and the defender of those states of central Greece, even the Boiotians, who had been unable to defend themselves. Yet if the price at Thermopylai was likely to be high, why should he hurry to pay it? It was the Boiotians, not he, who longed for the Sacred War which they had started, to be ended. To him, it really did not matter whether it ended this year, next year, or some other time. He judged the price too high, and turned away. Meanwhile Thermopylai could wait — for six years as it proved, when, the Phokians exhausted and the Athenians cajoled into a separate peace, it fell to him without a blow.

This well-known history illustrates some characteristics of Philip as a strategist that repeat themselves; an unusual capacity for patience and on occasion for accepting a reverse; a fine sense of priorities in which the foreground with its local immediacy and urgency is not allowed to predominate, but is seen in a true perspective within its frame of time and space; a preference for the political solution finally not a military one, the army playing its full part as a threat rather than a weapon of execution. So at Olynthos in 352 the reluctant ally is threatened but is not attacked.[40] So in the Olynthian War itself (349-8) the

51. The Thebans buried those of the Sacred Band that fell in the battle of Chaironeia in a communal grave (Polyandreion). It was enclosed by a perimeter wall on the north side of which a marble lion on a high pedestal (now restored) was erected.

52. The battlefield of Chaironeia, between Akontion and the northern slopes of Mt Thourion. The photograph shows the modern village of Chaironeia (on the site of the ancient city of that name) with the ruins of the ancient acropolis in the foreground.

51

Chalkidian League is crumbled in two campaigns in preference to one knock-out blow to the capital city itself.[41] Perinthos and Byzantion, both under siege by Philip at midwinter 340/39, a few weeks later are licking their wounds, but safe and no longer at war with him:[42] those sieges needed to be quick ones, and when he did not succeed quickly, Philip allowed no false pride to keep him there losing time, money, men, everything that mattered, when more important things, first in "Scythia", next in Greece, needed his presence more. Though Demosthenes once included excessive personal φιλοτιμία among his qualities, and perhaps rightly, there is no sign that he ever let it make a fool of him as a general.[43] In the final war in Greece his march on Elateia was a bolt from the blue, but he paused then and relied on diplomacy to undermine the organized resistance which did in fact follow; an error of judgment. Chaironeia itself was a decisive victory, but he did not pursue or follow up the defeated Greeks, for whom he had a political solution well short of humiliation and subjection in store. Even Sparta, isolated and at his mercy in 338, was let off with a military demonstration and allowed to survive as an interesting and useful political anomaly.[44]

But it was Athens most of all that evoked Philip's strategic and political interplay at the highest level. As we have seen, the "war for Amphipolis" (357-46) began when he was ready for it, not before. His own objective was to remove Athens as a threat to Macedonia by annexing her allies or dependencies in the area, potential bases for interference or domination in the future as they had often been in the past: Amphipolis, Pydna, Potidaia, Methone. In three years this was achieved. That the war continued for eight years longer was owing to the Athenian unwillingness to abandon their claims, and to Philip's threat to their possessions in the Thracian Chersonese as his conquests in Thrace spread eastwards. Strategically Philip held the whip hand, since the Athenian naval power could not damage him in any important way, and their land forces were quite in-

capable of challenging his own. Yet it was from this position of strength, and at the moment of an important victory ending the Olynthian War in 348, that Philip initiated the moves for peace with Athens which ended their war too.[45] In ancient Greek warfare it was hardly ever the victor who sought peace. Philip's motives here compel attention, and they are best explained by noticing his treatment of Athens in the years that follow. The Athenians became his allies in 346, and from this time he saw them in relation to a high strategy which embraced all Greece and the Aegean and beyond it. The Persian empire with its rich western provinces was by far the most attractive area for expansion now that he had fully realised his own great strength.

To overrun Persia by invasion based on the Aegean already had invited the ambitions of a Persian prince, Cyrus, and two Spartan commanders, Lysander and Agesilaos; with the lesson, as it seemed, that there was nothing to stop Greek-style infantry if supported by a numerous cavalry and the ancillary arms, and especially by a modern siege-train, from invading Asia and occupying a good slice of it permanently. At any time after the great Thessalian *coup* of 352 probably, and certainly long before the summer of 348 when he first proposed peace with Athens, Philip must have known that already his own powers greatly exceeded those of Cyrus and of the Spartans of the 390s. If a power so weak as Sparta could seriously think itself strong enough to attempt something permanent in Asia, he himself owed it to himself to follow their lead, profiting from their mistakes. To succeed, it was only necessary to make sure that none of the Greeks stabbed him in the back once he had quitted Europe for Asia, and that none of them offered themselves as bases for the Persian naval counter-attack against his rear, which could be expected with just as much certainty now as by Agesilaos when he had left home in 396. It was for this that the Athenian alliance was needed. The other Greeks did not need to help him, so long as they did not hinder him: they must be neutral at least.[46] But

Athens must help actively, give him the firm superiority in naval power that must never be in doubt once he had left Europe and committed himself seriously overseas.

It is this that seems to account best for Philip's preferential treatment of Athens in the later years of his reign, even in the terms of his separate peace treaty with her in 338.[47] Whether in the years of warfare with her earlier (in the late 350s) he ever contemplated a serious challenge to Athenian sea-power himself, must be left uncertain. The Macedonian resources in timber and in money made it possible, and though there was no native seafaring tradition, he could perhaps have relied for this on those Greeks of the north who came under his control, at Amphipolis and at Pagasai especially. But the squadrons of Philip which we do hear of in action seem to have been small and unable to offer battle with Athenian squadrons when they met.[48] It seems that he must have accepted deliberately this limit to his powers, with the corollary that his own naval strategy, when the war against Persia called for it, must be designed to be carried out with Athenian support.

The war against Persia is to be seen as the crown of his achievement as a general, even though he did not live to conduct it himself. The basis of power which he had built up in Macedonia itself (the army its τεκμήριον) and in Greece (the League of Corinth) was sufficient for the purpose. If he himself had led the invasion of Asia, he might well have been content with more limited objectives than Alexander's later, remembering that even a Herakleid, Temenid king, ("not being a bird") could not be in two places at once, and therefore had better set a limit to the territories he claimed to control. (Or would he have given Alexander a free hand as time went on, even to remotest Nephelokokkygistan?) Whether Philip was the best general of the fourth century B.C. before Alexander, is not quite easy to say; but he was certainly one of the best four (not one of whom survived him). Certainly, too, he was Epameinondas' best pupil. Though he never faced truly first-rate commanders in opposition, the missing chapter of his record as a tactician might still place him very high, if we had it, among the generals of all time. In the last resort, however, Philip could do no more than win, and keep on winning. His high standing as a general contributes its full share towards our estimate of him as a personality and a king.

PHILIP AND THE AMPHICTYONIC LEAGUE

The great plain of Thessaly, seemingly so distinct from Macedon, is not so distinct in fact, for there is easy enough access in three places, above all by the Volustana Pass by which the upland canton of Perrhaibia can be penetrated from Macedon and the middle valley of the Haliakmon is open to Thessaly. Given strong control in the one or the other, expansion north or south was inevitable. At the end of the fifth century king Archelaos, the most successful of Philip's predecessors, had controlled Perrhaibia and intervened in Larisa, taking hostages to guarantee its submission. In the first four decades of the fourth, the position was reversed. Philip's own father, Amyntas, had needed Thessalian help in the expulsion of Illyrians and seems to have been in a somewhat subordinate condition as a result. In his speech to the mutinous army in 324 Alexander spoke of the Macedonians "having been at one time scared to death of the Thessalians", and Jason of Pherai in the 370s was able to talk as if Macedonian resources were his for the taking.[1] The vulnerability of Macedon from the south was underlined in the 360s when the Theban chiefly responsible for the expansion of Theban influence into Thessaly, Pelopidas, was called in to arbitrate between the king and a pretender, events firmly fixed in Philip's mind, for part of the settlement was that he was taken to Thebes as a hostage.[2] So Philip knew well that if he did not dominate Thessaly, Thessaly would seek to dominate or unseat him, and one of his earliest acts was to move against Larisa. Whether he occupied this city is unclear, but it may be presumed that he established firm control over Perrhaibia. Macedon was safe.[3]

Defence came first and foremost, but the wealth and military resources of Thessaly must shortly have come to mind. In the fifth century the Thessalians had been, according to Isokrates,[4] the most prosperous of the Greeks, and their wealth was reflected in the large numbers of their cavalry, much sought after and much feared. In an expansive moment, Jason of Pherai could assert that Thessaly, when united, could produce six thousand horse and ten thousand hop-

lites. A more conservative estimate was three thousand horse, but, whatever the truth, in Greek terms their strength was very great, and Philip must have seen that Thessaly could make an immense difference to his military power.[5] In the army of Alexander their cavalry constantly played a vital part in his successes. In the period when Philip was still building up his military power, Thessaly must have seemed a most desirable acquisition.

Indeed in the ambitious plans of Jason of Pherai in the later 370s the possibilities of Thessaly were made plain. He was said to have had the resources necessary to maintain a mercenary army of six thousand, and while his control of the port of Pagasai no doubt enabled him to profit from all of Thessaly, since Pagasai was the only outlet for Thessalian exports, the revenues of the whole were considerable enough for Demosthenes in 349 to be able to declare that Philip depended on them for paying his own mercenaries.[6]

Until 353 Philip was preoccupied with matters nearer home, but in that year he embarked on his plans to bring all Thessaly under Macedonian domination. Political divisions gave him his opportunity. The long-standing rivalry of Larisa and Pharsalos had given way in the late fifth century before the rise of Pherai and the ambitions of its rulers to rule all Thessaly. A bloody battle in 404 was a presage of their intentions, which reached their peak, in the 370s, in the grandiose plans of Jason, who, having subordinated Pharsalos and then having got himself appointed to the somewhat mysterious office of *Tagos* (Commander of Thessaly), even planned to attack Persia.[7] He was murdered in 370, and his successors proved unequal to carrying through what he had begun. But somehow the office of *tagos* became hereditary to the rulers of Pherai, and their pretentions did not abate. Alexandros, in particular, provoked the Thessalians into seeking to defend themselves by forming a new federal constitution with an *Archon* (Ruler) at its head and by submitting to Theban suzerainty, and, although he was mur-

dered in 357 and his successors seemed less menacing, the mercenary army of Pherai was maintained and the opposition to Pherai needed support from outside. As Thebes became preoccupied with her own troubles in Central Greece, the way was open for Philip.[8]

In 353, summoned by the Thessalians to help defend them against Lykophron, the latest of the Pheraian tyrants, Philip marched south to a campaign of varied fortunes. Lykophron had summoned his allies, the Phokians. Philip defeated and expelled a small Phokian force, commanded by Phayllos, whereupon his brother, the master of Phokis, Onomarchos, came with his full army, and Philip, outnumbered and twice defeated (the only reverses he is ever recorded to have suffered) retired to Macedon, "like a ram" as he said "to butt the harder next time."[9] In 352 he returned, but no longer merely as an ally. The Thessalians in their federal assembly elected him *archon,* an office held for life, and armed with this new authority he set about the final destruction of the power of Pherai. Lykophron again summoned the army of Onomarchos and a great battle ensued, called in modern times the Battle of the Crocus Plain, which was effectively to determine the condition of Thessaly for a century and a half. Little is known of the battle save that it was on a plain near the sea, which only the western side of the Gulf of Pagasai seems to suit, an area remarked on by the geographer Strabo for its crocuses, and that it was utterly decisive. Over six thousand of the Phokian army, including Onomarchos himself, are said to have been killed, and over three thousand taken prisoner and slaughtered, the sort of defeat that Greek warfare had not previously known. Phokian influence in Thessaly was ended for ever. Philip then moved against Pherai, which surrendered. By mid 352 Philip was in effect master of all Thessaly.[10]

In theory, of course, Thessaly continued as an ally of Macedon and was later to be a member of the League of Corinth as part of autonomous Greece. The facts were quite otherwise. When their *archon,* the king of Macedon, bade, the Thessalians had no alternative to obedience. This gave Greek politicians like Demosthenes grounds for presuming that the Thessalians groaned under Philip's servitude, but it seems not to have been so. The Thessalians were willing partners in his plans as long as he took care to see that those plans did not offend their prejudices (and so his treatment of Phokis had to respect the ancient Thessalian hostility). For the rest, they were content. In 344 he carried through an administrative reform, whereby the tetrarchic organisation of Thessaly was restored. It led Demosthenes to presume that there would be great unrest, but he was quite wrong. Only briefly, after Alexander's death, during the Lamian war when it looked as if Macedon would not succeed in reducing the Greeks, did the Thessalians waver. The truth was that the landed barons of Thessaly found the values and life of the Macedonian court entirely congenial and the people of Thessaly either could not, or did not, dissent.[11]

The Battle of the Crocus Plain ended the struggle for Thessaly. It also marked the intervention of Philip in the Third Sacred War. The Phokians had occupied Delphi and "borrowed", as they claimed, the sacred treasures. Philip chose to regard them as sacrilegious, ordered his troops to wear into battle laurel wreaths, "and so, as if the god (Apollo) were the commander, went into battle; at the sight of the insignia of the god the Phokians, in terror from their awareness of their crimes, threw away their arms and fled...".[12] Philip had, in short, under the guise of piety taken sides in the ten-year war which was to

53. *The narrow vale of Tempe, between Mts. Olympus and Ossa, is one of the natural approaches to Thessaly from Macedonia. Through it flows the river Peneios. The Macedonian victory on the Crocus Plain in 352, when the forces of Pherai were crushed, allowed Philip to exercise decisive control over Thessaly. The Macedonians are said to have marched against the sacrilegious Phokians and their allies from Pherai wearing wreaths of laurel (the attribute of the Delphic God).*

end, as he foresaw it could, with his being securely established in Central Greece, and free to intervene wherever else he chose.

The war originated in Phokian resistance to Theban ambitions. Even before the death at Mantineia in 362 of Epameinondas, the architect and builder of the Theban hegemony, the Phokians, whose territory marched with Boiotia, had begun to chafe at Theban power. This was clearly intolerable to Thebes, and means were sought to deal with it. In itself Phokis was small and could easily be dealt with by the Boiotian army, but Phokis could seek help from Sparta, Athens and Pherai, and the position for Thebes was further complicated by the fact that Phokis was a member of the Delphic Amphictyony and, if Thebes did not respect her treaty with Phokis, she would herself be liable to reprisals from the whole Amphictyony. This ancient religious organisation of the peoples of Central Greece included the Dorians and the Ionians, represented in historical times by Sparta and Athens, and despite the membership of the Thessalians, whose ancient enmity with Phokis had been frequently renewed, Thebes had to make sure of the approval of a majority of the Amphictyons meeting at Delphi. She deemed her moment had come in autumn 357 when, with Athens preoccupied with war against her allies, Alexandros of Pherai assassinated and with a majority of Amphictyons known to support her, she had, on bogus grounds, secured that heavy fines were laid on both Sparta and Phokis. As could be expected, neither paid. So the fines were doubled in the spring of 356, and Phokis responded by occupying Delphi, erasing the offensive decrees, and announcing that she would take charge of Delphi and its affairs.[13]

From such petty bickering and mean Theban politics, the fatal war began. It got off to a wretched start. Greece was not interested in furthering Theban ambitions. Phokis fortified herself with alliances with Athens and Sparta, and it was not until autumn 355 that Thebes was able to get the Amphictyony formally to declare war on Phokis.[14] Even then, the only member to make any serious effort was Thessaly,[15] but it was the Thessalian interest that was decisive. For not only did it draw the Phokians into supporting the tyrants of Pherai but, also it meant that Philip, in supporting the Thessalians and from 352 as *archon,* had to play his part.

There was, however, one serious obstacle, *viz.* the geography of Thermopylai. In the fourth century it was still pretty much what it had been during the Persian invasion of 480, a narrow strip of land at the foot of steep hills, in places no more than a cart-track's width. If it was defended, it could not be forced, and if the mountainous path into Phokis itself was occupied, Phokis was impenetrable to Philip. In 352 after the Battle of the Crocus Plain, Philip spent some time on the affairs of Pherai, and then advanced the one hundred and forty kilometres to Thermopylai. Phokis was ready. The battle had destroyed her army and its leader, but not her will to resist. Her allies were summoned, and, although Sparta was too late to help, five thousand Athenians came by sea in time to confront Philip. He withdrew, having learned his lesson. Next time he would secure that passage was not denied him.[16]

For six years Philip left the war to take care of itself, while he consolidated his power in Thrace and Chalkidike. The Thebans fared badly. Three Boiotian cities were seized by the Phokians and Boiotian territory ravaged. Clearly help was needed, and Thebes appealed to Philip, who signified his continuing piety by sending a few troops. More was impossible until a way could be found of penetrating Thermopylai.[17]

He found it in Phokian exhaustion. The succes-

54. The conquest of Thessaly was of vital importance to Macedonia. It brought Philip the wealth and military forces of that area (mainly cavalry) and furthered his designs in Southern Greece. The illustration shows a grave stele from Pelinna depicting a Thessalian horseman wearing a chiton, chlamys and helmet. Mid 4th century B.C. Paris, Louvre.

sive war leaders had maintained the large mercenary army they needed to confront Thebes by dipping ever more deeply into the treasury at Delphi. Disputes arose about how the money was being used, and for a period the last leader, Phalaikos, was removed from office and inquiries begun. But the Phokians needed the mercenaries and the mercenaries needed their pay, and by early 346 Phalaikos was restored to power, albeit at a loss how to use it.[18]

It is not attested but must be presumed that Phalaikos too made overtures to Philip. Philip prepared to march south with the full Macedonian army and the Thessalians, and the projected campaign was known of in Greece well in advance. So he must have been confident that Phalaikos would not oppose his entry into Phokis. As we shall see, those in Phokis most deserving of severe treatment were very leniently treated by Philip. There must have been a secret agreement between the two rulers to the effect that, whatever settlement was made of the Sacred War, Phalaikos and his mercenaries would not be brought to book for their actions. Consistently with this, when the Athenians and the Spartans offered to share in the defence, Phalaikos rebuffed them both. Aischines attributed this to blindness. An exchange of winks with Philip is a much more likely explanation.[19]

As will be described in a later chapter, the attitude of Phokis forced Athens to seek for peace, but the next scene of importance for the settlement of the Sacred War was the congress of Greeks in Pella in the early summer of 346. The Athenians arrived simply to administer to Philip and his allies the oaths of allegiance to the newly-made Peace of Philo-

55. General view of the Sanctuary at Delphi. The seizure of the oracle of Apollo by the Phokians and their subsequent "borrowing" of the treasures of the God to meet the needs of the Third Sacred War provoked an outcry amongst the Greeks. Philip, intervening, was able to appear as the "pious" avenger of the God, to advance his political aims and increase his prestige in the eyes of the Greeks.

krates. They found there Thebans, Spartans, Phokians, Thessalians, and others, almost "from the whole of Greece," and it is clear that the congress had been called by Philip to settle the Sacred War.[20]

Philip's mastery of diplomacy was amply displayed. There were public sessions, it would seem, but also private sessions, in which he saw in turn the parties to the dispute and did everything that he could to make the Phokians think that there would be a peaceful solution, not a military intervention. Aischines the Athenian argued that only the guilty persons amongst the Phokians should be punished, not the whole state, and pleaded for a settlement which would punish also Thebes for her alleged wrong-doing. Philip kept his own counsel, but encouraged both sides to hope, and "told them not to prepare for war nor to fear there would be war."[21]

The expedition set off southwards, allegedly first to finish off the siege of Halos which lay at the southern end of the Crocus Plain. The various embassies accompanied him, the Phokians with no idea of what would shortly befall them. Just north of the Crocus Plain in Pherai, Philip finally swore to observe the Peace of Philokrates[22] and, as will be described later, the Athenian embassy was free to hurry home with the grim news that Philip's army was dangerously near Thermopylai. They found that the opponents of Phalaikos in Phokis had at last perceived where his policy must lead them and had appealed to Athens to come and prevent the Macedonians passing Thermopylai. But it was all too late. Before Athens could act, the news came that Philip was in control of Thermopylai.[23] There can be only one explanation of how he had got there. He must have split his army; half marched towards Halos with the unwitting ambassadors in train; half moved directly south, through Lamia and straight to Thermopylai. In 352 Philip had had to turn back. In 346, by skilful diplomacy, he had ensured that there was no one to resist. Nothing shows better his mastery of politics and strategy than the penetration of Thermopylai in 346.

Through Thermopylai, with his large army Philip confronted Phalaikos and his mercenaries. That is, the avenger of sacrilege, who six years earlier had sent his troops into battle wreathed in laurel, the symbol of Apollo, confronted the heir to the power and the guilt of those who had robbed Apollo's temple, himself guilty and at the head of those who had profited. The Thebans were coming from the south. The guilty men could have been utterly destroyed. No battle, however, took place. Phalaikos and his mercenaries were allowed safe conduct to where they wished. It was the clearest proof that there had been collusion.[24]

Philip then turned to the problem of the Phokians themselves who, even if they did have, as Demosthenes claimed, ten thousand hoplites and one thousand cavalry, were well outnumbered and wholly at his mercy. From the outset of the campaign Philip must have been doubly clear that Phokis must suffer for its wrongs. First, for his larger designs he needed Thessalian help and he could not afford unrest in Thessaly itself. The price was abundantly plain; the Thessalians were "from olden times enemies of the Phokians" and would be content with nothing less than harsh treatment for Phokis. Secondly, if he was to gain the goodwill of the Greeks, Phokis must be punished. In itself the occupation of Delphi did not necessarily earn the disapproval of pious Greeks, but, when the Phokians began to borrow from the temple treasures on such a scale that the money was hardly ever likely to be restored, it became plain temple-robbery, the penalty for which was at Athens death and probably so generally. Indeed when later it came to debate in the Amphictyonic Council, the Phokians' neighbours, the Oitaians, actually proposed that all male Phokians of military age should be thrown over a cliff, and one fourth century writer found divine retribution for Athens and Sparta, which had been contaminated by alliance with the law-breakers, in their defeats at the hands of Antipatros long afterwards, just as he saw divine favour in the rise of Philip who had piously

56. *One of the methods employed by Philip to impose his authority in Southern Greece was to secure control of the Amphictyonic Council. In 336 after the Macedonian victory at Chaironeia, the members of the council issued a new coin, one side of which showed Apollo, seated on the Omphalos with his lyre and a laurel branch, and a tripod in front of him. The inscription is ΑΜΦΙΚΤΙΟ. Athens, Numismatic Museum.*

56

gone to the help of the oracle. There could be no question, therefore, that Philip had to deal severely with Phokis if he was to win the favour of pious Greeks.[25]

Philip showed himself a true statesman. He consulted the Boiotians and Thessalians whose advice was doubtless for extreme measures. Philip's decision was to assemble the full Amphictyonic Council and in theory to let it decide, though in fact his influence could be widely felt and used to decisive effect.[26] In this way the extreme course demanded by the Oitaians was avoided. Inevitably, the Phokians were deprived of any share in the control of the temple or any further part in the Amphictyonic Council, and those in exile who had had any part in the temple-robbery were pronounced accursed; in similar mood, the Phokians were forbidden to arm themselves until the plundered money had been repaid (which would at the rate first proposed have taken nearly one hundred and seventy years). All the cities of the Phokians were to be destroyed and their populations dispersed into hamlets of no more than fifty families each, and no less than two kilometres apart. The result was no doubt "a dreadful and pitiful sight", as Demosthenes declared it in 343, but it was much less awful than what the Phokians could have expected. Before any of these decisions were taken, Philip had himself and his descendants declared members of the Amphictyony and accorded the two votes previously held by the Phokians, and it is perhaps not too much to suppose that both formally in the Council and informally behind the scenes Philip's influence was for moderation. He had set out to compose the quarrelling parties, not to destroy them. He had gained the good-will of the Greeks. The slaughter of the Phokians might in retrospect have been held against him.[27]

Demosthenes constantly asserted that Philip had strengthened the power of Thebes in that he had not broken up the Boiotian state, of which Thebes was the largest part and hence master. The charge is hollow. In the Common Peaces of the 360s the Greeks in congress had recognised the legitimacy of the Boiotian federal constitution, and to have broken it up in 346 would have been to renew discord in Central Greece. The same prudence of Philip's guiding hand was shown here by the Amphictyonic Council as in the treatment of Phokis' two partners, Athens and Sparta. Despite earlier threats of reprisal, neither state suffered any diminution of status in the Amphictyony, and there was no attempt at fining. At all points the settlement was prudent and moderate. Athens was even pressed to share in the deliberations. She declined and was invited to assent to what had been decided, an invitation which perhaps she could not refuse. But her status was undiminished.[28]

At the autumn festival of 346, Philip presided over the games. Did he think that in a sense he also presided over Greece, that the Delphic Amphictyony would serve as an instrument for controlling Greek affairs? When Athens was invited to assent to the settlement decreed by the Amphictyonic Council, Demosthenes in his oration *On the Peace* argued that to decline to do so could bring on Athens war against the Amphictyony with Philip at its head. This may have been exaggerated, but it may well reflect the view that Philip took of his new position. The dispositions of the Amphictyons were aimed, in the view of one fourth century historian, "at Common Peace and Concord amongst the Greeks". If Philip had felt that more was necessary, he would have secured it. Instead, after the autumn festival he returned to Macedon, to prepare, according to the same historian, for war against Persia, as if his work in Greece was done.[29]

Philip's work in Greece was only done if the Peace of Philokrates with Athens endured. But, as will be discussed in a later chapter, the war-party at Athens was resolved that it should not endure, and it became clear to Philip that he would have to intervene again. In later summer 340 he declared war, and the only area in which the conflict could be resolved was in Greece itself. He might regret this but had no reason to fear. He still held Thermopylai, and so could enter Greece whenever he chose. But in early 339 the Thebans surprised the garrison of one of the towns in the pass and Philip faced anew the problem of how to get at his enemy.[30]

It has been held that Philip's control of the Amphictyony enabled him to return to Greece. The president of the Amphictyonic Council throughout this period was the Thessalian Kottyphos, who it may be presumed was the man whom the *archon* of Thessaly, Philip, wished to preside. In the course of 340/39 a petty wrangle developed over the working of "sacred" land by the Lokrians of Amphissa, and in early summer 339 the Amphictyonic Council declared war against them and appointed Kottyphos to command. The campaign was ill-supported, and at the autumn festival Philip was formally summoned to conduct the war.[31] It is claimed that all this was contrived by Philip's man to give Philip an excuse for coming into Greece. The claim is absurd. Philip needed no excuse. He was at war with Athens and would come in his own good time, whatever the Amphictyonic Council did or did not vote. Only if the result of the alleged machinations had been that the Amphictyons declared war on Athens, could it have been suspected that Kottyphos' purpose was to gather support for Philip in his war. But no such declaration was made. The petty Amphissan War was a side-show and was dealt with by Philip while he sought by diplomacy to avoid the final conflict with Athens at Chaironeia.

Control of the Amphictyony had helped in a quite different sense. The severe terms inflicted on Phokis in 346 appear to have been modified. As early as 344 there were rumours that Philip intended to re-establish Elateia, the capital city of Phokis. By 339 it had been restored; when exactly is not known. But no Amphictyonic decree supervened to insist on what had been decided in 346. Philip had decided that Phokis should be to some degree restored. After 343 the garrison installed by Philip is not heard of again. The compliance of the Amphictyons must have been secured.[32]

The policy bore fruit. What enabled Philip to come into Greece in 339 was not the appointment of Philip to the command against Amphissa. That did nothing to secure his entry into Greece. The decisive thing was the attitude of Phokis. The Thebans could bar the way through Thermopylai. The Phokians welcomed him coming into Phokis by the mountain route. Once in, he was able to build up his army and his supplies and prepare to deal with Athens, and with anyone else who opposed him, by diplomacy or battle.

PHILIP AND MACEDONIA'S NORTHERN NEIGHBORS

Historians of classical antiquity often cite an old adage that one of the earliest and most enduring contributions of Macedonia to Hellenic civilisation was her role as a great shield against a more northern barbaric world, for only twice were the cities of Greece to the south forced to endure barbarian invasions. This statement supports another common observation, that Macedonia was one of the great march states of history. Situated on the edge of Balkan civilisation, it was forced repeatedly to repel barbarian incursions. The long experience hardened the populace to military service and its incumbent hardships — eventually helping to produce the military machine for which that nation was justifiably famous.

The survival of Macedonia, pressured by barbarians, let alone by the military forces of more advanced Greek *poleis* to the south, was not always obvious. At the accession of Philip II in 359 most observers, barbarian or Hellenic, would have doubted her chances. The Illyrians to the west of the state had won a conclusive victory against Perdikkas III, Philip's brother, killing the king and 4,000 Macedonians in battle. The loyalty of Upper Macedonia to the Argead monarchy was seriously shaken, and it was widely believed that Bardylis, the Illyrian chieftain, was consolidating his forces for further conquests. An attack on Macedonian possessions by the Paionians to the north under their chieftain Agis seemed imminent. The Thracians to the east under their national king Kotys could well be expected to take advantage of the national emergency also.

Frontier problems had both an historical and a geographical aspect for any Macedonian king. Historically, from the earliest days Illyrian raids were a major problem. The Illyrians, a separate Indo-European people, inhabited the basins and mountains in the high lake country of the central Pindos spine of the southern Balkans westward to the Adriatic coast and northward to the Dinaric Alps and the area of modern Dalmatia. They were simply a congerie of tribes mostly still in a war and raiding society. From

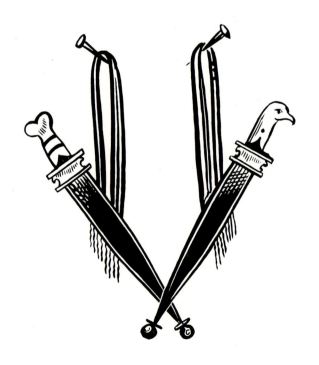

time to time "national" leaders would emerge in the sense that one individual's success in leading his own tribe or folk in raiding caused other tribes to attach themselves to him. Thus, the power of chieftains such as Bardylis was ephemeral and depended solely on their continued success. Once defeated, their conglomerate power vanished to await the proven abilities of some future successor. No sustained peace was possible; for no true state or states existed within Illyria. Macedonian kings simply had to hold their border tightly against continued attempts to wrest the points of access along it.

The very earliest records of Macedonian history suggest frontier problems with Illyria, even though the early Argead domain could not have extended beyond the Bermion range. Thucydides tells us that Perdikkas II in the fifth century could not control western Macedonia because of local dynasts and the fear of Illyrian incursions. In the early fourth century Amyntas III, father of Philip, was forced out of the country once and perhaps twice by Illyrian raiding. The situation deteriorated to where Amyntas had to pay tribute and send Philip as a boy to the Illyrians as a hostage. This episode, followed by the defeat and death of Philip's brother Perdikkas III in 359, surely attests the gravity of the Illyrian problem. Down to Philip's reign Macedonian policy consisted of paying money and giving hostages. As serious a dilemma as the Illyrian frontier posed, it was still a specifically Macedonian problem not well perceived by the general Greek world.

The Paionians to the north and Thracians to the east caused further concern. The Paionians, located along the Axios river at its confluence with the Erigon (Cerna), were not numerous enough to be a threat by themselves to Macedonia. Nevertheless, their strategic position and that of their shadowy neighbors, the Agrianians, along two major invasion routes made their control mandatory. Thrace was a very large area noted for its resources in metals and men. The Thracians, a separate Indo-European people, had had some of their tribes driven from the Macedonian plain by the Macedonians themselves. Like the Illyrians in the fifth century they, too, had invaded Macedonia. The Thracian threat was very great, if only because of the potentially enormous armies a domineering king could muster. Fortunately for Macedonia, the Thracians generally fought with each other or with the Greek colonies and their supporters along their coasts (Aegean and Black Seas). Before Philip, Macedonian kings had tried to maintain a frontier along the Strymon against the Thracians but were really not successful.

The geographical aspect was as problematic as the historical. The heartland of the Argead monarchy was the Macedonian plain. To the west the plain was circled by the first natural barrier, the Bermion mountain range. Beyond it were further valleys and mountain ridges, inhabited by first the Makednic peoples, and eventually by the Illyrians. Macedonia, like a proverbial onion, was surrounded by successive rings of mountains. A strong king would wish to control as many rings as possible to attain a defense in depth. Thus, achieving a strong defensive perimeter meant dominating the successive mountain ridges and their passes. The Bermion range is pierced by three passes: the two above Beroia and Naoussa and, most critically, the pass above Edessa. These passes afford access to Eordia (the basin of Lake Bokeritis). The ridge beyond this basin is breeched by the pass of the Kirli Dirven (near Klidi) which gives access to the large plain area of the Prilep-Monastir-Florina gap (ancient Deuriopos, Pelagonia, and Lynkos). Although this gap abuts the high Peristeri range, again, control of the passes is critical. To the south there is easy access to the other Makednic areas of Elimeia and Orestis (via the Kleisoura pass to the plain of Kastoria). But, due west and to the north lies the more open country of Lakes Prespa and Ochrid (Lychnidos), inhabited in antiquity by at least a part Makednic, but more nearly Illyriote, population. Before Philip, control of the narrows of the Erigon leading to Styberra and Pelagonia, and the Peristeri passes (Diavat, Pisoderi,

Vatochori) must have been critical. The failure of Perdikkas III in this area clearly demonstrated a need for still greater depth in the ring defense system. To achieve control meant confronting the recently victorious Illyrians again.

Paionia lay astride the age old Axios-Morava invasion route (via the Kačanick gap). Its capital Stoboi was quite exposed in the open valley at the confluence of the Erigon and Axios. The mountain pass defense system of western Macedonia could not apply here because Makednic cantons (Pelagonia) could be penetrated via the Erigon. Lower Macedonia had some protection via the defile of Demir Kapu, but this too could be outflanked. An effective defense would have to be obtained by using Paionia as a buffer state. This, of course, implied that Macedonia would draw Paionia into her orbit and in the long run keep the Paionians just strong enough to accomplish Macedonia's purpose. In general, the Paionians on the Axios between Stoboi and Skopje would control access to the pass of Tranupara (Kratovo) leading to the upper Strymon basin. Beyond that the mysterious Agrianians, allied more informally, would also help block the natural routes toward Sofia in what is now Bulgaria.

The incorporation and defense of Thrace posed still further geographical problems. The area was a large one — by ancient routing nearly 700 kilometers from Pella east to Perinthos on the Sea of Marmara. The ridge of the Rhodope range in the south curves eastward following the northern Aegean coastline and is pierced by numerous passes and rivers (Strymon, Nestos, Hebros). Inland the Haimos (Balkan) range further north parallels the Rhodope and the Danube River beyond and is characterized by similarly rugged features. These ranges are blocked just east of the Strymon River by the north-south line of the Rila and Pirin Planina. Thus, the valley between the ranges is difficult of access from Macedonia. This valley, drained by the Hebros (Maritsa) River, opens naturally to the east towards the Black Sea and the eastern Aegean. From the Macedonian point of view

the valuable areas were the river basins and plain areas such as Daton (Drama) along the north Aegean. Again, as in western Macedonia, to hold these areas meant controlling the appropriate passes above or beyond them. Unfortunately, the topography of these highlands was even more irregular. Though the main mountain systems (Rhodope, Haimos) ran east-west, the basins and plains were also divided by steep north-south ridges.

Logically, any Macedonian advance into Thrace would follow the already established ring defense system. The first invasions would be eastward into the basins and plains along the Aegean Sea. This area would be defended by controlling the appropriate passes through the Rhodope range. In time, the valley (Hebros) between the Rhodope and Haimos ranges, the Haimos ridge itself, and finally the Danube beyond would be added systematically to the widening perimeter of defense.

As we examine Philip's campaigns in these border areas, we shall see that history and geography were combined expertly with military force and political settlement to achieve a new frontier policy — a policy of prime importance to Macedonia, but hardly of note to Philip's critics far to the south.

At the time of the death of Philip's brother Perdikkas III on the Illyrian frontier in 359, Macedonia was not only threatened by the barbarian Illyrians, Thracians and Paionians, but also with murmurs from the Chalkidic League and outright intervention from Athens. Clearly, the new ruler needed time to organize. The Paionians and Thracians were soon mollified, Athens and the Chalkidic League brought to agreements. Yet, it is obvious that the Illyrian threat was the most serious due to the defeat and death of Perdikkas. The sources tell us that Upper Macedonia was "slave to the Illyrians" and their leader Bardylis. Philip did not face the Illyrians until the next year (358). This has caused speculation as to why the Illyrians did not press their victory. Some have thought that Philip made a temporary treaty with the Illyrians, but there is no evidence for such a thing. It is more likely that, given the amorphous nature of the Illyrian alliance, Bardylis was more interested in consolidating his gains than pressing further for the moment.

The ethnic origins of Bardylis himself are a topic of much debate. Some have thought he was a chieftain of the tribe of the Taulantinoi; others, more recently, have insisted he was the head of the Dardanians. Yet, the former group had lived along the Adriatic littoral (on the Albanian Myzequeja) and had never threatened the Macedonian frontier. The Dardanians did become fierce enemies of Macedonia during the Antigonid period, but no source suggests them as a national enemy this early. Rather, considering that Bardylis could put 10,000 troops into the field and that this figure is only to be matched by later Illyrian kings who enjoyed the support of many tribes, it is quite likely that Bardylis' real power came from a multi-tribal alliance rather than a specific ethnic identification. One source claims he was a member of the obscure tribe of the Hylloi from Dalmatia. Another says that although of humble origins, he rose to power because of his reputation as a raider. Whatever his origins, when Philip marched against him in 358 with the troops of Lower Macedonia, Bardylis was sufficiently confident because of his previous victory to propose a peace treaty. Philip could not accept this offer. Strategically it would have left Bardylis in control of the important passes. Upper Macedonia would naturally fall into his sphere of influence, if it had not done so already. Lower Macedonia would have to return to the old

57

57. The Paionians, who inhabited the area around the middle and upper Axios river, constituted a serious threat to the northern border of Macedonia, which Philip countered sometimes by diplomacy and sometimes by military campaigns. The illustration shows a silver coin of the Paionians with a horseman. Athens, Numismatic Museum.

58

58. Silver coin of the Paionian king Patraos. Athens, Numismatic Museum.

system of paying tribute to sustain itself. Philip needed a clear victory to re-establish the monarchy.

The battle with Bardylis took place west of Herakleia in Lynkos (perhaps near the later site of Nikaia, a way-station on the Egnatian Way and close to the critical Diavat pass through the Peristeri range). We are told that 7,000 of the 10,000 Illyrians perished and the remainder were pursued by Philip's cavalry. Bardylis, reportedly ninety years old at the time, is heard of no more. However, Philip then married an Illyrian princess, Audata, who took the Macedonian name Eurydike. Philip's first marriage probably was to ensure an arrangement with Bardylis or his successor.

Despite the crushing defeat, some Illyrians still had hopes of disposing of the new warrior "upstart" from Pella. In 357 Grabos, another Illyrian chieftain, (perhaps from the tribe of the Grabaioi or the Taulantinoi) attempted an alliance with the Chalkidic League. When that failed to come to fruition, Grabos, Lyppeios the Paionian, and Ketriporis the Thracian allied themselves with Athens (summer 356) in hopes of confining Philip's growing power. Philip decided to deal with the allies individually. Parmenion was given the task of defeating Grabos, which he accomplished in August of 356. Philip heard the news of the victory over Grabos, of his victory at the Olympic games, and of the birth of Alexander all on the same day.

Parmenion was clearly an important figure from one of the Upper Makednic cantons, quite likely Pelagonia. His victory over Grabos was significant even beyond this. Parmenion's campaign demonstrated that Upper Macedonian princes were now firmly committed to the Argead monarchy. Considering the importance of the Upper Macedonian tribal contingents to the later armies of Philip and especially Alexander, it is all the more obvious why Philip took the Illyrian threat so seriously. His response was not chosen simply to establish a satisfactory frontier against the Illyrians; but in reality to attempt to force unity on the Makedonians them-

selves. Philip had no further difficulties with the up-country princes. His Illyrian wars and Parmenion's victory had seen to that.

In the years after 349 Demosthenes and then Isokrates allude to Philip's engaging in severe fighting and a general reordering of affairs within Illyria. It is difficult to say exactly when he did so, but it parallels his general reorganization of frontiers in Thrace and Paionia as well. Philip campaigned in Thrace in 352/351 and it is likely that Illyria felt his weight in 351/350. Demosthenes charged Philip with a ruthless transport of populations. Isokrates, his ally, argues that Philip pacified the region and made it tribute-paying. From these statements it appears that Philip had determined on a particular frontier policy which involved moving peoples about to achieve it.

Recent discoveries in southern Yugoslavia and Albania have given us a better idea of just where his new border lay. One must also keep in mind that his authority extended much farther than Macedonia proper. To widen his defensive base, Philip extended his immediate frontier around the Petrina range and its passes. Presumably the new line would run from Mount Golenitsa above Pelagonia southwestward across the Erigon narrows to Mount Plakenska and the northern shore of Lake Ochrid. The critical defense points here are the passes along the Erigon to Pelagonia and the Pylon pass across the Petrina range. From there the boundary extended south along the eastern shore of Lake Ochrid and then along the peaks of the Petrina range south of Ochrid and west of Lake Prespa. At that point the frontier turned east around the southern tip of Mikra Prespa on to the entrance of the Vatochori pass and south past the pass leading to Mesopotamia. Thus, he clearly protected Pelagonia and Lynkos against further incursions by enlarging the frontier. Philip did not stop here.

Forts and city garrisons were positioned ahead of the frontier itself to dominate the lake country, especially the communication routes. We find evidence of Philip's military construction at sites dominating access to the Black Drin valley, the Wolf's pass above Lin (Claudanon) and the Tsangon pass on the Devoll. There were likely many others. He transported numbers of Macedonians to the area and forced the Illyrians westward. This emigration was not an attempt simply to create an ethnically acceptable population, but also to introduce an agricultural and fishing economy into the lake country. Clearly, he wished a buffer zone along the Albanian mountains to add to his margin of defense. Nor was he content as yet.

Philip had allied with Arybbas of Molossis in 357 to gain Epeirotic cooperation against the Illyrians. Then, in 350, Philip invaded Epeiros and brought back his young brother-in-law Alexandros to Pella for education and forced Arybbas to accept a lesser position as regent. Finally in 342 Philip forced Arybbas out of Epeiros and installed Alexandros on the Molossian throne in Epeiros. Of course, there were many reasons for Philip's decision to dominate the Epeirotic confederacy, but one of them had to be that Epeiros would furnish a secure southern frontier line. Thus, he could be assured of a solid line of security from northern Pelagonia on to the Ionian seaboard.

The range of Philip's eventual sphere of influence in the central Balkans is shown in two wars against distant leaders. The first was in 345 against an Illyrian, Pleuratos. Pleuratos was a common name among the rulers of the Illyrian Ardiaioi along the Dalmatian coast and the Scutari (Skodra) region. The second war was waged in 337 against a Pleurias. The name Pleurias is perhaps attested among the Dardanoi or Autariatai on the upper White Drin. The battlegrounds of these wars are not known, so that Philip may not have fought in the homelands of these peoples, but rather in the high lake country to prevent their access to his new buffer zone. Indeed, when Isokrates remarked in 346 that Philip was master of all the Illyrians except those who lived along the Adriatic, he may have meant that Philip dominated all the Illyrian tribes of the central Balkans. He probably made them tribute paying and

subject to recruitment for auxiliaries. There do not seem to have been Macedonian governors or local interference beyond his frontiers, but he did dominate the superior routes of communication with fortified positions and garrisons. Indeed, military domination of the lake country gives any serious government offensive power across the peninsula as far as the Adriatic. By his actions Philip made Macedonia safe from western attack. He was the first king in her history to do so, and his policies set the precedent for succeeding Macedonian rulers.

Scholars are indefinite concerning the ethnic origins of the Paionians and their northeastern neighbors the Agrianians. The Paionians seem to have had considerable Thracian and Illyriote stock with Hellenic elements among them as well. At the accession of Philip the Paionians, under a single leader Agis, began pressing down the Axios river in hopes of finding more fertile territory. No significant threat in themselves, they were simply one additional problem of the year 359. At first, Philip persuaded the Paionians to retire by bribing them. Within the year Agis died and Philip used the occasion to mount a swift campaign against them. The defeated Paionians were forced to accept allegiance to Philip, to maintain the frontiers, and to offer military service when required.

In 356 Agis' successor Lyppeios did join with Grabos and Ketriporis the Thracian in an alliance with Athens against Philip, but Athens did nothing. Grabos' defeat broke up the alliance. Presumably Lyppeios returned to Philip's system. However, following Philip's reverses in Thrace (353), he apparently passed through Paionia in 352 on route to Pella to shore up his defenses. He had no further troubles here.

Little is known about the Agrianians to the east of the Axios and above the upper Strymon basin. They could have become allied to Philip as early as 352 or even before. We hear of no formal campaigns. However, considering Philip's interest in the Hebros river basin in 342/341 the routes via Agrianian territory would be of prime importance and the allegiance of the area long since assured. Further, on his return from the Danube in 339 Philip encountered no resistance after crossing the Haimos (Balkan) mountains. Surely the Agrianians were part of the frontier alliance system.

Of greater difficulty is a description of Philip's Thracian policies. Campaigning in Thrace occupied most of his career. Traditionally Macedonia had reached only as far as the Strymon, thereby incorporating Thracian tribes between the Axios and Strymon rivers. The area provided some buffer for Macedonia, but still left three major routes of access: the pass of Rentina in the south; the route via the Kumli, Dov Tepe pass, and Lake Doiran to the Axios; and, the Strumitsa route. The first could easily be blocked, the latter two had been used by invaders before.

The activities of the Thracian kings were a constant worry. In the first year of his reign Philip managed to forge a treaty with the king of Thrace Kotys (or his immediate successor Berisades), but by 356 coastal Thrace had broken up into three kingdoms; Ketriporis in the west (Strymon-Nestos), Amadokos in the center (Nestos-Hebros), and Kersebleptes in the east (Hebros-Black Sea coast). The internal squabbling caused by this division initially alleviated the pressure on Philip. Subsequently, however, as each king sought Macedonian or Athenian support for his cause, Philip was re-involved continually.

When Philip seized Amphipolis on the lower Strymon (357) Ketriporis began attacks on Greek towns in the plain of Daton (Drama). One of these towns, Krenides, appealed to Philip for aid. His response was to put an end to Thracian incursions, annex the area, and refound Krenides as Philippi. This town became a model royal colony and marks a solid step in stretching Macedonia from the Strymon to the Nestos (Mesta). Ketriporis reacted the following year by joining the brief alliance between Grabos, Lyppeios and Athens. More importantly the success in taking Krenides encouraged Philip to continue an-

nexing the Greek towns along the coast, especially those allied with Athens. In 355 and 354 Neapolis (Kavala), Abdera and Maroneia fell. Though the latter two were in the territory of Amadokos, Philip avoided going inland against him. He also made a pact with Kersebleptes, king of eastern Thrace.

While the Phokians were defeating Philip in Thessaly in 353, the Athenian commander Chares forced Kersebleptes to renounce the alliance with Philip and join Athens. Curiously enough this threw Ketriporis and Amadokos into Philip's camp. Philip now acted decisively. In 352 and 351 Philip pressed

beyond the Hebros to Heraion near Perinthos on the Sea of Marmara. This campaign did not result in Philip's annexing territory past the Nestos. However, it did throw Athenian plans to dominate the Straits into turmoil and pressed the kings of Thrace closer to Philip. This outer area was becoming a firm buffer. Yet, the work was not accomplished and Philip would have to re-employ this procedure.

Athens could not be expected to remain quiet while Philip rearranged the Thracian coast to his liking. By 347 she had won over Kersebleptes again and was aiding him in the construction of coastal fortifications. In a brilliant three month campaign (March-June, 346) Philip and Antipatros defeated Kersebleptes once again and forced him into an alliance. The new coastal bases were removed. By this

59. From early times northern Greece was a major meeting ground for the forces of the Greek and barbarian worlds. The scene on this bronze plaque from Olynthos illustrates these two opposing worlds. It shows a naked Greek youth on the left and on the right, a barbarian leader holding a sceptre and wearing a typical barbarian headdress. First half of the 4th century B.C. Thessalonike, Archaeological Museum.

59

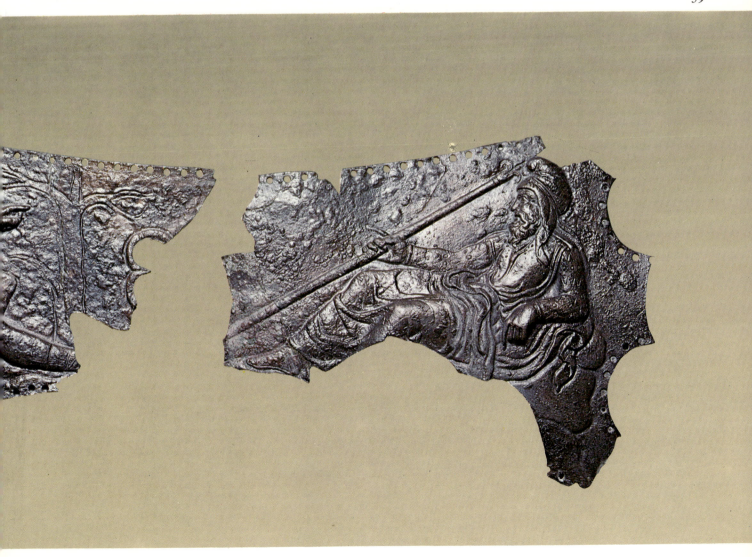

time Philip had annexed the territory as far as the Nestos. Then he forced Teres, successor of Amadokos into his camp and, with Kersebleptes, he had a double buffer beyond the Nestos.

Between 346 and 342 Philip was occupied in Illyria and Epeiros along with the extensive diplomatic activity with Athens. By 342, however, conditions in eastern Thrace had changed considerably. Not only was Athens attempting to break Kersebleptes' loyalty, but a newly reconstituted Persian Empire was rapidly restoring its authority in Asia Minor. Would the Persians attempt to reclaim their former possessions in Thrace? Philip realized the old alliance system with the Thracian princes was no longer adequate. Thrace would have to be held directly. Also, the Thracians would have to be buffered by alliances with Scythian and Celtic tribes in the north to prevent outside interference.

The fighting continued from summer 342 into the winter of 341. Both Teres and Keresebleptes opposed him. Knowing Philip meant direct conquest this time left no other choice. In addition to occupying the coastal fortresses, Philip now began a series of military colonies in the Hebros valley. Drongylos, Kabyle, and Masteira are noteworthy in the lower Hebros basin. Upriver in the valley between the Rhodope and Haimos Philip founded Beroe (Stara Zagora) and Philippolis (Plovdiv). A tax of one tenth of the produce of the land was permanently levied on central and eastern Thrace. The mines were opened to exploitation and the Thracians were forced to serve as auxiliaries in Philip's armies. After Teres and Kersebleptes capitulated in the summer of 341, they were removed from power and replaced by a "general of Thrace" appointed directly by Philip from among his Companions. Some resistance lasted into 340 and both Antipatros and Parmenion were occupied completing the conquest. A rebellion broke out among the Maidoi (supported by the Dentheletai) on the upper Strymon east of Mount Kerkine in 340, but the young Alexander advanced east along the Bregalnitsa River, suppressed the rebellion and

founded Alexandropolis, a new military colony, to dominate the region.

Coastal and central (Hebros valley) Thrace were now firmly under Philip's control. The area as far as the Nestos was part of Macedonia; the rest was under a military governor. Surrounding the new holdings with firm alliances would complete the ring defense, thus assuring freedom from external barbarian attack while Philip faced the immediate Athenian threat and then the long-term Persian problem.

As early as 342 Philip decided to protect his burgeoning central Thracian ventures by advancing north through the Shipka pass to make an alliance with Kothelas, king of the Celtic Getai in the area between the Haimos range and the Danube. Quite typically, Philip cemented the alliance by marrying Meda, daughter of Kothelas. In 341 at the end of the reduction of Thrace, Philip advanced to the Black Sea coast and north to the mouths of the Danube (Dobrudja). Some Greek coastal colonies allied with him, marking the beginning of a coastal alliance system to protect Thrace. The Graeco-Macedonians generally called the indigenous Black Sea peoples Scythians. Though the term normally meant steppe nomads, here evidently it referred to the local farmers and herders. In the winter of 340/339 one of these Scythian kings, Ataias, who controlled much of the Dobrudja and area north of it asked Philip for aid. Philip sent troops, but they were rudely rebuffed. Thereupon, Philip decided his arrangements along the coast were insufficient. After coming to terms with Byzantion and Perinthos in the spring (339), and faced with war against Athens and Thebes, Philip advanced to the Dobrudja, defeated and killed Ataias, captured some 20,000 prisoners, and advanced west along the Danube. On the Danubian plain the Celtic Triballoi attacked him. Philip was wounded and the army lost most of its booty. Still Philip extricated himself and returned via the Isker valley (the area of Sofia down the Strymon to the Strumitsa and the Axios valley). Clearly, problems remained in the alliance system north of the Haimos which was to become one of Alexander's first tasks after assuming the throne. For the meantime the alliance and control of the passes amply protected Macedonia and Thrace from northern pressure.

If the early days of Philip's reign were devoted to meeting the problems of immediate security, they were rapidly met. Once boundaries were created, Philip moved to extend these borders to well-defined natural frontiers. He protected these by creating a circle of influence beyond, using diplomacy, political and marital alliances, or war. The reign is marked by successive interventions to achieve this. In the west the frontier depended on control of the difficult Peristeri and Petrina ranges and the Lychnitis and Dassaretis lake basins. Additional alliances and fear secured Macedonia's influence as far as the Adriatic. In the north defensible passes and the Paionian /Agrianian dependency offered security. To the east Macedonia as far as the Nestos was protected by the high Pirin-Rila and Kerkine-Belasitsa-Dysoron ranges, the Nestos and Strymon river basins, and the hard Akontisma and Rendina passes. To the north and east lay a military district as far as the Straits, offering a *cordon sanitaire* between Philip and the Persians. Philip had definite plans about the Persian presence. Although the work of creating an outer perimeter in the north of Thrace (Danube basin) was not really complete, Philip's greatness as a strategist is nowhere better demonstrated than on his frontiers. His brilliant victories against more civilized peoples, the Athenians, Thebans, or Phokians, for example, are better attested. But, to the Macedonian people, Philip became the father of the nation by defining frontiers and demonstrating the success of defense in depth. The loyalty of the people and aristocracy to Philip was well deserved. Alexander was to become an international hero, but Philip was the great national king.

PHILIP
AND ATHENS

From the start of his reign Philip saw clearly that war with Athens was inevitable. Under the Athenian Empire in the fifth century the whole of Chalkidike and the seaward cities of Thrace and of Macedon itself had been under Athenian rule, and in the fourth Athens constantly dreamed and schemed to recover her power. In 368, shortly after the eclipse of Spartan power at the battle of Leuktra, she set about the task. Her immediate objective was Amphipolis which controlled large resources of mines and ship-building timber,[1] but there was no reason to suppose that Athens wanted no more than that. In 359 an Athenian naval force landed a rival claimant to the throne on the coast of Macedon. Clearly the former Athenian policy of seeking Macedonian subservience was not dead, and success at Amphipolis would in all likelihood be followed by attempts to resume control elsewhere. In any case, Philip wanted the city for himself. Not only its economic advantages moved him, but also its strategic importance; it controlled the route eastwards into Thrace. So, in 357 when Athens was preoccupied with the revolt of some of its major allies, he seized the city, and war with Athens began.[2]

Amphipolis was not Athens' only objective. The Thracian Chersonese (the Gallipoli Peninsula) had been an Athenian possession and in 365 she set out to wrest it from the Thracian kings. Although militarily she made little progress, by 352 the easternmost king, realising that he would need allies against Philip, ceded it to Athens, and from that moment Athens had constantly to fear that Philip might take it. Thus even while she schemed to attack in the west of Thrace, she was on the defensive in the east.[3]

Philip had one great asset which he exploited to the full. He had no fleet and wisely did not seek to create one. Athens with a large fleet could not afford to maintain a substantial naval force in the north Aegean and had to rely on sending out expeditions when they were needed. However, for anything up to three months from the middle of June the Etesian winds, as the ancients called the modern Meltemi,

make navigation from south to north difficult and dangerous, occasionally impossible. So, by choosing that season for his campaigns, Philip, with the aid of his efficient corps of engineers, could assault and take cities before Athens could seek to prevent him.

The truth was that war in the north was hopeless for Athens. In the fifth century when she was rich and powerful, she had been unable to retake Amphipolis. In the fourth she was poor, and Macedon became rich and militarily strong. It is no surprise therefore that in the 350s she accomplished by arms practically nothing while Philip year by year built up his army and extended his empire.

In 349 a new phase began. The city of Olynthos in Chalkidike was itself rich and populous and stood at the head of a confederacy of thirty-two cities, capable of becoming a serious obstacle to Philip's progress. In the 350s, being opposed to the recovery of Athenian power in the north, it stood in uneasy alliance with him,[4] but in 352 it made peace with Athens,[5] thoughts of alliance in the future not being excluded. From that moment the whole state was doomed and in 349 Philip struck.[6] The Chalkidians appealed to Athens for help, which was promptly agreed to, and the war in the north became the more urgent for Athens. If Olynthos fell, Philip would be invulnerably strong.

The Athenian best known to us for his support for the Chalkidians is Demosthenes, best known because his masterly *Olynthiac Orations* have survived, though there is no reason to think that by 349 he had attained a position of any importance in Athenian affairs. In that year he was only thirty-five years of age, and little regarded. His earliest speeches were written for others to use in the courts, but when in 352 and 351 he began speaking in the assembly, his arguments showed merely a youthful lack of judgement or else a determination to oppose for the sake of making his mark. Neither his speech *For the Megalopolitans* (352) nor that *On the liberty of the Rhodians* (351) suggested that he possessed great strategic or political insight, and his *First Philippic* of

the same year, which argued for a more effective prosecution of the war in the north, and which was later to become famous as a sample of his great rhetorical powers, contained no real answer to the problem of how to stop Philip; ravaging Macedonia and sending help to doomed cities could win for Athens nothing but disaster.

The politician to whom he opposed himself was, it would appear, Euboulos, who is so shadowy a figure in the sources available to us that history has generally made a caricature of him. At the end of the war with the allies in 355, Athens was nearly bankrupt. Her revenues had dropped to a mere third of what had once been deemed necessary for the running of the state, and Euboulos undertook the supervision of financial recovery.[7] His method was to stimulate commerce and to make it difficult for the revenues to be squandered on costly and inessential wars.[8] In this category he clearly placed the war for Amphipolis. Popular sentiment forbade its abandonment, and perchance fortune might remove Philip and restore the city to Athens. So the war was allowed to continue, but it had largely to pay for itself, principally by plunder. This did not mean, however, that he abandoned Athens' vital interests. If Philip sought to penetrate Thermopylai, Athens would play her part, as she did in 352. If he threatened the Chersonese, help would be sent, as was planned in 352 and secured in 351. It is puppetry, not history, to represent him as seeking peace at any price. His policies paid off. The finances of the city steadily recovered, and Athens entered the final war in 340 in a financially strong condition.

The Chalkidian appeal was nonetheless a crisis. If Athens did nothing to help, the Chalkidians might submit to Philip in despair, but if they could not save themselves, there was little that Athens could do even to postpone the end. So, sensibly enough, small forces were sent out in autumn 349 and early 348, mere encouragement for the Chalkidians. But Philip picked off the cities one by one, and as the campaign moved towards its climax in an assault on Olynthos itself, the Chalkidians sent a final desperate appeal for help.[9] It found Euboulos for the moment in eclipse. He had just sponsored an Athenian expedition to Euboia,[10] which had come to disaster in the morass of Euboian politics, and his opponents, one may suppose, had their way. A large force of Athenian hoplites and cavalry was voted, but delayed by the weather, a singular piece of good fortune for Athens. They could not have prevented the Macedonian assault, and could only have been captured or killed.[11]

In late summer 348 Olynthos fell. The Chalkidians were appallingly treated,[12] and Philip was ready to move to carry the war into Greece itself, as indeed was long ago to be expected. It had been Demosthenes' fondly held belief that if Athens did not fight Philip in the north, she would face him in Attica, but his judgement was wrong. The truth was that Philip would settle with Athens willy nilly, unless he could be kept out of Greece, and Athens' only hope was to reserve her efforts for the defence of Greek liberty with the help of allies within Greece. The war in the north had seemed to the Greeks the last flicker of Athenian imperialism for which they had no sympathy whatsoever. Now it was over. The real conflict was about to begin.

Events of 352 had made clear to Philip that if Thermopylai was held and Phokis hostile, Greece was impenetrable. Political guile would be necessary, but the divisions of central Greece offered him rich possibilities. As already described, the Sacred War was staggering to an end. The Thebans were without hope of deciding the issue on their own, but the master of Phokis, Phalaikos, was also in desperate straits. He had all but exhausted the treasures of Delphi and could look forward at no great interval to being unable to pay his large mercenary army. Between the two, Philip saw he could insinuate himself into Central Greece, and this would spell disaster for Athens in one way or another. Thebes appealed to him for help, and it became known in Greece that Philip, aided by the Thessalians, planned intervention. What was not known, but is to be presumed,

was that Phalaikos, as has been argued in a previous chapter, had secretly negotiated with Philip a happy issue out of the trouble in which he was ensnared.

As long as Athens believed she could count on Phokis, she had nothing to fear; Thermopoylai could be blocked and access to Phokis denied. But in early 346 she learned that Phalaikos declined to be defended by Athens, or indeed by Sparta, Phokis' other ally, and, for all that Athens could do, the highway into Greece and so into Attica itself was wide open to Philip. Athens had to seek peace.

The tangled negotiations which resulted in the Peace of Philokrates began. Athens sent an embassy to Pella, which included Aischines and Demosthenes, and terms were discussed.[13] From the outset it was clear that Athens would have to sign away all claim to Amphipolis if Philip was to be kept out of Attica. The embassy returned to Athens followed shortly by a Macedonian embassy, and at the end of a dramatic two-day debate the Athenians voted to accept the Peace. The Macedonians administered the oath to the representatives of Athens, and the same ten Athenian ambassadors set out for Macedon to receive the oath from Philip and his allies.[14]

So far the peace making seemed straightforward, but on this second embassy a wholly changed situation presented itself to the Athenians. While they waited for Philip to return from a lightning campaign to secure his control of the easternmost part of Thrace, embassies assembled from the major states of Greece, from Thebes, Sparta and Phokis, and it was clear that the end of it all would not be as simple

60. *Amphipolis, an Athenian colony in the strategically important region at the mouth of the Strymon river, was the meeting point where Ionian and Attic artistic traditions fused with conservative local elements. Moreover the city retained economic and political connections with the peoples of the hinterland, thereby contributing to the spread of Greek culture. The terracotta bust of the young woman in the illustration was produced at the end of the 4th century in one of the figurine workshops which flourished in the city. Kavala, Archaeological Museum.*

as the Athenians had expected. Preparations for a Macedonian campaign southwards were afoot and the ambassadors were probably aware of them. Discussion arose, Demosthenes wishing to warn his countrymen that all had miscarried and that they must abandon the Peace, his opponents preferring to stay and do what they could to obtain a peaceful settlement in Central Greece which would render Macedonian military intervention unnecessary. With consummate skill, Philip kept all parties guessing. The military preparations were, he declared, for dealing with the little city Halos in south-east Thessaly, for some time under siege; he saw the representatives of each side in the Sacred War separately, hinting at a settlement that would content them; the oaths were delayed, and the army moved south with the various embassies in train; the Phokians even believed that they would suffer no harm.

At Pherai, a little to the north of Halos, Philip and his allies finally swore to observe the Peace of Philokrates and the Athenian embassy were free to hasten home with the news that Philip and his army were alarmingly near to Thermopylai.[15] They found there a Phokian embassy appealing for help, for in fear of what Phalaikos might do the Phokians had turned against his policy of rejecting Athenian aid. In view of what the ambassadors had to say, there was no question about what to do; Phokis had to be defended if possible. The Council passed a Recommendation to the People to that effect. But by the time the People met, the news had come that Philip was "in the Gates". Phokis could not be saved.[16]

Philip had tricked the Athenians. They had expected that having obtained the Peace Philip would not intervene in Greece, but that if he attempted to do so and Phokis were willing to be defended, they would have the option of abandoning the Peace, and of going and keeping him out. Instead, Philip did not swear to the Peace in Pherai until units of his army were in position to deny the Athenians that option. The settlement of the Sacred War followed. A Macedonian garrison was installed in Thermopylai. If the Greeks were ever minded to fight Philip, they would have to fight within Greece itself. The whole affair had been a masterpiece of politics and strategy.

There was, however, another side to it all. From the very outset Philip had insisted on alliance with Athens as well as peace, and time would show that he had already formed the plan of attacking Persia, for which he would need the naval power of Athens. This was not clear beyond cavil in 346, but time would make it so, and Philip might have sought to defend his trickery in such terms.

The events of 346 greatly divided opinion in Athens. Demosthenes, who had been Philokrates' right-hand man in the negotiation of the Peace, in bitter fury at having been tricked by Philip, turned his whole heart and mind to ending the Peace and undoing the damage which his policy had done. Indeed at the crucial assembly, when the news that Philip was already in control of Thermopylai and all hopes of keeping him out of Phokis were plainly ended, Demosthenes had even wanted the Athenians still to march out (though, it is only fair to state, some find it impossible to accept that Demosthenes could have followed so mad a course). He was laughed at and shouted down, and from that moment of humiliation onwards he never ceased to accuse of black treachery those had had the sense to accept the inevitable.[17] The charge was ridiculous. Aischines and his supporters knew as well as Demosthenes that Athens had been tricked and that the prospects for Greek liberty were grave, but, when Philip withdrew from Greece in the autumn, they began to hope that something good could come out of the disastrous peace. Thus by a curious twist the man who had made the peace, Demosthenes, turned to attacking Aischines, the man who now wished to maintain it.

The uneasy peace lasted until autumn 340. Demosthenes lost no opportunity to attack it and to assert that Philip was exploiting it to his own advantage. In 344 his attacks became so virulent that Philip and his allies protested to Athens and invited the Athenians to propose amendments to the Peace.[18]

Demosthenes and his supporters used the occasion to demand the return of Amphipolis, which they must have known Philip never would or could concede.[19] Nevertheless for a period of nearly two years the possibility of amending the Peace remained open and opinion at Athens evenly divided; Aischines, prosecuted by Demosthenes in 343 allegedly for what he had done in 346 but in truth for what he wished to do in seeking to maintain the Peace, was acquitted by a narrow margin, a fair index of public opinion.[20] But Demosthenes and the war-party hammered away at Philip and the Peace, and early in 342 negotiations with Philip were finally broken off.

Demosthenes argued constantly that under pretence of peace Philip was in fact constantly intervening in the affairs of the Greek states, giving clandestine support to his own supporters. His speeches are peppered with allegations both general and detailed, and, if we had only Demosthenes to rely on, his view would inevitably be accepted.[21] Fortunately there is extant a speech delivered in early 342 by a fellow member of the war-party denouncing Philip but curiously silent about his alleged interventions and one may infer that by that date Philip had not infringed the Peace either in the letter or in spirit.[22] Whether after that date and before the declaration of war in September 340 Philip did intervene, is disputed. If Demosthenes is to be trusted, Philip seriously threatened Athens by sending mercenaries to support his friends in Euboia until in 341 two Athenian expeditions ejected them.[23] But it is at least doubtful. His bitter denunciation in the *Third Philippic* of May 341 concluded with a lame demand for embassies to be sent all round Greece; if the picture he has painted was true, it was time for actions, not words. The reverse is perhaps the truth. It was the policy of Demosthenes that turned Euboians to seek Philip's aid, and even so they received virtually none. (However it must be made clear that no other paragraph in this chapter would be more hotly challenged by those historians, who, believing Demosthenes alone to have been on the side of the angels,

tend to credit all he says).

The aim of Demosthenes was simple. He wanted war. In June 342 Philip began his final Thracian campaign, and though he was at first fighting far from the Chersonese, Athens naturally feared for her possession. An Athenian general, Diopeithes, had been stationed there earlier in the year and had begun to collect a mercenary army. But he did not wait on the defensive.[24] He attacked the territory of one of Philip's allies, and, when Philip wrote to Athens protesting,[25] Demosthenes argued that Diopeithes must not be recalled, that Philip was virtually at war with Athens, and that legal niceties were out of place. Demosthenes had his way, and resumption of war was rendered the more certain. But it was always the same. Indifferent to truth or falsehood, Demosthenes did all he could to secure that the Peace of Philokrates was denounced. When Philip, for reasons that can only be conjectured, laid siege to his own allies, Perinthos and Byzantion, an Athenian force was at hand to help them,[26] and by September 340 Philip had had enough. He wrote to Athens declaring war, and promptly snatched the Athenian corn-fleet.[27]

Was Demosthenes right in all this? Philip and Macedonian power were certainly a menace and had to be opposed, but it was not obvious how this could effectively be done. There was then, as earlier, nothing that Athens could do to harm Macedonia or detain Philip in the north. He kept control of Thermopylai; the road to Athens was open whenever he cared to take it. Some have thought that Demosthenes all along believed that, when Philip came south, the Thebans would join in opposing him. But the evidence suggests the contrary. When Demosthenes began to seek a resumption of war, the Thebans were more likely to assist than to hinder Philip, and not until he was on the very border of Boiotia in 339 did Demosthenes do anything to secure a Theban alliance. The truth is rather that Demosthenes trusted in Fortune, and after the final defeat he declared that Fortune, not his own policies, had failed Athens.[28]

61-62. *Olynthos, the head of the Chalkidian League, was a wealthy and populous city. Excavations there have uncovered both public buildings and luxurious private residences adorned with mosaics of black and white tesserae, among the earliest discovered in Greece. Left: Bellerophon, mounted on Pegasus, killing the Chimaira. Right: detail from a large mosaic with Dionysiac motifs, from the "House of Good Fortune" (Agathe Tyche).*

The war began with what seemed to be a success for Athens. Philip abandoned the sieges of Perinthos and Byzantion, and winter 340-339 saw him fighting Scyths on the Danube.[29] The truth may rather be that, when he did not take the cities at the first rush, Philip preferred to settle with Athens and to leave the Bosporos and Hellespont till later; if Athens fell, they would not prolong resistance. The attack on the Scyths was necessary to round off his Thracian campaign, but by late summer 339 he was free to move south. In one important respect his position had deteriorated. While he was fighting the Scyths, the Thebans snatched control of Thermopylai from his garrison, and so he had anew to face the problem of how to get in to Greece. But Philip had prepared. Phokis was now ready to receive him and he by-passed the Gates. (Astonishingly, the Thebans made no attempt, as far as we know, to block his passage over the mountains, but, even if they had, no doubt Philip would have been military prepared to force his way).

The news that Philip was in Phokis and could only be checked by arms from marching into Attica caused consternation and near despair in Athens. Demosthenes' earlier attempts to form a Hellenic alliance against Philip had largely proved abortive.[30] In early 342, when Philip had been active in Epeiros making his final arrangement of the affairs of the Molossian kingdom, there had been general alarm in Greece lest he advance further southwards. Demosthenes had persuaded the Athenians to send a force to Akarnania and there was intense diplomatic activity which bade fair to produce a general alliance. But when Philip did not even advance the few miles necessary to capture Ambrakia, which he could have easily taken, the movement petered out and even alliances actually formed by Athens shortly afterwards mostly fell apart. In 341 Demosthenes did indeed gain an ally which it was important to deny to Philip, viz. the Euboians, but a combined land army was still lacking, and when in 340 he answered Philip's declaration of war, he concluded by proposing that Athens

should set about the formation of a general Hellenic alliance. At the battle of Chaironeia, Corinthians, Achaeans, Megarians and a few others did fight beside the Athenians. How and when their aid was enlisted remains obscure, but it is certain that the real prerequisite of any defence of Greece, viz. alliance with Thebes, had not been attempted, perhaps not even thought about. So the news that Philip was already in Phokis was indeed alarming. It was even possible that Philip would secure Theban neutrality, if not Theban aid.

Demosthenes was the man of the hour. He proposed and himself effected alliances with Thebes.[31] Within a few days the Athenian army was in Thebes on its way north to join the Theban army near the borders of Phokis, and so the scene was set for the battle which would decide the future of Greece.

That was late in 339, but the battle of Chaironeia did not take place until the end of August 338. Philip no doubt needed to assemble his full army and supplies, and there were minor operations in the winter about which we are very poorly informed. But the long delay before the battle can only be explained by supposing that Philip hoped by diplomacy to resolve the situation. The Theban-Athenian alliance however stood firm, and resolution by armed conflict was inevitable.

Philip's army numbered over thirty thousand foot and two thousand cavalry, probably fewer than his opponents.[32] The Greek position too was strong, extending obliquely across the valley of the Kephisos, with one flank resting on the river, and the other on hills to the south. Outflanking was therefore impossible and, because of the obliqueness of the Greek line, frontal assault difficult. The only things that can be said for certain are that the Macedonian cavalry on the left flank, commanded by the eighteen-year old Alexander,[33] delivered the decisive blow against the Thebans on the right of the Greek army and that the result was unprecedentedly decisive. The flower of the Theban army, the Sacred Band, was cut to pieces, and of the six thousand

Athenians present one thousand were killed and two thousand taken prisoner, and there was no question of continuing the struggle.[34] How exactly Philip achieved this result may be reflected in a story preserved in a late military writer, who speaks of Macedonian withdrawal on the right flank and a reckless and disastrous pursuit by the Athenians.[35] If this is correct, it cannot be the case that there was a breach in the Macedonian line, for the Greeks would have exploited it and the outcome of the battle would have been different; the Macedonians must, rather, have executed the brilliant and complex manoeuvre of a controlled wheel, for which they had been carefully trained by their king. Whatever the truth of this story, when the day ended all Greece was at Philip's mercy.

Philip was merciful to Athens. Although he was to treat Thebes with severity, he released the Athenian captives without ransom before he had even negotiated the so-called Peace of Demades that shortly followed. He meant to use Athens, not to render her useless.[36]

In accordance with long-standing custom in Athens, a Funeral Oration was delivered at the beginning of winter in honour of the fallen, and, as a mark of the esteem of his fellow-citizens, Demosthenes was chosen to deliver it. The speech is preserved, a conventional piece with nothing of real interest apart from a claim, made in passing, that the battle had been lost because the Theban commanders were incompetent. Demosthenes' real *apologia* came in his oration *On the Crown*. A supporter of Demosthenes had proposed that Demosthenes be honoured with a crown in recognition of the unfailing excellence of his policies and of his actions. The de-

63. *The Chalkidian League, made up of 32 cities headed by Olynthos, was a significant political force in northern Greece during the 4th century B.C. The illustration shows a tetradrachm issued by the League with the head of Apollo on one side and the lyre on the other. First half of the 4th century B.C. Athens, Numismatic Museum.*

cree was challenged by Aischines and after long delays, the case was heard in 330. In what is surely the supreme achievement of Greek rhetoric Demosthenes justified himself before his countrymen and posterity.

The speech is as remarkable for what it does not discuss as for what it does. There were parts of his career which he preferred to pass over in silence, but for the rest his theme was that it was not he, but Fortune, that had failed Athens, that he had been the patriot who saw through Philip and his black designs, and his opponents traitors who had been bribed into opposing the patriotic cause, not just Aischines and his ilk in Athens but all Greek politicians who had favoured concord with Macedon. Since that moment in 346 when Demosthenes had been laughed at and shouted down in the assembly, he had constantly denounced his opponent as corrupted by Philip, and this is the view that posterity has largely accepted. Although Polybios in the second century had made answer and rebutted the attack on Demosthenes' famous Black list of traitors,[37] the Demosthenic view prevailed in antiquity; the success of Philip was due above all to bribery of corrupt politicians.

It probably was not so. None of Demosthenes' opponents at Athens was ever found guilty of accepting bribes, and although we are in no position to assess the precise truth of his allegations about other cities, there is no reason to take them more seriously than his allegations about Aischines. The real causes of Philip's success lay elsewhere. First and far above all there was his strategic genius. He was the true heir of Epameinondas and he realised to the full the military possibilities suggested by that great soldier's developments in the art of war. Secondly, there was his political genius, whereby he was able to exploit the petty rivalries of the Greek states. As Polybios remarked, they looked to Philip to protect them and there was no other power that either would or could. By posing as saviour here and avenger there, he prevented the Greeks uniting in defence of the liberty of all. Finally Macedon was a national state far richer and far more populous than any Greek city-state. When Philip realised its potential, it was inevitable that the world of the independent city-state would pass away. Its rise to empire was facilitated by the Greeks but in the long run was not to be stopped by mere city-states. They had to unite either against him or under him. Independence as they had known it was no longer possible.

PHILIP AND THE SOUTHERN GREEKS: STRENGTH AND WEAKNESS

Prior to Philip's accession the Macedonian state had been expanding by a process of conquest, interrupted from time to time by periods of restraint or even retrenchment. Under Philip's rule, Macedonia went beyond the bounds of mere expansionism and suddenly became an imperialist power.

The written sources attribute Macedonian imperialism exclusively to Philip's determination. In the present state of our knowledge it is impossible to determine whether his aims coincided from the very beginning either with those of a particular group, or with the wishes of a broader section of the Macedonian people. We can conjecture, however, that, even if Philip's determination had been the original motivating force, it must have carried with it in no time at all an increasingly large section of public opinion. This ever growing support is not to be ascribed solely to his indisputable authority as a ruler, but also to his followers' anticipation of personal gain — an anticipation which must have seemed more and more well-founded with every new success. Clearly, without the support of public opinion and the co-operation of prominent elements and groupings of Macedonian society, his achievements would have been considerably less impressive. Nevertheless, it is equally certain that the scale of his accomplishments was closely related to the relative strength of Macedonia and her allies on the one hand and the rival powers on the other; the congruence of favourable and unfavourable circumstances attending either side also played an important role. It would not be extravagant to claim that not only the effectiveness of Macedonian actions but even the very impulse behind them resulted from an awareness of their superiority in force and from the fact that circumstances acted in their favour. To fully appreciate, therefore, Philip's actions and his achievement as a whole, we must assess the conditions prevailing at the time, the relative strength of either side and the advantages and disadvantages on both sides.

Philip attempted to assert himself as the leading power in the Greek world at a time when, of the three states that had formerly held this position, Sparta had retired from the arena; Thebes no longer played a leading role and Athens was desperately trying to arrest her decline. Sparta had been crushed by the Boiotians twelve years before Philip's accession to the throne, had lost roughly half her territory, was suffering a decline in manpower, and was no longer protected by a ring of dependent allies. The conditions that had favoured the rise of Thebes and the Boiotian League, of which she was leader, were ephemeral. The signs that the city was incapable of maintaining itself in the position which it had reached, manifested themselves a mere three years before the beginning of Philip's reign in Macedonia. Moreover, Philip had not threatened the interests of Boiotia but, on the contrary, had been allied to the Boiotians for many years. The Boiotians became disenchanted with him and entered into alliance with the Athenians only at a very late date, when Philip was in a much stronger position than ever before. Athens clashed repeatedly with Philip from the very beginning, because she continued to have interests in areas bordering on Macedonia that were swiftly captured by the Macedonian monarch, and in the Straits, towards which he was advancing.

Athenian reaction to Philip passed through three phases covering the years 359-355, 355-346 and 346-338. 1) Down to 355 the majority of the Athenian populace was imperialist-minded. When, in 359, under very unfavourable external circumstances, Philip assumed power as regent for his nephew, a minor, the Athenians sent military assistance to one of his rivals. Philip attempted to reduce the fervour of their hostility by removing the Macedonian garrison from Amphipolis, which he knew the Athenians coveted. After he had defeated his rival, he freed the Athenian prisoners of war and proclaimed his desire to conclude a treaty with Athens. In 357, however, he captured Amphipolis, having pre-empted Athenian intervention by a promise that he would surrender the city to them, if they handed over to him the town of Pydna on the coast of Macedonia, which was independent and allied with Athens. The Athenians fell into the trap: they failed to send aid to Amphipolis, thinking that they would gain the city without effort, but did not foresee that if they attempted to treat Pydna as an Athenian possession, this would provoke a reaction

amongst their other allies. Considering that meanwhile Athens' most important allies had already revolted, and she was at war with them, this lack of foresight is unaccountable and proved fatal. Discontent amongst her allies mounted, and Athens found herself embroiled in a war that permitted Philip to acquire Pydna as well as Amphipolis in a very short space of time. Xenophon and Isokrates were both opposed to the extreme democrats who had long supported an imperialist policy. The inability of Athens to crush the revolting allies gave them the opportunity, or the courage, to proclaim that Athens was treating other Greek states unjustly and should abandon her violent attacks on cities unwilling to follow her lead.[1] The desire for empire had such a strong hold on public opinion, however, that the Athenians were moved by it to the foolhardy decision to support the Persian satraps of western Asia Minor, who were in revolt against their king. Factors operating in favour of this decision were the Athenians' lack of funds to support the war against their former allies, and their belief that the Persian King would be compelled to order Maussollos, satrap of Caria, to withdraw his support from the rebellious allies.

2) The king of Persia responded by threatening war. Disillusioned, the Athenians abandoned their attempt to coerce the seceding states and gave their support to politicians who put forward a new programme: in future, Athens would refrain from aggressive action and would react only when vital Athenian interests were jeopardised. From the subsequent course of events, it seems that these interests lay a) in Euboia, which acted as a protective buffer to Attica and could be used as a base for attacks on it, if it fell into the hands of a hostile power; b) at Thermopylai, in the event that a power further to the north attempted to force the pass; c) in Chalkidike and other areas of the north Aegean where the Athenians still had interests (timber for ship-building, allies); d) on the shores of the Hellespont, partly because Athenian cleruchies still existed there, but mainly because one third of the grain consumed by the Athenians passed through the Straits. At home, the new political programme aimed at revitalising the private sector of the economy, increasing public re-

64. Athens came into conflict with Philip from the very beginning of his reign, since the city continued to have interests in some parts of the north Aegean that quickly became the target of the expansionist policies of the Macedonian ruler. Athenian military forces were both fewer and inferior to those of Philip; Athens also lacked commanders of any distinction. The illustration is of a relief base from the Athenian Akademeia dating from the first half of the 4th century B.C. An Athenian warrior on horseback wearing a chlamys and petasos, is about to run his enemy through with his spear. Athens, National Archaeological Museum.

65. Philip's army was unquestionably superior to those of the other Greek states. It was commanded by Philip himself, one of the greatest military organisers and generals of all time. The Macedonian king had, moreover, introduced innovations in structure, equipment and tactics. He had imbued his men with fighting spirit and had created strong bonds with them. The balance of power thus tilted steadily in favour of the Macedonians and against the Greeks of the south. The illustration shows a relief of a gravestele from Pella, a Macedonian warrior, the work of a local craftsman dating from the end of the 5th century B.C. Istanbul, Archaeological Museum.

venue and carrying out public works. A law was also passed providing that the balance of the regular revenues be transferred to the Theoric Fund, out of which disbursement was made for tickets to the theatre which were allocated free of charge to the citizens, and from which small sums of money were distributed at some of the festivals. The same law, or perhaps a second law supplementary to it, gave powers to the committee responsible for the finances of this fund to supervise the conduct of the other state officials. The pretext for this second measure was to prevent wastage of other revenues; in reality it aimed at increasing the income accruing to the Theoric Fund; the end result, however, was to make those responsible for the Fund the general controllers of the entire public economy. Euboulos, who was Chief Commissioner of the Theoric Fund for eight years, became more powerful than any other archon and appears to have governed Athens from behind the scenes. He succeeded in increasing the annual regular public revenue from 130 talents during the Social War to 400 talents in 339. His main achievement, however, was to swell the Theoric Fund over which he presided, and was therefore able to distribute greater sums of money to the citizens. This policy curbed the imperialist, aggressive inclinations of the Athenian *thetes*. Before the introduction of the new measures concerning the Theoric Fund, and more specifically before they had begun to bear fruit, the *thetes* had always voted in favour of armament and war, and had supported the seizure of foreign territory and attacks on foreign powers. They had had their reasons: on the one hand they themselves did not have to bear the costs of war — which were mainly met by the exaction of special taxes paid by the richer Athenians — and on the other, war offered greater opportunities for employment and the possibility of the award of a plot of land *(kleros)* in areas outside Attica. Under the new dispensation, however, a good number of *thetes* were reluctant to vote in favour of military expenditure since this would entail a reduction in the funds accruing to the Theoric Fund. To guard against the possibility that this check on aggressive tendencies be rendered ineffective, a law was passed involving the death penalty for any-

one who ventured to propose that the balance of the regular budget be used for any purpose other than to swell the Theoric Fund. Despite all this, the party in power in Athens from 355 to 346 did not neglect armaments or shrink from war, even with Philip. When the latter approached Thermopylai in 352 the Athenians swiftly dispatched a force of 5,000 infantry and 400 cavalry, all of them citizens, to reinforce the Phokians who were holding the pass. The scale and speed of this action suggest that it was unanimously supported by the politicians who at that date held the stage in Athens. In 348, these same politicians proposed Athenian intervention in Euboia, even though in the meantime Athenian forces had been sent to aid the Olynthians against Philip. One year later, after Philip had vanquished the Olynthians, Euboulos proposed that the Athenians should take the initiative in establishing a broad alliance opposed to the Macedonian. His motion was accepted by the assembly and embassies were despatched to a number of cities to secure this end.

At the time Demosthenes was an opponent of this policy; in 353/2 he urged Athens to ally with Megalopolis against Sparta,[2] and in 351 to send a military force to assist the Rhodian democrats in returning to their city.[3] He had apparently failed to grasp the fact that the balance of power between Philip and the Athenians demanded that the latter concentrate all their attention on the Macedonian king and avoid embroilments in other areas where they had no vital interests. By implication it is also clear that Demosthenes was still aligned with the old imperialistic policy of Athens. A few months later, however, he

66. *At Chaironeia Philip fought against the Athenians supported by the Boiotians. Earlier in the 4th century the Boiotian League had assumed a leading role in southern Greece. The League was Philip's ally for many years, and only turned against him at the last moment. The illustration shows the grave stele of Mnason, a Boiotian warrior. It is a remarkable example of a notable though rare technique; incised outlines and details and light colouring help the figure to stand out against the dark-coloured stone. Thebes, Archaeological Museum.*

delivered the *First Philippic,* in which he inaugurated his efforts to galvanise the Athenians into turning the whole of their attention and all their resources against Philip. His basic policy was enunciated in a series of speeches delivered between 353 and 347: the Athenians should not fail to defend any of their territories or interests threatened by Philip, should come to the aid of any city attacked by him, and should lend encouragement to those who, having gone over to his side, showed an inclination to secede from him.[4] Considering the efforts of the Athenians to be insufficient, he castigated their inertia and procrastination, and their failure to execute, (or their incompetent execution of) the decisions they had agreed upon, and repeatedly appealed for a more intensive and consistent economic and military mobilisation.[5] It is from a number of passages in Demosthenes that we learn that the recent laws concerning the Theoric Fund were a major factor contributing to the inadequacy of the Athenian reactions. As early as 351 he was commenting sarcastically that the Athenians spent far too much on festivals and that they always managed to take the decisions relating to them in good time.[6] Shortly after, this, however, in 349 and 348, while urging the Athenians to act decisively and aid the Olynthians to withstand Philip's attack on them, he spoke more openly against the laws concerning the Theoric Fund. He refrained, however, from officially proposing that they be revoked since he would have risked incurring the death penalty to no good end, but he dared go so far as to imply that the responsibility for their abolition lay with those who had introduced them.[7] At the same time he was severely critical of the fact that, at a time when foreign affairs were taking such a dangerous turn, the state officials concerned themselves — in accordance with the policy of Euboulos' group — with whitewashing the battlements and constructing roads, fountains and other works of little importance. He also referred to indications that men in public office were enriching themselves and censured the people for remaining content so long as the officials of the Theoric Fund distributed money to them and organised processions to their satisfaction.[8] In this way Demosthenes attempted to disseminate the idea that the laws favouring the Theoric Fund were preventing the city from taking decisive action against Philip; and he publicly exposed Euboulos and his followers as responsible for these laws. By these means he sought either to compel the instigators themselves to propose the abolition of the laws or to reduce their political influence and make them eventually lose control over public affairs. Demosthenes was also critical of the proposal that the Athenians should intervene in Euboia,[9] clearly because, in his view, it would divide the Athenian forces at a time when they should be concentrated in Chalkidike where the fate of Olynthos was being decided. It was a moot point, however, whether the survival of Olynthos was more vital to the Athenians than the loss of Euboia. Unhappily for them, they were able neither to protect Olynthos nor to prevent Euboia (with the exception of Karystos) from seceding from the confederacy. Finally, Demosthenes foresaw that the Athenian attempt to form an anti-Macedonian alliance was doomed to failure unless Athens by her actions convinced the other Greeks of her determination to resist Philip.[10]

3) The secession of Euboia, the capture of Chalkidike by Philip and the failure of attempts to form an anti-Macedonian alliance all undermined the prestige of Euboulos and his friends, who ceased to sway the majority of the Athenian people from 346 onwards. Their place was taken by Demosthenes, Hypereides, Hegesippos and others. Demosthenes did not oppose the conclusion of peace with Philip in 346, but he strove to achieve better terms for the Athenian allies and criticised the incompetence and treachery of a number of the Athenian negotiators. He regarded the peace itself as simply an interval that would allow the Athenians to recover their power so as to be able to resume the contest against Philip on more favorable terms at a later date. Accordingly, for a number of years he avoided the extreme positions held by other politicians opposed to Philip. The faction that believed that the Athenians would sooner or later have to wage total war against Philip was opposed by a group that supported the consolidation of the peace; the chief representative of the latter view in the political arena was Aischines. Isokrates stood outside

67. Demosthenes' political role is much discussed. For some he is the incorruptible patriot, defender of freedom and democracy, while others see him as the blinkered politician, incapable of estimating the changing times and the need for unity amongst the Greeks, which was ultimately achieved by Philip. The illustration shows a Roman copy of the lost statue of Demosthenes by Polyeuktos (280 B.C.). Musei Vaticani.

68. *Hypereides, whom the ancients considered an orator second only to Demosthenes, was also a member of the anti-Macedonian party. He was the main prosecutor of Philokrates, the man responsible for the Peace of 346 B.C. The bust of Hypereides is a copy of a 4th century original. Copenhagen, National Museum.*

68

active politics; he was still obsessed with the idea he had long held that the Greeks should reconcile their differences in order to wage a concerted war against Persia. He now saw in Philip the man who could realise these aims and addressed himself directly to the Macedonian. Thus after 346, the influence of the politicians who favoured a more active opposition to Philip was counterbalanced by the emergence of an opposition supporting the adoption of a friendly attitude towards him. In the end, the anti-Philip faction prevailed, its crowning achievement being the conclusion of an alliance which was joined even by Boiotia, which had been hitherto hostile to Athens and had been Philip's ally for a considerable time. As the final confrontation with Philip drew nearer, the Athenian assembly passed a law transferring the balance of payments from the Theoric to the Military Fund (339).

It is by no means inconceivable that the Athenians would have opposed Philip more actively before this date had the Boiotians not been hostile to them and allied with their enemy. They were obliged by this circumstance to retain the biggest part of their army in Attica to guard against the contingency of an attack by an enemy with whom they shared a border, even though the latter were in turn threatened from the west by the Phokians, who were Athenian allies. The enmity between the Boiotians and the Phokians also went back to that phase of the Sacred War which preceded Philip's involvement. Philip had already clashed once with the Phokians. The Macedonian monarch had undertaken to defend Larisa from the attacks of the tyrants of other Thessalian cities. The latter sought the aid of the Phokians. It was willingly given to them, because Phokis needed as many allies as she could get to face the coalition of Lokris, Boiotia, the Thessalian League and a number of its dependent states which had declared war on her. Though numerically inferior to their enemies, the Phokians, having seized Delphi and appropriated the treasuries, raised a powerful mercenary force, with which they captured some Lokrian territory and were waging an evenly balanced struggle against the Boiotians. Philip defeated the first expeditionary force sent into Thessaly by the Phokians (354), was in turn defeated by the full force of the Phokian army in the following autumn, but one year later achieved a crushing victory (352). This brought him the following advantages: the Thessalians declared him *archon* of their league which meant that he became commander-in-chief of their forces and was also able to dispose of certain funds that were placed at his disposal; at the same time he became an ally of the Boiotians and of some of the other states in Central Greece. The Phokians, of course, were allied with Athens and Sparta, but this counted for nothing with Philip; for the Athenians were already his enemy and the Spartans were in no position to harm him. After their defeat at the hands of Philip, the Phokians confined themselves to their own territory and to lands they had captured from neighbouring states. They continued to prove a formidable foe to their neighbours, including the Boiotians: but they no longer represented an obstacle in Philip's path; later, he simply crushed them once he had freed himself from other distractions and had neutralised the Athenians by concluding peace with them in 346.

Having briefly outlined the conditions that favoured the imperialist policies of Philip, we may now examine the relative strength of the opposed forces in the light of our present knowledge and assess the strengths and weaknesses of the Macedonian and his rivals.

No attempt will be made to compare the territorial extent of the population of Macedonia with the other leading Greek states. Territory in itself does not constitute strength, and our knowledge of the population of the ancient Greek states is very fragmentary; it consists for the most part of estimates based on calculations that are far from certain, with the result that widely differing hypotheses have been propounded. It may be safely stated, however, that Macedonia was much more extensive and much more populous than any other Greek state even before the rise of Philip, and that these assets became more marked as a result of his conquests.

Macedonia was also much richer than any other Greek state, most of its wealth deriving from mines. As early as Alexandros I (485-440), the mines of Dysoros yielded 360 talents of silver annually. Philip

acquired further mines: in 358 at Damastion, south and southwest of lake Lychnitis (Ochrid); in 357 in the area around Pangaion; and in 356 to the east of Philippi. This last region produced an annual income of over 1,000 talents of gold. Macedonia had bronze and iron mines, too, which probably also belonged to the state. Customs dues were a further source of state revenue. As commander in chief and later as *archon* of the Thessalians, Philip exacted dues on the harbours and markets of the League, as well as the tax paid to the League by the surrounding tribes — the Perrhaibians, the Magnesians, the Achaians and the Dolopians. We may now turn to the public revenue accruing to Athens. During the Social War (357-355) the regular annual income fell to 130 talents. After the revitalising of the public economy by Euboulos, it rose by the year 339 to 400 talents per annum[11] — scarcely 4/10 of the yield of one of the mines owned by Philip and perhaps 1/10 of his total revenue. The regular income of Athens was earmarked for the expenses incurred by the administration, for public works, for providing for the poor and for the Theoric Fund. The costs of arming and of the conduct of war were met from other sources. With the exception of the *thetes*, the citizens were obliged to furnish themselves with their own hoplite equipment, and all those above a certain level of wealth had to maintain a warhorse. The richest citizens of all were responsible for equipping warships and paid special taxes to cover other items of expenditure. Some idea of the size of this expenditure may be derived from the following details: the expedition of 5,000 infantrymen and 400 cavalry sent by the Athenians to Thermopylai in 352,[12] which stayed in the field only a few weeks, cost 200 talents.[13] The following year Demosthenes calculated that about 8 talents per month were required merely to feed 2,000 infantrymen, 200 cavalrymen and 2,000 oarsmen, the complement of 10 triremes.[14] We have no information on the public finances of other Greek states.

In vital campaigns against his Greek rivals Philip was able to mobilise the following forces: in 352, 20,000 infantry and 2,000 cavalry; in 340, a total of 30,000 men; in 338, 30,000 infantry and 2,000 cavalry. These included Macedonians, Thessalians and other allies.[15] In case of need, he had a safety margin, in terms of both men and resources, that would have enabled him to conscript three times as many Macedonians and perhaps four times as many Thessalians, as well as to hire thousands of mercenaries. The largest forces put into the field against Philip by the Boiotians and the Athenians, in 338, were 11,000-12,000 infantry and 800 cavalry and 10,000 infantry and 600 cavalry respectively — numbers which were very close to the totals that could be mustered by Boiotia and Athens when all the men capable of serving were mobilised. The second most important mobilisation of the Athenians against Philip was their attempt to stop him at Thermopylai in 352. In 351, on learning that Philip had laid siege to Byzantion, they detached a force of 10 triremes and the sum of 10 talents; and in 349 and 348 they sent aid to Olynthos that consisted initially of 2,800 mercenary peltasts and 30 triremes, followed by 4,000 mercenary peltasts, 150 Athenian cavalry and 18 triremes, and finally 2,000 Athenian hoplites, 300 Athenian cavalry and 17 triremes. It is worth noting that the 4,000 mercenary peltasts, 150 Athenian cavalry and 18 triremes sent in 348 had to be withdrawn from the Hellespont, an area upon which the Athenians depended for their survival. The Phokians succeeded in mustering an army much larger than that of the Boiotians or the Athenians by hiring mercenaries with funds that they had appropriated from the treasuries at Delphi. Before the outbreak of the Sacred War they had 5,000 men. In 354, the second year of the war, they had 10,000 and by 353 the number had risen to 20,000 — a force with which they defeated Philip in Thessaly. Their force the following year was the same size, but they lost 9,000 men, either killed or taken prisoner. In the last year of the war, continuous losses and the dwindling of the resources in the treasuries had reduced them to 8,000 men.

Philip's army was superior to that of any of the other Greeks in terms not only of numbers but also of quality. Moreover, it was commanded by Philip himself, one of the greatest organisers and army leaders the world has ever seen. Parmenion, the second-in-command, was also a general of exceptional capabilities. Under them served first rate senior and junior officers. Philip had introduced a number of innovations in the organisation, equipment and tactics of the army which had improved its efficiency. The soldiers were imbued with fighting spirit and were connected by strong ties of loyalty to Philip; they were trained to carry out swift forced marches and to execute battle plans with great precision.[16]

None of the Greek powers with whom Philip clashed were in a position to inflict any damage on Macedonia. The Phokians were encircled by hostile states and were held in contempt as desecrators by the Amphictyonic League. On the three occasions on which they made a drive to the north they reached southern Thessaly; the second time they defeated Philip, but the third they were comprehensively crushed. The Athenians, despite their possession of a fleet, were unable to prevent Philip from subjugating their allies along the north coast of the Aegean. On the other hand, their fleet made them vulnerable to Philip, since the sources of timber for their shipyards were Chalkidike and other areas that came under Philip's control. One third of the cereals consumed by the Athenians, plus a significant proportion of their trade, passed through the Bosporos, towards which Philip advanced ever closer with each successive conquest. Also in this area there were many Athenian cleruchies, the settlers of which were faced with the dilemma either of suffering at the hands of Philip or of fleeing back to Athens.

Philip always became acquainted accurately and swiftly with the various currents of public opinion in both friendly and hostile cities, as well as the decisions taken by them, the motives dictating these decisions and the degree of decisiveness that activated his foes. All this information was acquired with ease because all affairs were discussed publicly in the

69. *Aischines was the great opponent of Demosthenes who repeatedly accused him of serving Philip's interests; modern historians believe that Aischines' policies were perhaps more clear-sighted than those of his great rival. The original of this bust dates from the end of the 4th century B.C. Aischines' composure contrast sharply with the disturbed though determined expression of Demosthenes. London, British Museum.*

popular assemblies, and he had a large number of informers, while the states hostile to him did not possess the means to prevent information from being passed on. In contrast, neither the Athenians nor the citizenry of any other state opposed to him ever knew his intentions or the forces at his disposal, since he was solely responsible for decision making, at most exchanging views with a few trusted friends. The speeches of Demosthenes reveal that not even he was able to form a proper assessment of Philip's economic and military resources, of his powers of leadership, of the devotion of his subjects or the loyaly of his allies. Indeed, we read that Macedonia was weak[17] and vulnerable[18] from a military point of view; that Philip's soldiers, both the foot-companions and the mercenaries, enjoyed an exaggerated reputation;[19] that the Athenians had a stronger military force and more abundant economic resources than Philip;[20] that the Macedonians were weary as a result of continuous warfare and strongly desired peace;[21] that all commercial transactions between Macedonia and foreign powers had come to a halt;[22] and that the Thessalians, the Paionians, the Illyrians and other peoples were on the point of revolt.[23] That all these were inventions of Demosthenes to inspire courage in the Athenians seems highly improbable; at the most we may suppose that to this end he exaggerated the somewhat mistaken information he had received or the groundless opinions that he had formed. Conversely, had he been fully aware of the strength and resources at Philip's command, he would not have urged the Athenians to interfere in the dispute between Megalopolis and Sparta in 353/2, or to embroil themselves in the Rhodian civil war (351); nor, after the Athenians had suffered at the hands of Philip's fleet very close to the coast of Attica, would he have advocated that they should confront the Macedonian with a strike force of only 10 triremes, 2,000 hoplites and 200 cavalry, three quarters of whom were mer-

70. *The Agora at Athens was the centre of the city's public life. Towards the middle of the 4th century, the democratic institutions, the emergence of incompetent and corrupt leaders, the growth of a pessimistic outlook and an increasing individualism put Athens at a disadvantage in relation to the dynamic new society of Macedonia.*

cenaries, and a reserve of 50 triremes and an equal number of horse transports and supply ships. Generally speaking, it may be claimed that the relatively small scale of the Athenian mobilisations against Philip were dictated not only by the limited possibilities of the Athenian economy, and from the need to retain in Attica a force large enough to beat off a Boiotian attack, but also from an underestimation of Philip's forces. It may be that, had these forces not been so underestimated, the Athenians would have pursued a different policy and not repeatedly deployed inadequate forces that resulted only in adding the loss of allies and strategic positions to the wastage of economic resources and human lives.[24] The Athenian attitude in 344 was certainly unrealistic; they misinterpreted a friendly proposal from Philip as an indication of weakness on his part.

Philip was able to plan for the long term: he made all his decisions alone, calmly and without delay. In Athens, decisions were made by a show of hands in the popular assembly, after it had heard reports on the state of affairs, speeches by orators propounding a variety of ideas and a number of differing proposals; the atmosphere was always emotionally charged as a result of the disputes between the orators, and the problems were clouded by the arguments advanced by the speakers themselves and the political groups who supported them. Demosthenes complains that there were speakers who lacked any original ideas and who were simply concerned to win the favour of the people, always posing the questions "What do you want? What should I propose? What can I do to please you?"[25] From Demosthenes, too, we learn that the various political groupings made use of claques present in the assembly to shout approval of their favourite speakers and that, as a result, the rest of the citizens were pulled in different directions.[26] Isokrates also censured the mutual recriminations on the part of the orators, the general disorder that prevailed on the speakers' platform and the violent reactions of the crowd.[27] We might add here that many Athenians were reluctant to vote in favour of proposals that involved financial sacrifices, the reduction of the allocation to the Theoric Fund, the conscription of citizens (as opposed to mercenaries) and other sacrifices. As a result, the decisions taken were ill-considered, referred only to immediate contingencies and changed constantly. Philip himself was able to exploit the emotionally charged atmosphere of the Athenian assemblies in order to achieve the reactions he required by making timely diplomatic gestures and proposals. He was also greatly assisted by the fact that, whereas his own diplomacy was of a secret nature, that of the Athenians was unavoidably open.

Moreover, Philip, answerable to no one, could pick the most favourable moment to effect his decisions, amending them, if necessary (or advantageous) as he went along. By contrast, the decisions of the assemblies, in Athens and in other Greek states, whether democratic or oligarchic, were executed by magistrates, generals and ambassadors who were held answerable for their failure to carry out orders, even ill-judged orders, or for the failure of measures decided upon too hastily.

One of Philip's greatest advantages was his own character and quality. Naturally, the same man at the head of a weak state or faced by a different congruence of circumstances, could not have achieved as much; nor can one claim that his achievements could have been possible if the Macedonians had not been attuned to his policy. It is equally beyond dispute, however, that he himself made Macedonia as strong as it could be, given its population, resources and numbers of men of military age; he rid the state of internal weakness,[28] neutralised the disadvantages of the monarchic system and made the best possible use of its advantages. He strengthened the martial spirit of the Macedonians both by moral encouragement and material incentive. His army performed better than any other army of the period under the same conditions, and he spared it from losses whenever he could by using diplomacy,[29] propaganda, his own personal magnetism and bribery. He was also adept at making the most of his opportunities and at exploiting the rivalries and inadequacies of his foes. None of politicians and generals at the head of the states opposed to him could compare with him. Even Athens suffered from a lack of politicians and generals of any calibre. Demosthenes' political acumen fell short of his patriotism and did not match the energy he expended, after 346, in an attempt to prepare the Athenians for a decisive confrontation with Philip and to find allies for Athens. Hypereides had even less political competence, and Hegesippos was a narrow-minded fanatic who induced in the Athenians a mood of ill-timed intransigence. Three Athenian generals from the period of the confrontation with Philip are frequently mentioned: Chares, Charidemos and Phokion. The first, advanced in years, was an experienced general but of the old school. In 353, in command of a naval squadron in the north Aegean, he fell victim to one of Philip's ruses; however, he defeated some of Philip's mercenaries at Kypsela on the Hebros and captured Sestos. He faced Philip for a second time in Chalkidike in 349, where he was again unsuccessful. As a result he was stripped of his command and served with a lower rank at the battle of Chaironeia. Phokion was a mediocre general, but an exemplary citizen and an obedient officer: despite the fact that he was a professed anti-democrat he obeyed the laws and carried out his duty. Perhaps because he was pro-Macedonian, he never served against Philip but was always used in other missions. Charidemos was not an Athenian by birth. He first saw action as a young mercenary hoplite and distinguished himself as a mercenary officer in the service of the Athenians during the decade 370-360, for which he was awarded Athenian citizenship. Shortly afterwards, however, he offered his services to other masters, in the Troad, and seized the opportunity to capture a number of cities on his own behalf. Soon he was collaborating with Athens' enemies and even defeated an Athenian contingent and imposed humiliating terms on it (359). Despite all this, the Athenians welcomed him back to the city in 357 and elected him general — a striking testimony to the lack of competent generals in Athens. In 349 he headed a squadron of reinforcements sent by the Athenians to Olynthos and spent his time in frivolous pastimes. As for the other generals of this period, we have only scant comments, all unfavourable, and no names. They refused to risk their lives in battle, though they perpetrated actions punishable by death; when tried they were acquitted and re-elected, to repeat their crimes.[30] Others neglected the struggle against Philip in order to pursue their own private wars.[31]

Clearly a number of the advantages enjoyed by Philip and the disadvantages that told against the Athenians, set out above, stemmed from their respective constitutional systems: the Macedonian monarchy on the one hand and the Athenian democracy on the other. It should not be inferred, however, that either the monarchic system of the Macedonians or the democracy of Athens were in themselves contributing factors to the outcome of the struggle. If this were the case, monarchies would always defeat democracies under equal terms. To this generalisation may be added specific arguments relevant to the case in question. Macedonia had been a monarchy long before the rise of Philip yet the monarchy had been a source of weakness rather than strength since it gave rise to dynastic strife. Conversely, at an earlier period, the democratic constitution had been a source of strength to Athens. It had scarcely been introduced when the Athenians successfully beat off attacks by Sparta, Boiotia and Chalkis (507-506), and Herodotos properly attributes these successes to the new constitution.[32] At a later date, Athens, still under democratic rule, repulsed alone the first Persian invasion (490); she also contributed more than any other Greek state to frustrate the Persians' second attempt (480); she also founded and led both the First and the Second Confederacy. The accusations[33] hurled against the Athenians by the Corinthian ambassadors in Sparta in 431 are diametrically opposed to the complaints of Demosthenes about his fellow citizens and strangely enough, striking similar to his branding of Philip. The institutional and functional defects in the Athenian democracy were not so pronounced during those periods; further, any damage arising from these defects was made good by other, positive features. During the struggle with Philip the flaws in the constitution had increased for reasons that cannot be discussed here, and the damage caused by them was irreparable. In contrast, the Macedonian monarchy had been strengthened by Philip, who made good its weaknesses and was able to exploit all its advantages in the pursuit of his expansionist and imperialist designs.

The foregoing comparison reveals that Philip was far stronger than the Greeks in all aspects of strategic importance, a factor which gave him a considerable safety margin. He did not need to use his manpower or his material resources to the full, and could clearly have achieved the same results had his superiority been much less pronounced. Naturally, a more mediocre or less ambitious personality would have achieved far less given the same human and material reserves; but it is clear that in Philip's case the awareness of his overall superiority, combined with favourable circumstances, spurred him even further and further, for it is the nature of the ambitious to aspire to greater and greater feats when the resources at his disposal permit more than he has achieved.

Contrariwise, the limited nature of the resources at the disposal of the Athenians and the unfavourable congruence of circumstances combined to undermine Athenan morale, divided public opinion and sapped the will to resist of large sections of the citizen body; the resulting climate of pessimism was severely damaging to Athenian institutions and produced a dearth of competent politicians, facilitating the rise of incompetent and corruptible elements to the leadership. When a society is beset by a series of reverses and gripped by pessimism, the individual becomes less and less inclined to make personal sacrifices for the sake of the public good, and looks increasingly to his own self-interest. Under Philip, Macedonia was a dynamic and optimistic society, the individual members of which were fully conscious of the importance of their own personal contribution to the realisation of the aims of the society as a whole.

The result was that on the one side efforts were intensified and the fruit they bore added further to the general feeling of dynamic confidence, while on the other the reserves of energy were continuously decreasing as a result not only of being expended in a hopeless struggle but also of being squandered by corrupt officials for purposes of their own. The balance of power thus tilted steadily in favour of Philip and against the southern Greek states that attempted to resist him.

PANHELLENISM: FROM CONCEPT TO POLICY

In 338 Philip crushed the combined forces of the southern Greeks at Chaironeia. Immediately after the battle he dispelled their fears by inviting them, together with other Greek states, to sign a peace treaty and participate in a campaign against Persia under his leadership. Thus Philip was at last able to embark on the practical implementation of both parts of a Panhellenic programme which he had started working out some years before. It was a programme which had been conceived and promoted by a number of Greek intellectuals and which Jason, tyrant of Pherai, had fully intended to put into practice with the first part slightly different.

For various reasons, which it is beyond the scope of this book to consider, the Greeks had always formed themselves into a large number of small, separate states ever since the dawn of their history. This political fragmentation had some beneficial effects: democratic forms of government came to predominate more rapidly than they would otherwise have done, for example, and it was much easier for able citizens to rise to positions where their talents could be put to good use. But at the same time it was also responsible for continual outbreaks of hostilities between one Greek state and another. Each sought to expand at the expense of the others; those which gained the ascendancy established oppressive hegemonies over the rest; the victims of aggression stopped at nothing to protect their integrity, their autonomy, their very existence. All this warring caused serious loss of life and destruction of property, resulting in increasing poverty which was the main cause of the wars. In short, Greece was trapped in a vicious circle of suffering.

Yet, despite their disunity, the Greeks quite early acquired a sense of national identity. Moreover, they took pride in their origins, as they deemed themselves endowed with qualities or virtues which raised them above other peoples, whom they scornfully referred to as barbarians. But this national consciousness and ideology, although alive and productive on an intellectual plane, functioned only occasionally as a political factor. The examples are few: a) the concerted resistance of the mainland Greek states to the Persian threat at the beginning of the fifth century; b) the rallying of the Athenians and their allies in the second quarter of the same century in support of the Asia Minor Greeks against the Persians; c) the support given to the Greeks in Asia Minor and Cyprus by the Spartans and their allies early in the fourth century. On the other hand, there were occasions when the Spartans, the Athenians or the Boiotians were not above calling for, or accepting, assistance from the Great King in a war against other Greek states. Furthermore, a great many Greeks, political exiles or poverty-stricken citizens of poor states, did not scruple to serve as mercenaries in the Persian armies.

But eventually it became clear to more and more Greeks that warring between them was fratricidal, that it arose over petty issues and that it provided no solution to the underlying problems. It also became obvious that if the Greeks befriended each other and united their forces, they could take territory from their common foe, Persia. These ideas, first formulated and propounded by political theorists, mostly orators, were subsequently adopted by some rulers. The theorists were the offspring of the cities of southern Greece; the rulers were monarchs of the Greek North.

Gorgias was the first publicly to denounce fighting between Greeks. He declared that their sufferings would be at an end if, united, they turned against Persia. He delivered two speeches to this effect, one at the Olympic Games of 392 and the other in Athens on the occasion of the public funeral of those fallen in battle. This was at the time of the Corinthian War which had broken out in 396, only eight years after the end of the long drawn-out Peloponnesian War. Gorgias was in a position to be an impartial observer of the Greek scene, for his loyalties lay with none of the Greek states then in conflict. Having lived in many different states, he had acquired a Panhellenic outlook. Both occasions chosen by Gorgias were favourable for the presentation of such ideas: the Olympic Games brought together citizens of different states, neutrals and belligerents alike, and hostilities were suspended for the duration of the Games. And the public funeral of the Athenians fallen in inter-state warfare created a psychological climate conducive to reconciliation between the Greeks and to the undertaking of a common war against a national foe.

The orator Lysias spoke in the same vein at Olympia during the Games of 384.[1] For two years peace had held, but this peace had been imposed on the Greeks by an ultimatum from the Great King who sided with the Spartans. In the eyes of Sparta's opponents this constituted blatant meddling in the Greeks' internal affairs by a foreign monarch, who, moreover, was the arch-foe of Hellenism. Other Greeks also shared this resentment. Lysias urged the Hellenes to unite against the Persians and against all tyrants, especially Dionysos of Syracuse. It reflected badly on the Greek nation, he said, that parts of it should be ruled by barbarians and other parts by tyrants, and all the more so because the reason for it was not that the Greeks were too weak to resist but that they wasted their energies fighting each other.

Lysias, despite his residence in Athens, his sympathies with the Athenians and his sufferings as a democrat under the Thirty Tyrants placed by Sparta in his adopted homeland, nevertheless believed that the Spartans had the best claim to lead the Greeks.[2] It may seem surprising, on the face of it, that this suggestion should have come from Lysias, and especially so as he made it at a time when Sparta, with the support of the Great King, was lording it over Greeks or threatening to do so. Still, during those years, a union of Greeks would have been unthinkable except under Spartan leadership.

By 380, when Isokrates' *Panegyrikos* was published, many other men of letters besides Gorgias and Lysias had publicly proclaimed the need for unification of all Greeks and for an all-Greek war against the barbarians.[3]

But the man who made the propagation of this policy the task of his life was Isokrates. He urged its adoption in two long discourses, the *Panegyrikos* (written between 390 and 380) and the *Philippos* (written in 346), and more briefly in various letters. The prologues to his letters to Dionysios of Syracuse (367) and to Archidamos, king of Sparta, (356) have survived, and so have the full texts of two letters to Philip of Macedon, one of 344, the other of 338 (the authenticity of the latter is questionable). We have evidence of letters from Isokrates to Agesilaos, king of Sparta (also of questionable authenticity), and to Alexander, son of Jason, and he is believed also to have written to Jason himself.[4]

Over a period of several decades Isokrates consistently propounded the same basic ideas, even at times using almost identical phraseology,[5] although as time went on he shifted his support from one potential Panhellenic leader to another, besides re-working his arguments and revising certain details of the programme. At no time did he actually put forward any specific proposals on crucial issues, his main concern being with the general need for Greek unity and the launching of a joint crusade against the barbarians.

The gist of his argument was as follows. Poverty is the curse of Greeks; it underlies every kind of conflict, be it discord between cities or discord within cities. The breakdown of inter-state relations, the animosity between rich and poor and the deterioration of political aims are evils that go hand in hand with poverty. In all this quarrelling and feuding the points at issue are so petty that even the victors do not stand to benefit, for their losses outweigh their gains. The way for the Greeks to alleviate their poverty and bring their internal strife to an end is by conquering the barbarians in Asia and seizing their territory; and there is nothing to prevent them from doing so, if only they make up their differences and join forces with each other. These are the basic arguments of Isokrates, which he maintained steadfastly.[6] He also blamed misfortune as a contributory cause of internal instability: many Greeks, banished by their fellow-citizens after internal disputes, plotted to return by means of force; those in power lived with the fear of being the next to be defeated; the exiles and the poverty-stricken outcasts often ended by becoming mercenaries, and when some Greek city fell into their hands they sacked it ruthlessly, ravished the women and sold the captives as slaves.

In the *Panegyrikos* and in his letter to Archidamos Isokrates merely cites these as evils which would be eradicated once the Panhellenic programme was under way. In the *Philippos,* which is a later work, their continued existence forms the basis of a new argument in favour of putting the programme into practice: if this situation is allowed to worsen, he says, the established social order will be fatally endangered.[7] The *Panegyrikos,* finished under the humiliating circumstances of the peace imposed by the Great King, exudes Isokrates' indignation over the undignified position of the Greeks. The interference of the Great King in Greek affairs, the readiness of the Greeks to curry favour with him and the return to Persian rule of the Greek cities in Asia Minor all contributed to feed his anger.[8] Liberation

of these cities is included amongst the aims of the programme in his letter to Archidamos,[9] but not in the *Philippos* or his later writings.

Isokrates anticipated the moral objections that might be raised to his proposals for a war of conquest in Asia and tried to refute them in advance. It is right, he said, that wealth and power be removed from those who have more of both than is due to them;[10] and it is equally right that the arrogant be humbled.[11] After all, the Persians are our enemies by nature and heredity alike. In past times they have harmed us, and even now they are plotting against us.[12] It is a disgrace, therefore, to sit back and do nothing, for the Great King has no army capable of confronting us. He tacitly admits as much himself by employing Greek mercenaries as soldiers and officers.[13] It is a disgrace, too, to fight on his side against other Greeks, or to help him to put down rebellions among his subjects. None of this redounds to our credit, when, with minimal effort and no danger at all, we could take everything he has.[14] Other arguments of Isokrates pivot on the idea of the Greeks' inherent superiority over the barbarians: the barbarians are cowardly[15] and are worth less than the Greeks who are in distress.[16] It is shameful that barbarians should be more prosperous than Greeks;[17] that although individual Greeks have barbarians as slaves, the Greek people collectively allow themselves to be reduced to servitude by the barbarians;[18] and that the barbarians, who are effeminate, inexperienced in war and corrupted by luxury, have produced men who aspire to rule over the Greeks.[19] Another of Isokrates' arguments in this vein is concerned with the relative merits of Greeks and Persian royal families: it is a disgrace, he says, that the descendants of Herakles (i.e. the kings of Sparta and Macedon) have a humbler title than the descendants of Cyrus, who was exposed as an infant by his own mother.[20]

71. Twenty years of warfare and diplomatic negotiations culminated, on the eve of Philip's death, in the founding of the League of Corinth. This marked the realisation of the ambitions to which he had devoted his whole life. Most of the northern Balkan region had been subjected to Macedonian authority and the majority of the Greek states were bound to him by a complicated network of alliances. The map shows the political allegiances of the Greek states at the death of Philip.

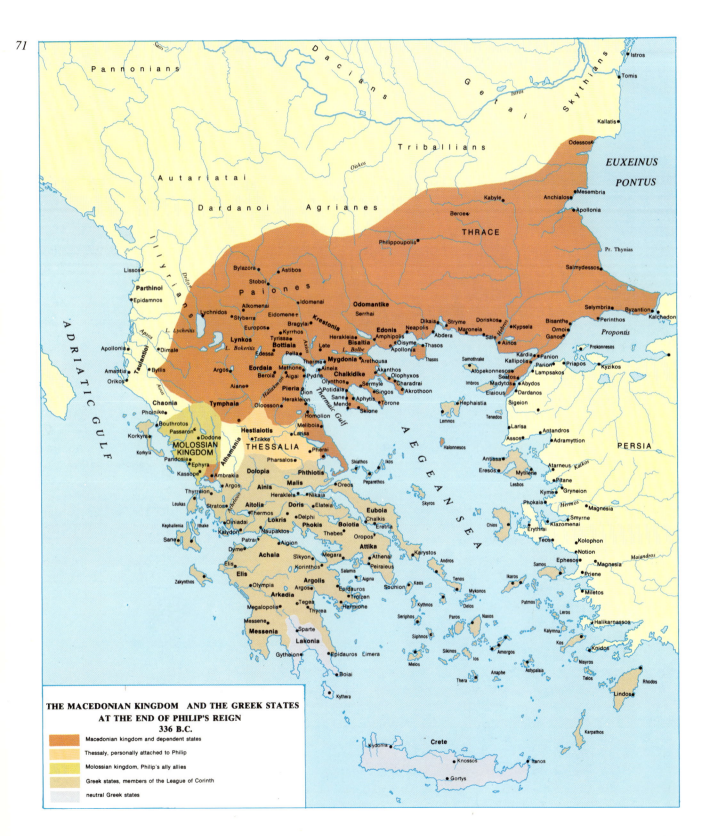

THE MACEDONIAN KINGDOM AND THE GREEK STATES
AT THE END OF PHILIP'S REIGN
336 B.C.

Macedonian kingdom and dependent states

Thessaly, personally attached to Philip

Molossian kingdom, Philip's ally allies

Greek states, members of the League of Corinth

neutral Greek states

Concord among the Greeks, Isokrates goes on, is a necessary prerequisite for any campaign against the barbarians,[21] for without internal peace the conquest of Asia is not feasible (here he cites the case of Agesilaos, who had to cut short his campaign in Asia to deal with Sparta's enemies in Greece).[22] Conversely, the conquest of Asia will consolidate peace among the Greeks.[23]

In the *Panegyrikos*, written (as already mentioned) between 390 and 380, Isokrates proposed that the all-Greek alliance should be under the joint leadership of Athens and Sparta, although he went to great lengths to prove that the Athenians were better qualified to be the leaders. Later on, however, he turned successively to a number of different rulers:[24] to Jason, tyrant of Pherai (before 370); to Alexandros son of Jason; to Dionysios, tyrant of Syracuse (367); to Archidamos, king of Sparta (356); and finally (from 346 on) to Philip. That Isokrates turned to autocratic rulers for the execution of the Panhellenic programme shows his disillusionment with both Athens and Sparta as potential leaders and his faith in absolute rulers (as being charismatic personalities) and in the monarchy as an institution (because of its effectiveness). However, he admonishes the recipients of his letters to reserve their autocratic tendencies solely for the barbarians and in no case to attempt monarchic rule over the Greeks.[25]

Isokrates gave specific reasons for each of the monarchs he chose as potential leaders of the Panhellenic movement. Writing to Dionysios of Syracuse, he founded his appeal on the fact that he had the most powerful army and the greatest prestige among the Greeks.[26] In his letter to Archidamos he supported his choice by adducing the latter's royal status and high repute.[27] His choice of Philip was based on broader grounds: he was a descendant of Herakles;[28] he had the natural talents of a man destined to achieve great things;[29] he had already achieved much that seemed "beyond hope or reason", and this heralded further exceptional success;[30] he had a force unmatched anywhere in Europe;[31] he had no ties with any of the Greek city-states and so he could consider all Greece his homeland.[32] Of all the many rulers whom Isokrates had tried to interest in his Panhellenic programme, Philip alone had the personal qualities and the objective advantages demanded by the task.

What was this task? Only in the *Philippos* do we find a few hints. Philip should take the initiative to bring the Greek states into unity and concord.[33] He himself should take the first step by becoming reconciled with his adversaries,[34] and then use his powers of persuasion to make the rest of the Greeks follow his example.[35] The use of force was ruled out: he was not to seize Greek cities, nor was he to impose himself on the Greeks as a monarch. For monarchy was not for the Greeks.[36] Then, again strictly by exhortation, he should secure the cooperation of the Greek cities in a campaign against the barbarians,[37] of which he would be the supreme leader.[38]

When Isokrates was writing the *Philippos,* he was more certain than ever that concord among the Greeks really was a practical possibility. The first to be persuaded to cooperate should be the four largest cities: Athens, Sparta, Argos and Thebes. They would not oppose this move, for their arrogance and intransigence had been sapped by their misfortunes.[39] The other cities would then follow suit.

At this time Isokrates was at his most optimistic that the campaign would not only materialize, but also be successful. In the *Panegyrikos* he had pointed out that the armies of the Great King were in no position to stand up against the Greeks. He had cited examples from the past[40] and had stressed the fact that the Great King was "a ruler of disaffected subjects."[41] In the *Philippos* he referred again to the inferiority of the Persian troops[42] and to the cowardice of the barbarians,[43] and at the same time he presented fresh arguments based on the contemporary situation: the Great King was faced with revolts of many of his subject peoples,[44] whereas Philip could build up a strong mercenary force composed of the Greek exiles and indigents from whom the Great King habitually drew his own mercenaries.[45]

As regards the extent of the Greek conquests, Isokrates was an extremist, though his thinking on the subject was full of inconsistencies. This is clear

72. *Isokrates gave the most consistent and most eloquent expression to the ideal of Panhellenic unity. He wrote a number of speeches and many letters urging its implementation. His objective was to unite the Greek states in a common campaign against the barbarians. The original of this bust of the Athenian orator dates from the 4th century* B.C. *Naples, Museo Archeologico Nazionale.*

from his various proposals: the Greeks should subject all the barbarians,[46] or as many barbarians as possible,[47] they should conquer the whole of Asia,[48] or the whole of the Persian Empire, or at least Asia Minor as far as the Cilicia-Sinope line (this last proposal had already been made by others).[49] Greek colonies should be established in the conquered regions and the landless peasants and exiles could be sent to live there.[50] The natives were to become *perioikoi*[51] or helots.[52] Isokrates was wise enough not to work out any plan for the division of the conquered Asiatic territories between Philip and the Greek cities.

How, we may ask, did Isokrates envisage the subsequent course of events? From the spirit running right through his exhortations, and from the few hints in the *Philippos*, it may be surmised[53] that he expected cooperation among the Greeks to continue after the Asiatic territories had been won, for the conquest would remove the causes of friction between them.

Isokrates never advanced any concrete political or constitutional proposals on which Philip's cooperation with the Greeks would be based.[54] Attempts by modern scholars to read such a meaning into certain passages of the *Philippos* involve stretching the evidence.[55] The more they reconstruct his political ideas, the more inconsistent they make Isokrates appear. Only very general political ideas can safely be attributed to Isokrates in the context of his Panhellenic programme. He did not aim at the formation of a unified Greek state but would have been content with a reconciliation between the existing Greek cities and their peaceful coexistence thereafter. Accordingly he condemned both the imposition of one city's dominion over another and the subjection of Greeks to the rule of a monarch. This last point he states expressly in the *Philippos*, where the Macedonian king is admonished not to try to dominate the Greeks[56] but to pay heed to public opinion[57] and to win the affection of the Greeks.[58] The cities should remain independent. No longer would their existence and their interests militate against those of Hellenism. Philip was to be responsible for maintaining the balance between the cities and the nation. He was to incarnate and represent the nation, his relations with it being governed by some form of charter. He would thus be the guarantor and instrument of the new order, but not its master. Macedonia and the Asiatic territories awarded to Philip after the conquest would remain outside the terms of this new order, which was to refer solely to the relationship between Philip and his allies, the Greek states. Philip would continue to be king of Macedonia according to the traditional laws of the Macedonians, and he would have sovereign power over the barbarians.[59]

Isokrates had a number of imitators.[60]

By 375 Philip's precursor Jason, the tyrant of Pherai, had annexed to his state a large part of Thessaly and some adjacent lands to the southwest, and had built up an exceedingly strong army which included a large number of picked mernenaries. He planned to become *tagos* of all Thessaly in order to move on to a still bolder plan:[61] having under his command more foot-soldiers, more peltasts and more cavalry than any other army in Greece, he would form alliances with other states and break the hegemony of Sparta and Athens, and then he would lead an expedition into Asia at the head of a Panhellenic army. He was certain that he could defeat the forces of the Great King, for the King's subjects were schooled to be slaves rather than trained for physical endurance. Moreover, the *myrioi* of Cyrus and the tiny army of Agesilaos had demonstrated the superior quality of the Greek soldiers.[62]

The last part of Jason's programme and his reasons for optimism recall parts of Isokrates' *Panegyrikos* published in 380. Whether Jason was influenced by this treatise of Isokrates or by his own teacher Gorgias, or by both, and to what extent, we cannot say for sure, but he must have got from Gorgias the idea of a Panhellenic expedition to Asia, if nothing else. Where Jason's designs ran contrary to the ideas expressed in Isokrates' *Panegyrikos*, and presumably also to the content of Gorgias' *Olympikos*, was in his plan to challenge the leadership of Sparta and Athens and establish Thessalian hegemony over Greece by force of arms. As we have seen, Isokrates had urged the Greeks to stop fighting each other and to entrust the leadership of the Panhellenic movement jointly to the Spartans and the Athenians. When he learned of Jason's plans he sent a letter, the text of which has not survived. We may presume, however, that his object in writing to Jason can hardly have been to persuade him to unite the Greeks and lead them against the Persians, for Jason had already proclaimed his intention of doing so, but rather to advise him not to use force against other Greeks, just as he was later to counsel Philip. After gaining control of all Thessaly and becoming *tagos* of the Thessalian *koinon*, Jason had intended to preside over the Pythian Games in the summer of 370 and to strengthen the Amphictyonic Council, over which he had great power because, as *tagos* of the Thessalians, he controlled not only their votes but also those of the states dependent on them. He was assassinated, however, before he could carry out his plans.

Quite by chance, Philip took his own first steps towards the realisation of the Panhellenic ideal from the point that Jason had reached. He, too, became leader of the armies of the Thessalians (353) and afterwards their *archon* (the office of *tagos* having by then been abolished). During the Third Sacred War, against the sacrilegious Phokians, he placed his army at the disposal of the Amphictyonic Council. After the defeat of the Phokians he became a member of the Council and master of its decisions (346). Eventually he managed to cajole the Greek states into some sort of cooperation and to assume the leadership of a Panhellenic expedition against the Great King (337). Soon after that, however, his life came to an abrupt end at the age of 46, when he was assassinated like his Thessalian forerunner. There are indications that Philip had had both the ultimate objectives of his Panhellenic policy in mind for some time before he was able to start pursuing them in practice.[63] But it is equally apparent that at an earlier stage he never lost sight of those interests even when he was pursuing the two inter-related objectives of the Panhellenic programme.

The internal strengthening of Macedonia and the successive extensions of its boundaries belong to Philip's strictly Macedonian policy; but his consistent refusal to be tempted into extending his kingdom to the south of Mt. Olympus and the Kambounian range and his whole attitude towards the southern Greeks were dictated by the aims of his Panhellenic policy. North of the natural boundary between Thessaly and Macedonia, Philip added to the Macedonian state not only barbarian, but also Greek territories; whereas south of that border he sought not to annex more land to his realm, but rather to pave the way for an all-Greek alliance and for his recognition as its head. Furthermore, his behaviour towards defeated Greek states varied greatly according to whether they lay north or south of this same dividing line. To those that lay north of the border he was ruthless: transportation was the least of the punishments that he meted out to the people of Methone and the cities of Chalkidike; some of the Olynthians he reduced to helotism, others he sold as slaves; and the lands of these same cities he divided up amongst the Macedonians.[64] This was in strong contrast to his treatment of states lying south of Macedonia: he resolutely stepped in to save the Phokians from extermination, even though by doing so he displeased his allies,[65] and he showed unexpected clemency to those defeated at Chaironeia, notably the Athenians.[66] He himself justified this leniency to friends who advised him to seize southern Greece by saying that he preferred to be known for a long time as a benefactor than for a short time as a despot.[67] Long before the Battle of Chaironeia he had repeatedly shown Athens his desire to be on friendly terms with her.[68] Summing up, we can say that Philip worked with unwavering determination and consistency for the expansion of Macedonia within the limits he had set for himself at an earlier stage. Beyond those limits he showed himself equally determined to avoid any unnecessary shedding of Greek blood or waste of Greek wealth, and to do nothing that might make him appear to be a conqueror. Rather than to domineer, Philip tried to gain the ascendancy in southern Greece with the consent, or at least the toleration, of the majority of the Greeks and to run counter to their wishes as little as he could.

Philip's plans to campaign in Asia became known in 342.[69] However, there is reason to believe that his conciliatory policy towards Athens even as early as 346 was in some measure dictated by the value he placed on her fleet in an eventual war against the Great King.[70] We shall never know what Philip actually had in mind as the ultimate objective of his Asiatic policy, since he was killed before he had a chance to start putting it into practice. If he saw the conquest of Asia as an extension of his Macedonian policy, we may assume that he intended to annex the Asiatic territories to the Macedonian kingdom; if he saw it as an extension of his Greek policy he would presumably have founded Greek cities in Asia, which in due course would have become signatories to the Greek pact of 337; and if he saw it as a purely personal affair, he would have ruled there as absolute monarch, as Alexander and the Hellenistic kings were to do later.

As for the motives that led Philip to plan a campaign in Asia, it may fairly safely be said that the Macedonian king would neither have conceived the idea nor launched the expedition for the sole purpose of relieving the sufferings of the southern Greeks, as Isokrates entreated him to do. Had this been his aim, all he had to do was to encourage the southern Greeks to establish colonies in Thrace. This would have killed two birds with one stone, as it would have accelerated the economic and cultural development of that newly conquered region. We must therefore assume that there were many motives for his projected adventure in Asia, and that they probably complemented each other. Philip's personal ambition must have been one of them. The Macedonians' increasing tendency towards aggressive expansionism must have been another. It need hardly be said that strategic reasons must also have played a part: the security of Philip's acquisitions in Thrace demanded, if not the destruction of the Persian Empire, at least the pushing of its boundaries as far east as possible. Lastly, the factor that may finally have turned the scales was his realisation that expansion into Asia and his own continued supremacy in southern Greece were inextricably interlinked. A successful campaign in Asia, with the participation of contingents from the southern Greek states, would rule out the possibility of diplomatic or military intervention by the Great King in Greek affairs, this being a well-tried policy invariably pursued by the Persians whenever a power emerged west of the Aegean that was capable of threatening their interests. At the same time, such an expedition would make it difficult for anti-Macedonian elements to solicit Persian support. Finally, it would turn the attention of the restless and dissatisfied to new interests, full of excitement and promise.[71]

We should note three important points which are elucidated under (a), (b) and (c) below. First, it was in Philip's interests not to add territory to the Macedonian state; secondly, he had the power to make up his own mind on the subject and thirdly, he was able to exert an influence that virtually amounted to suzerainty over the unannexed territories. (a) Macedonian kingship was not absolute monarchy: it was a monarchy restricted by tradition, usage and precedent.[72] Yet these restrictions did not apply beyond the boundaries of Macedonia. From the time Philip was declared commander in chief and later archon of Thessaly, he was the first Macedonian king to acquire any experience in exercising authority unrestricted by Macedonian laws. (b) In inter-state relations, Philip represented the Macedonian state and made decisions that were binding upon it, while its citizens exercised no control whatever over his actions. All Greek monarchs, whether kings or tyrants, had this right. Under ancient Greek law, states ruled by a monarch were identified with the monarch, just as those without a monarch were identified with their citizens. Thus, in a treaty, a signatory state without a monarch is referred to by the name of its citizens (the Athenians, etc.), but one with a monarch by the mere name of its ruler (Amyntas, Jason etc.), even the monarch's style (king of Macedonia, tyrant of Pherai) being superfluous.[73] (c) Because of the strength of the Macedonian army at his disposal, Philip could exert as much influence as he liked outside the Macedonian state. He could even have established a personal state, wherever he wished and as large or small as he wished.

From 346 onwards the trend of Philip's Greek policy can be followed easily. At the same time his growing interest in the idea of an Asiatic campaign begins to be apparent. In 346 he had his way over the issue of retribution against the Phokians and also over the question of re-organising the Amphictyonic Council, which he re-convened. He raised no objection to the infliction of heavy penalties on the Phokians, but despite the risk of displeasing his allies (which he did), he opposed the Theban and Oitaian demands for annihilating them. His attitude is explicable not only when viewed within the context of his policy of sparing the southern Greeks, but also as a means of preventing the Thebans from benefit-

73. As links between Macedonia and Southern Greece became increasingly close, the local Macedonian traditions mingled with those of the major artistic centres of the period. The relief gorgoneion in the picture is a typical example of mixed influences and traditions; it was the attachment for the movable handle of a krater-situla found at Stavropolis near Thessalonike. Second half of the 4th century B.C. Thessalonike, Archaeological Museum.

74

THE PACT OF THE HELLENIC LEAGUE 337 B.C.

```
. . . . . . . . . . . . . 26 . . . . . . . . . . | . . . 6 . . .
[Ὅϱκος. ὀμνύω Δία Γῆν Ἥλιον Ποσε]ιδῶ Ἀ[θηνᾶ]-
[ν Ἄϱη θεοὺς πάντας καὶ πάσα]ς. ἐμμενῶ [....]
[. . . . .⁸ . . . . καὶ οὐ λύσω τὰς σ]υνθήκας τὰ[ς..]
[ . . . . . . . . . ¹⁸ . . . . . . . . . οὐδ]ὲ ὅπλα ἐποί[σω ἐ]-
[πὶ πημονῆι ἐπ' οὐθένα τῶν] ἐμμενόντων ἐν τ-
[οῖς ὅϱκοις (?) οὔτε κατὰ γῆν] οὔτε κατὰ θάλασ-
[σαν οὐδὲ πόλιν οὐδὲ φϱο]ύϱιον καταλήψομ-
[αι οὐδὲ λιμένα ἐπὶ πολέ]μωι οὐθενὸς τῶν τ-
[ῆς εἰϱήνης κοινωνούντ]ων τέχνηι οὐδεμι-
[ᾶι οὐδὲ μηχανῆι οὐδὲ τ]ὴν βασιλείαν [τ]ὴν Φ-
[ιλίππου καὶ τῶν ἐκγόν]ων καταλύσω ὀδὲ (sic) τὰ-
[ς πολιτείας τὰς οὔσας] παϱ' ἑκάστοις, ὅτε τ-
[οὺς ὅϱκους τοὺς πεϱὶ τῆ]ς εἰϱήνης ὤμνυον,
[οὐδ' αὐτὸς οὐθὲν ὑπενα]ντίον ταῖσδε ταῖς
[συνθήκαις ποήσω οὐδ' ἄλ]λωι ἐπιτϱέψω εἰς
[δύναμιν· ἂν δὲ τις ποῆι τι] παϱάσπονδον πε-
[ϱὶ τὰς συνθήκας, βοηθήσω] καθότι ἂν παϱαγ-
[γέλλωσιν οἱ ἀδικούμενοι (?) ] καὶ πολεμήσω τῶ-
[ι τὴν κοινὴν εἰϱήνην (?) παϱ]αβαίνοντι καθότι
[ἂν δοκῆι τῶι κοινῶι συνεδ]ϱίωι καὶ ὁ ἡγεμὼ-
[ν παϱαγγέλληι καὶ οὐκ ἐγκ]αταλείψω. το[..]
[. . . . . . . . . . . .²³ . . . . . . . . . . . . ].. [....⁸....]
```

74-75. Representatives of all the Greek states assembled at Corinth for the conference called by Philip in order to conclude a "common peace". This marked the realisation of the ideal of Panhellenic unity. Above: the text of the oath taken by the members of the League of the Greeks in 337 B.C. preserved on a fragmentary inscription found on the Acropolis in Athens. Opposite: gilded clay disc with a relief bust of Athena Parthenos, one of the deities by whom the oath of the alliance was sworn. 4th century B.C. Thessalonike, Archaeological Museum.

ing by the total destruction of the Phokians.[74]

The Amphictyonic Council was of considerable political importance, thanks to the powers it wielded and the prestige it enjoyed. In the past only the strongest states, such as Sparta, had been able to flout its judgements. Now that Philip was behind it, no state, however powerful, would be able to stand up against it. Philip had already placed his army at the disposal of the Council, and it was thanks to his intervention that the Phokians had been defeated. Now he was about to become the head of the Council itself. This he did by introducing a few, but effective, changes. The Council expelled the Phokians and awarded their seat to Philip and his heirs. It also temporarily deprived Sparta of its membership and gave its votes to other Dorian states. The fact that Philip was admitted as a member of the Council, rather than the Macedonians, is interpreted by some scholars as an indication that the Greeks did not recognise the Macedonian people as Hellenes, though they were prepared to accept the Macedonian royal family. But, as we have observed, states ruled by monarchs were identified with their monarchs: the Macedonians therefore could not have a seat on the Council; it belonged only to their king. Philip's membership was thus tantamount to the membership of the Macedonians. It was another matter that Philip, if he wished, could in practice pursue a personal policy within the framework of the Amphictyony. With his own votes plus those of the Thessalians (whose *archon* he was), of the peoples subject to the Thessalians and of some other states as well, Philip was able to control the Council. It is interesting to note that not only did Philip not have the Athenians expelled from the Amphictyonic Council, despite the fact that they had been allies of the Phokians, but in 343 he actually saw to it that the Athenians carried the vote in a dispute they had with the Delians. Before that, he had shown the importance he attached to public opinion in Athens by sending envoys to reply to the charges of Demosthenes and other hostile orators, who had accused him of not keeping his promises.

In 344 Persian envoys arrived in Athens with an offer of an alliance. The Great King probably saw in the rise of Philip a potential menace to his empire. Although at that time the Athenians were looking for allies against Philip, they rejected the Persian proposal. Philip, in ignorance of their refusal, immediately sent an embassy to Athens to forestall a pact between the Athenians and the Great King and, if possible, to mollify the Athenians' hostility towards himself. The central point of his message was that he would consent to a change in some of the peace terms. The Athenians then made excessive

demands in the belief that Philip was in a difficult position. Philip's reaction was twofold: he made overtures himself to the Persians and, as a counterpoise to Athens, established governments well-disposed to himself in a number of Greek cities. A few years later he wrote to the Athenians that his offer in 344 had been a well-intentioned gesture designed to settle the differences between them to the advantage of all Greeks.[75] This move must therefore be regarded as a pointer to the Panhellenic policy he was to adopt after his victory at Chaironeia.

Philip's rapprochement with the Persians was short-lived. Hermias, tyrant of Atarneus and Assos on the west coast of Asia Minor, started secret negotiations with Philip. The latter's prompt response shows how keen he was to seize this opportunity of obtaining a foothold in a region where he was planning to act. But the goings-on did not escape the notice of the Great King's spies. Persian intervention was immediate: Hermias was defeated, taken prisoner and put to death in Susa in 342. Thus the Great King learnt of Philip's plans. The full support given by the satraps of Asia Minor to the city of Perinthos, which they supplied with mercenaries, arms, food and money when it was besieged by Philip in 340, must be seen as a direct Persian response to the threat posed by Philip.

It was not long before the southern Greeks, too, got wind of Philip's intention to invade Asia. Demosthenes hinted at in 341,[76] when he was intensifying his efforts to rally support for a broad coalition against Philip. That coalition, joined even by the Thebans, who in doing so broke their alliance with Philip, was crushed at Chaironeia.

That this victory paved the way for Philip's Panhellenic expedition to Asia did not escape the Athenian orator Demades, one of Philip's opponents, at the time captive in the victor's camp. Demades, taken aback by the sight of Philip wandering about drunk and savagely expressing his joy over his victory and his scorn for those he had defeated, was bold enough to rebuke him thus: "O King, are you not ashamed of behaving like Thersites when fortune has

76. *Relief head of a Silenos, decorating the central boss (omphalos) at the bottom of a silver kalyx. It was found in grave Z, Derveni and is dated to the second half of the 4th century* B.C. *Thessalonike, Archaeological Museum.*

entrused you with the role of Agamemnon?"[77] Philip could not fail to grasp the implications of this unflattering comparison between Thersites, the ugly, provocative and antipathetic anti-hero of the *Iliad,* and Agamemnon, the most powerful of all the Achaian kings and their commander in chief in the Trojan War. Demades' allusion brought Philip to his senses, for it reminded him of the role he had set himself to play. Breaking away from the influence of drink and of his primitive excesses, he rose to meet the challenge and devoted himself single-mindedly to the pursuit of his well thought-out policy, which was to be implemented in two stages.

Philip's first step was to establish relations with his defeated enemies and settle a number of other Greek matters of local importance. He allowed the bodies of the Athenians who had fallen in battle to be cremated with due honours. A few days later he communicated his peace terms to the Athenians — terms of unprecedented generosity. He would free the captives without ransom and return the ashes of the dead; he would allow Athens to keep Skyros, Lemnos, Imbros and Samos and he demanded her cooperation in the suppression of piracy. The Athenians, astonished by his magnanimity, accepted without demur. Philip then honoured the Athenians by ordering no less a personage than the crown prince Alexander, with two leading Macedonian generals, to escort the ashes of those fallen in battle. Towards the Thebans he adopted a different attitude: not lenient, but not harshly vindictive either, even though the Thebans had broken faith with him. He released their prisoners of war, but only on payment of a ransom; he permitted the burial of the dead, but he demanded payment for the place of burial of the Thebans fallen in battle; Thebes was deprived of all the lands she had seized from other Boiotian cities and also of Oropos, the latter being awarded by Philip to the Athenians; he forbade Thebes to represent the Boiotians on the Council and the other collective bodies of the Amphictyony; and he planted a garrison at Cadmeia, the acropolis of Thebes. He also placed garrisons at Chalkis and Corinth and in Ambrakia. He obliged the Akarnanians to banish those of their compatriots who had fought against him at Chaironeia. He did not disband the federations of defeated states. The democratic governments in the Boiotian and Euboian cities, as well as in Corinth,

Troizen and Ambrakia, were overthrown, but they remained in power in Athens and in Achaia. Whether these changes came about at Philip's insistence or simply through the pressure of local political forces, we do not know. The mildness of Philip's conduct towards the defeated, which was in striking contrast both to the behaviour of other Greeks in comparable circumstances and to his own ruthless treatment of his northern enemies, is only explicable in the light of his Panhellenic policy. The relative harshness of his conduct towards the Thebans, in comparison with his general leniency, was due to the fact that they had broken their alliance.

Now that Philip no longer needed to worry about offending the Thebans, he was able to alleviate the situation of the Phokians by getting the Amphictyonic Council to reduce from thirty to ten talents the six-monthly instalments which the Phokians had to pay to the Delphic sanctuary by way of indemnity. He also assumed the role of arbitrator in disputes between Greeks who had taken no part in the recent war. In this capacity he favoured the territorial claims of the Argives, the Tegeans, the Megalopolitans and the Messenians against the Spartans, and he put military pressure on the latter to oblige them to conform. However, he opposed the demands for the annihilation of Sparta made by certain states friendly to him. Another of Philip's important actions was his restoration of the Arcadian League to its former size.

With these bilateral or local settlements accomplished, Philip now went on to far more important issues: the formation of a coalition of Greeks, under his leadership and the preparation of a Panhellenic expedition against the Persians.

At the end of 338 Philip invited the independent Greek states of the mainland and islands to send delegates to Corinth to discuss matters of common interest.[78] The choice of Corinth as the meeting place was designed to serve as a reminder of the conference held there by those who resisted Xerxes in 480 and thus to suggest that a similar task was to be undertaken by the Panhellenes. Nevertheless, it seems that the question of a campaign against Persia was not discussed at this conference, but only the terms of a "common peace". This term (koine eirene) was used by the ancient Greeks for every treaty of friendship, non-aggression and collaboration (occasionally also of mutual defence) signed by a large number of states, not necessarily former belligerents. It was also used to describe the situation which followed the signing of such a treaty. Many similar treaties had been signed before the "common peace" we are concerned with, beginning with the "King's Peace" or "Peace of Antalkidas" of 387/386.[79]

The clauses of this "common peace" were dictated by Philip and accepted by the Greek states who had responded to his invitation. Sparta was not amongst them. From a number of fragmentary sources[80] we learn that the signatories, who did not include Philip, were collectively styled "the Hellenes", and that they undertook the following obligations:[81]

1) not to compel any other state to join in the "common peace" against its will; 2) to abide by the treaties (but it is not clear which treaties[82]); 3) to respect each other's liberty, autonomy and territorial integrity; 4) not to make war against each other unless one of the signatories violated a clause of the agreement; 5) neither to interfere with the shipping of the other signatories or to oblige their ships to put into ports other than their destination; 6) to abide by the *dogmata* (resolutions) of the *synedrion* (the body of plenipotentiary representatives of the signatory states); 7) to carry out the orders of the *hegemon;* 8) not to give asylum to political exiles nor to assist them against the governments of their homelands; 9) to respect all constitutions in existence at the time of the signing of the pact, with the exception of tyrannies; 10) not to redistribute landed property, cancel debts or free slaves; 11) not to pass laws inflicting punishment by death or exile or confiscation of property for offences which until then had carried a lighter penalty; 12) not to commit hostile acts against Philip or his heirs; 13) to cooperate in suppressing any violation of the pact and punishing the offenders.

In comparison with earlier "common peace" pacts, clauses 6-12 are innovations. The institution of the *synedrion* has no precedent in a treaty of this type, but only in alliances and in the Delphic Amphictyony. The composition of the *synedrion* was

77. Handle - attachment in the form of a Siren from a silver hydria found at Torone in Chalkidike. The mythical being with the head of a woman and the body of a bird rests on a floral composition. End of the 5th century B.C. Thessalonike, Archaeological Museum.

also original in conception: instead of each state having an equal number of representatives, the numerical strength of each state's delegation was weighted in proportion to its population and its naval and military strength. We know[83] that the Thessalians had ten seats, the Phokians and the Lokrians three each, the Perrhaibians two; three other states whose names are illegible had five, two and one, the Zakynthians and the Cephallonians three between them, the Thasians and the Samothrakians two between then and a group of states in Central Greece between them five.[84] The position of *hegemon* was analogous to the role of guarantor that the Great King had reserved for himself in the Peace named after him.[85] But the analogy is somewhat strained, especially as we do not know exactly what was the scope of the *hegemon's* jurisdiction in the treaty of "the Hellenes".[86] The *hegemon* was, of course, Philip, who, as we can deduce from the known clauses of the treaty, was not himself a signatory, although he sponsored the pact. By remaining outside the treaty his position in relation to the signatories was similar to the archonship he held in the Thessalian League. Clause 8 forbade the giving of aid to movements aimed at overthrowing the governments of other signatory states. Clauses 9, 10 and 11 forbade the signatories to make any constitutional or even legislative changes concerned in matters of a social nature.[87] Most of the Greek states by this time had oligarchic regimes and governments friendly to Philip, but the democratic governments that remained, in Athens and in the cities of Achaia, were protected just as the others were. It would appear that Philip accepted this show of liberalism as the price to the paid for avoiding constant unrest in the few democratic states that remained. The installation of an oligarchic regime in Athens, especially, would have been opposed by the democratic majority and Philip's reputation as a peacemaker would have been sullied. The motives behind Philip's stipulations in clauses 8 to 12 were strictly political not social. By means of these clauses he hoped to stabilise the "common peace", both for its own sake and as a stepping stone towards his next objective, the campaign in Asia. The restrictions contained in these clauses were designed to frustrate any attempts to enlist the support of landless peasants, debtors and slaves against Philip by promises of land redistribution, cancellation of debts and freedom.[88]

Yet it is obvious that these same measures also served the interests of the affluent classes in the southern Greek states. The rich, being uneasily conscious of the increasing numerical strength of the poor and of their growing readiness to revolt, were inclined to support Philip. There were of course some noteworthy exceptions: one was Demosthenes, Philip's arch-enemy, whose father employed many slaves and who had himself amassed a large fortune, whereas Aischines, the leader of Philip's Athenian supporters, belonged to a poor family and had made his living by humble employment, for which he was derided by his opponent, Demosthenes.[89] Finally, clause 12 imposed on the signatories various obligations towards Philip and his heirs.

With its novel provisions, Philip's "common peace" seems stronger than any of its predecessors. Yet the surest guarantee of its duration lay in the institution of the *hegemon* and in the fact that it was Philip who held this position. For Philip was able to deploy against any violator not only the armies of the other signatories, the majority of which he influenced directly or indirectly (through the ruling parties, which owed their power to him), but also if need be, the whole might of his own army.

The next steps in Philip's pursuit of his Greek and Asiatic policies, insofar as the historical record is complete were: his proposal, put to a new conference of delegates from various Greek states, for a war against the Persians, ostensibly to avenge the sacrilege committed by Xerxes against the temples of the Greek gods; the acceptance of this proposal; Philip's election as *strategos autokrator* (commander-in-chief with full powers) over the united forces of the southern Greeks taking part in the campaign; and lastly the passage of a resolution, which defined as a traitor any citizen of a member-state who entered the service of the enemy.

Now it is most unlikely that such resolutions would have been carried if there had not already existed an offensive treaty containing, at the very least, the following stipulations: 1) that such and such states were allies; 2) that this treaty was concluded for the purpose of waging war against the Persians; 3) that a *strategos autokrator* would be at the head of the combined forces; 4) that the latter would be appointed by a body of representatives constituted in a certain way. The second and third of these clauses could not have been included in the treaty of "common peace" analysed above, not so much because there is no evidence for them (after all, they might well not have been included in the fragments that have survived), but because they are clauses of an offensive alliance rather than of a pact of "common peace". We must therefore assume that in addition to the "common peace" Philip also made an offensive alliance with the southern Greeks. This alliance would not have been made at the same time as the treaty of "common peace" (for then the latter would have been superfluous) but at a later date. When Philip dictated the terms of the "common peace" he judged the time not yet ripe to propose an offensive alliance that would oblige the southern Greeks to levy troops so soon after Chaironeia when their casualties still haunted their minds, their wounds still troubled their bodies and their defeat still rankled. We must therefore assume that this offensive alliance was drawn up at the same time as, or slightly before, the passage of the resolution concerning the Asiatic campaign: it could have been ratified first and the resolutions about the campaign passed immediately afterwards, or alternatively, the resolutions may themselves have been terms included in the treaty of alliance. It is very probable that treaty adopted the basic terms and institutions of the pact of "common peace". This, and the fact that the forming of the alliance coincided with passage of the campaign resolutions, might explain why the alliance is not mentioned in the sources as an event separate either from the "common peace" or from the resolutions approving the campaign in Asia and the election of Philip as *strategos autokrator*.[90] Philip would once again have refrained from signing the treaty of alliance himself, following both his own example in the "common peace" and the much earlier example of Athens at the time of the Second Athenian Confederacy.[91] It was a position which offered many advantages.[92]

The preliminaries completed, Philip was now free to embark on his Asiatic policy proper. In the spring of 336 he dispatched to Asia Minor a vanguard of 10,000 men, most of them Macedonians, liberated the Greek cities from the Hellespont oto the Maeander and captured some territory along the way. Had he not now been struck down by the assassin's knife, he himself would have followed with the main body of the Macedonian army and the allied contingents.

Many of Philip's actions were in accordance with what Isokrates urged him to do. He aimed consistently at the two goals of the Panhellenic programme. He tried to allay the enmity of the Athenians from 346 until the moment when they organised the alliance of southern Greeks against him. And he behaved to those he defeated at Chaironeia with a leniency which is only explicable if we see it as a move towards the realisation of the Panhellenic programme. He also tackled the unification of the Greeks before the expedition to the East. He did not force any state to join either in the "common peace" or in the offensive alliance. He respected the independence of all the separate states of the Greek mainland and the islands; he did not even limit their autonomy, save in a few instances where he deemed it necessary in the interests of his wider policy, which was to preserve social peace in the interests of the forthcoming expedition to Asia.[93] A passage in the text which has come down to us as a letter from Isokrates to Philip, written after Chaironeia, tells us that many were wondering whether or not Philip had actually been influenced by Isokrates, and that Isokrates himself was not sure what the answer was.[94] If the text is genuine, this testimony must refer to a time before the "common peace", and certainly to a period before the offensive alliance which publicly revealed the basic lines of Philip's thinking, thereby providing a much surer basis for comparison with Isokrates' ideas. If the text is not genuine, the wisest course is to refrain from giving a positive answer to a question that even today remains unanswerable. Some confirmation of Isokrates' influence on Philip can be deduced from the correlations noted above and by the chronological relation of the *Philippos* (346) to the subsequent activities of the Macedonian king, which have a close affinity to the precepts of the Athenian orator. But one may well ask: could Philip not have had the same ideas as Isokrates without necessarily having been influenced by him? Whatever the answer, this much is certain: the theorist was so much of a pragmatist that his precepts were not far removed from the deeds of the statesman; and the statesman was so much of a visionary that we may well wonder whether or not the inspiration for his deeds lies in the exhortations of the theorist.

MACEDONIA UNDER PHILIP

By every criterion open to our assessment the Macedonians were Greek. But the increasing modern interest, as archaeological evidence adds definition and depth to the somewhat hazy picture preserved in the ancient literary sources, is especially directed at the ways in which they differed from their contemporaries. Owing to its relatively isolated position on the northern frontier of the Hellenic region and to the peculiar circumstances of its historical evolution this distinctive society retained some features that seem unusual, often anachronistic, in the fourth century context — although perhaps not so out-of-place in Homer's heroic world. At the same time, in some respects, it could be thoroughly contemporary and thoroughly Greek. It is this lively and lusty blend both of the Balkan and the Aegean, and of the old and the new that gives the people of Macedonia their particular fascination and forms our central theme in this brief survey of their society in Philip's reign.

In modern Macedonia the political and social influences of past decades and centuries have left their traces in, among other things, some intermixture of Greek dialects and remnants of non-Greek languages. Just so in the fourth century the population movements of two centuries and more had bequeathed a legacy including a variety of language and dialect. However, although some of the earlier inhabitants, overrun during the expansion of the Macedonians out of the Pierian mountain areas of the south-west, must have spoken in Illyrian, Thracian and Paionian tongues, our evidence for the Makedones themselves – both those who had become the dominant political and cultural group on the central plain and to its east and those who had occupied the western mountains of Upper Macedonia – is that they spoke Greek.[1]

It is not surprising that the members of the Temenid dynasty, which traced its ancestry back to Temenos, a king of Argos, and thence to Herakles,[2] should have been Greek-speakers nor that they spoke it in a quite standard form. The same may have been true of the Bakchiad ruling house of Lynkos, which claimed Corinthian descent,[3] though our evidence is too poor to be certain. At the same time, if many — perhaps all — of the Macedonians were able by Philip's time to speak standard Greek, it is clear that they also spoke a Macedonian dialect of it that was somewhat different,[4] one which might still be familiar enough to serve in special circumstances — for example, as a watchword or in a distinctively Macedonian ceremony, but whose use was in general decline. The evidence is slight, but the indications are that this was, or resembled, the Aeolic form of Greek used, in mixture with other dialects, in Thessaly. The Macedonians of the western uplands who in the past had been related politically to the Epeirotic tribes west of the Pindos range, probably spoke a form of West Greek, similar to that used in Epeiros; but that too, especially following Philip's annexation of Upper Macedonia, will have moved in the direction of the standard form.[5]

Thus there was no apparent difficulty, for example, in the well documented communications between the Athenian and other envoys visiting Pella in 346 and the King and his retainers,[6] or indeed at any time in the known contacts of Macedonia with the main city-states to the south. Thus too the language of Alexander the Great's army was Greek; the 30,000 young Persians who were trained to take a part in it were taught "Greek letters and Macedonian weaponry".[7]

The organisation of Macedonia, of course, was not at all typical in fourth century Greece. Most obviously, its institutional framework was monarchic. Then, despite changes in past decades for administrative reasons, its cities were not *poleis* in the classical sense; above all, they were not autonomous, even in theory. It is for that reason, presumably, that Demosthenes could refer disparagingly to Philip as a "barbarian",[8] although to do so was misleading by reason of his, and his subjects', language. A half century earlier Thucydides implicitly classed the Macedonians with the barbarian peoples;[9] he also included the Molossians and Thesprotians of Epeiros, though their language, as inscriptions prove, was Greek too. Such a designation, which seems to equate barbarism with a tribal form of organisation, or non-*polis* organisation, rather than non-Greek language, entails too many contradictions to be helpful.

Macedonian religious institutions,[10] or at least those most in evidence, were very obviously Greek, the most important temples and festivals being dedicated to Zeus and Herakles. The main cult-centres of Zeus, so far as we can tell, were at the old capital of Aigai and at nearby Dion. As we should expect, bearing in mind the ruling dynasty's lineage, the cults of Herakles were especially prominent at the old capital and at its newer counterpart, Pella. Festivals in the Hellenic style were held to mark both regular and extraordinary occasions, like the festival of Zeus and the Muses at Dion, like the Olympian Games which Alexander held at Aigai or like the celebratory festival in which Philip was taking part when he was struck down in 336.[11]

To an observer one of the most striking characteristics of the Macedonians and their kings, apart at least from the constant military commitments of their own and others' making, was the pervasiveness of their day-to-day religious observances. The regular routine of sacrifice, offering and thanksgiving, seen most clearly in Alexander's better documented reign, was the king's responsibility, for there was no professional priesthood; so that he was also, in effect, chief priest.[12] The ritual observances are one thing, but beyond that we constantly notice, during Philip's reign, how carefully he took both his own and others' religious practices and beliefs into account — sometimes cynically, perhaps, but too consistently for it to be no more than that.[13]

Many social customs, naturally for a people so distant from the main centres, were alien to the classical Hellenic way of thought. They were the traditions and *mores* of a frontier people, whose survival against the marauding tribes of the Balkan area, not to mention the depredations of their Hellenic

78. *Detail of a painted stele, discovered 20 years ago in the fill of the Great Tumulus at Vergina. The female figure is rendered with consummate skill and is reminiscent of figures in Renaissance art. End of 4th century* B.C. *Veroia, Archaeological Museum.*

79. *Detail from a mosaic from the palace at Vergina, showing a mythical female figure.*

confrères, depended on toughness and belligerence. Even the king — or perhaps the king above all — was brought up from childhood to hunt wild animals, an often dangerous and very military skill with as much protocol and as much importance attached to success as would be found in most armies. Under normal circumstances he would take his place at an early age, as Alexander did, in his father's militia, to command sections of it as soon as he was able. Most importantly, he learned to command invariably from the front. Like his subjects the young prince was not "blooded" until he had put down his first enemy in battle.

It was a male-dominated society, even more so than the more civilized city-states of the classical world. Women, other than royal women at any rate, played a wholly subordinate role, even those of the royal family finding their main functions in providing heirs for the king or dynastic marriages for his allies. The royal family, at least, was polygamous, for the obvious reason that the male upbringing must have brought about, by its rigours, a high rate of attrition among princes; also because, although the people appointed the king, they always selected (while that remained possible) from the Temenid family and mostly the eldest surviving son, so that it was always essential to furnish that family adequately with heirs. Alexander, who somewhat irresponsibly declined to do so when it was most practical,[14] left the kingdom without an obvious focus of loyalty and so destroyed the dynasty.

It was a society governed by no written body of law. But, of course, we should not fall into the error of underrating the strength of oral law, understood and accepted custom, especially when we think how large a part is played by precedent and time-honoured practice in the most sophisticated and structured of modern legal and constitutional systems. The king as supreme judge (other than in capital cases, or perhaps only treason trials, which were adjudicated by a Macedonian assembly, or by the army when the king was on campaign) played an important part in this, but his actions here and elsewhere were expected by his subjects to be governed not by sheer strength but by what was traditionally proper in the behaviour of their rulers.[15]

There were occasions on which an assembly of Macedonians operated, at least (as we have noticed) in a judicial capacity to try certain capital cases[16] and, most interestingly, to appoint a new king, or perhaps to remove an existing one,[17] but there seems to have no constitutional power otherwise to oblige the ruler to do what he did not wish. On the other hand, it was traditional and proper for the king to be accessible to his people and for them, on occasion, to tell him their wishes remarkably bluntly.[18] His ultimate authority on nearly all matters — although, as Demosthenes almost wistfully observed, it gave him certain diplomatic and military advantages — was the feature most alien to contemporary Hellenic thought.[19]

The population of the kingdom was relatively large by Greek standards, there being perhaps as many as one million inhabitants in all; the Makedones proper will have comprised only a proportion, perhaps not an extremely high one, of these, descendants of the earlier inhabitants probably forming a substantial sub-citizen class. In this kaleidoscopic picture there is an element that stands out most clearly: the role of the royal court as a focal point for the cultural life of the kingdom. Indeed, when one notes the two different strands of material culture, the old and the new, surviving side by side in

80. The "Macedonian" tombs were subterranean buildings often with a temple-like facade, probably used as family vaults. The illustration shows a reconstruction drawing of the two-tier facade of the great tomb at Lefkadia, near Naoussa. It had Doric half-columns on the lower storey and Ionic on the upper, separated by false windows. It was lavishly decorated with painted and relief scenes. The panels between the lower half-columns contained a monumental representation of the Judgement of the Dead in Hades. From left to right the dead warrior, Hermes the Escorter of Souls, and Aiakos and Rhadamanthys, two of the judges in Hades.

the archaeological remains –the one often somewhat akin to the Protogeometric and the other as modern as the best workshops of the Hellenic world could produce[20] – it seems fair to observe that the "modernisation" of the Macedonian people was a process operating from the centre outwards. Their awakening to the developments of classical Hellenism occurred as the result of a conscious interest on the part of the royal house, rather than primarily and directly through contact with other Hellenic groups.

The Temenid dynasty was obviously most attentive to its Hellenic heritage and fostered in this predominantly conservative society an appreciation of the most impressive, largely Athenian, work in contemporary thought and creativity. The most famous past patron of the arts had been Archelaos. He had been generous to his visitors, but we need not suppose that men of the stature of the tragedians Euripides and Agathon, the epic poet Choirilos, the painter Zeuxis or the musician Timotheos of Miletos were attracted alone by financial reward. There is no reason to suppose that this savagely sophisticated people was any less intriguing or refreshing to them than it is to us.

Not all of the reigns are well enough documented for us to know how seriously most kings took such things. But certainly in the brief five-year reign of Perdikkas III (365-360), Philip's elder brother and predecessor, the tradition seems to have been maintained. He was advised by men as distinguished as Kallistratos, on finances, and Plato's pupil Euphraios (in fact even, though by letter and not in person, by Plato himself), presumably on questions of statecraft and government. Which artists visited his court we do not know. But at any rate it was as part of an established tradition that Philip offered his patronage to some of the more outstanding men of his time in the Aegean world.

At Philip's court we may note first the central role of the theatre and related arts in the glimpses of its cultural life that remain to us. They were prominent in most, perhaps all, of the great celebrations known to us, not in isolation but in their typically Hellenic association with religious ritual and, often, athletic contests — for example, in the festivities of late 348 signalising the victory over Olynthos and the other cities of the erstwhile Chalkidian League. Most spectacular of those known, probably, was the magnificent festival of the arts mounted in July 336 at Aigai (providing, as it happened, the setting for Philip's assassination), with dignitaries and envoys in attendance from much of the Greek world. They were there not only for the ostensible reason, to celebrate the marriage between the princess Kleopatra and her uncle, king Alexander of Epeiros, but also to be caught up in the excitement of the early despatches coming home from the general Parmenion, then taking the first, successful steps in Philip's and the Hellenic League's, Asian campaign.[21]

Such lavish displays, however, were exceptional — although it is revealing that the Macedonians should have chosen to mark their festive occasions in such a way. But what is even more significant are the constant reminders we happen to be given that theatre and arts flourished at most or all times at Philip's court. When we discover prominent actors, men like Aristodemos, Neoptolemos and Thessalos, playing occasional political or diplomatic roles, rushing here or there as envoys, we may note that, as more or less stateless professionals of recognised standing, whose service of Apollo and itinerant style of life fitted them ideally for such communications, their choice was obvious enough.[22] But more important than that is the fact that such men seem to have been there at the court so regularly. It is this, even more than the great occasions, that makes it clear that to Philip and those around him the combination of the

81. Amongst the objects found in the Great Tumulus of Vergina were a large number of grave stelai like the illustrated, tomb-stones of common Macedonian citizens. The purely Greek roots of the inscribed names, and their manifestly Macedonian traits testify to the centuries-old Greek tradition alive in Macedonia.

savage and the sophisticated was a natural one by now, that the latter element was not just something contrived on great occasions to impress the gullible. The archaic elements attracted the sneers of Macedon's opponents, but the Olympian superciliousness of a Demosthenes or a Theopompos should not seduce us into thinking of Philip and his retainers as no more than brawling, unlettered ruffians.[23] We find, for instance, in Antipatros, one of Philip's two most distinguished generals and administrators, a man at once capable of writing a history (now lost) of Perdikkas III's Illyrian wars and cultivated enough for the great Aristotle, who was to name him executor of his will, to devote nine books of letters to him.[24]

The reign saw the influx of many non-Macedonian Greeks into the life of the court and army. Some took up Macedonian citizenship; others did not. Among those who came and stayed were two outstanding young men, the Cretan Nearchos, later known for his account of the exploratory voyage down the river Indus and thence by sea to the Persian Gulf, which he commanded on Alexander the Great's orders in 326 and 325, and Eumenes of Kardia,an educated man who served as Philip's secretary from 342 and later, in his old age, wrote a history of the period after the death of Alexander.[25]

Many men of established reputation were to be found at court at various times. In the late 340s the historian Theopompos visited Pella; indeed he may have been promoting himself for the post of Alexander's tutor given instead to Aristotle in 342.[26] His major work, a mammoth *Philippic History* in fifty-eight books, centred upon the reign of Philip, whom he described as the greatest man Europe had produced.[27] He was nevertheless as inclined as some others to misunderstand the customs of Macedonian society and there were times when his pen dripped vitriol; but it is a great loss to us that only fragments of his work survive. The famous orator Python of Byzantion, another (like Theopompos) of the distinguished pupils of Isokrates' school of rhetoric in

Athens, served Philip as diplomat and negotiator.[28] His old mentor, though he never visited Macedonia (born before the Peloponnesian War broke out he was little short of eighty at Philip's accession and ninety-eight when he died in 337), corresponded with the king on occasion and may have influenced some of Philip's thoughts on the settlement of Greece and the campaign into Asia.[29]

This was a time when theorists of government, disillusioned by the predilection of the Greek city-states for tearing each other apart and by the apparent weaknesses of both democracy and oligarchy, were much given to speculation about the possibilities for order and moderation under the government of an enlightened monarchy. Plato had theorised over the virtues of the Philosopher-king and it may be that those of his disciples who went to Pella conceived it to be part of their mission to try making a philosopher of Philip.[30] In 348, soon after Plato died and was succeeded as head of the Academy by Speusippos, Aristotle, the man who would be seen as the greatest of all Plato's pupils, left Athens. Whether he went at first to Macedonia is not clear; his father, a native of Stageira in the Chalkidike peninsula, had been the friend and physician of Philip's father, Amyntas III (c. 393-370), and it is likely enough. In any case he next spent two years or so in the liberal princedom of Hermias of Atarneus, in north-western Asia Minor, in the company of the fellow Platonists Erastos and Koriskos, then in 345, by that time married to Hermias' daughter, moved to Mytilene where he probably met and worked with Theophrastos.[31] Three years later, around the middle of 342, he was offered

82. Some very fine mosaic floors, in large buildings, were discovered at Pella. The illustration depicts a deer-hunt. It was the work of one Gnosis whose name can be read near the top, just below the border. The three dimensional quality of the figures, achieved by strong contrasts of light and dark, and the careful attempt to render perspective, reflect the contemporary achievement in the sphere of large-scale painting. c. 300 B.C. Pella, Archaeological Museum.

ΓΝΩΣΙΣ ΕΠΟΗΣΕΝ

ΚΥΝΗΓΙΟΝ ΛΕΟΝΤ
LION HUNTING SCE

83. *Floor-mosaic from Pella depicting a lion-hunt. Two youths, one on either side of the picture are raising their weapons and preparing to strike the lion which is rendered in perspective in the centre. It has been suggested that the two youths are Alexander, Philip's son, and his friend Krateros.*

84-85. A group of graves discovered at Derveni, 10 kms from Thessalonike, contained exceptionally rich grave offerings (jewellery, silver and bronze vessels, armour and weapons), objects of considerable importance for their high artistic quality. The most striking object is this large Krater exuberantly decorated. The body of the vessel shows a band of Bacchic revellers dancing around Dionysos and Ariadne. The volute handles are richly decorated with snakes, palmettes and acanthus leaves; the heads of four deities fill the space at the centre of the volutes; one of these is the head of Herakles. Thessalonike, Archaeological Museum.

and accepted the post of tutor to the young Alexander, then nearly fourteen years old.[32] (He was followed, then or later, by Theophrastos, who was to incorporate some Macedonian data in his writing on natural phenomena.)

Aristotle was not the prince's first tutor. Two earlier mentors in particular are known, one a stern disciplinarian named Leonidas, a kinsman of Alexander's mother, the other Lysimachos from Akarnania.[33] To sort out the respective influences of these two and Aristotle on the king-to-be is not really possible, though it is probable enough that the well known scientific interest of his adulthood were fostered by the last tutor. His love for Homer, his devotion even while on campaign to the works of the Attic tragedians, may find their seeds in his earlier instruction rather than alone in the tuition of Aristotle. But most of all they were probably the result of a familiarity with especially Athenian culture acquired during his boyhood at Philip's court.[34]

Alexander, perhaps by inheritance and certainly by upbringing, was a precocious boy. By the age of fifteen or sixteen, at some time during 340, he was to take over a heavy burden of responsibility in the administration of the kingdom during his father's continuing absence in Thrace and beyond.[35] In 342, though, on Philip's departure, Antipatros was appointed to govern the kingdom. Perhaps the tensions of the capital were inappropriate to the degree of concentration and reflection required by effective education. Perhaps, too, the steamy heat of Pella and its marshes did not conduce to such pursuits. At any rate Philip established Aristotle, Alexander and some others of the prince's age (no doubt some of the Royal Pages, including one or more of Antipatros' sons) at the old town of Mieza just below the modern Naoussa on the cooler slopes of Mt. Bermion. Aristotle's school was at the Nymphaion, a series of caves, colonnades and shady walks, recently identified, and here he taught his young charges and worked away at his own studies.[36]

Macedonia was in a way a kingdom with two

86. Detail from the Derveni Krater. A seated Mainad, one of the four statuettes that were attached to the shoulder of the vase close to the handles. Exquisite work of the second half of the 4th century B.C. Thessalonike, Archaeological Museum.

87. Detail from the Derveni Krater, showing Dionysos. A silver ivy tendril runs above the god's head. Thessalonike, Archaeological Museum.

88. *Gold wreath of olive from a grave at Derveni. 4th century* B.C. *Thessalonike, Archaeological Museum.*

89. *Gold diadem with a decorative motif consisting of a central palmette and spiral tendrils; from grave B at Derveni. Thessalonike, Archaeological Museum.*

90. *Gold myrtle wreath from grave D at Derveni. Second half of the 4th century* B.C. *Thessalonike, Archaeological Museum.*

88

capitals. Aigai (or Aigeai) was the old and Pella, from the reign of Archelaos, the new. But the former was more than just the earlier seat of the monarchy. It was as old as the very first expansion of the Makedones out of the nearby Pierian mountain area and figured prominently in several of the foundation-myths of the tribe. Its settlers were said, in one, to have been led there by a herd of goats; its name means something like "the place of goats". Throughout the Temenid period and later, it remained a kind of ceremonial centre of the kingdom; there the kings were buried and there many of the great occasions of state were set — including, for example, the festivities during which Philip met his death.[37]

Its identification has posed problems, mainly because of a tradition that its earliest name was "Edessa", which led to confusion with another Edessa in ancient Macedonia (= the modern town of that name), which was hence long supposed to be the site of the old capital. The actual evidence — not archaeological, for that has only recently come to light — pointed somewhat equivocally towards some other location. There were surviving references to both Aigai and Edessa, apparently as separate places. Next, Theophrastos had observed that in the area of the ancient city a curious reversal of wind-currents sometimes took place, so that while the prevailing wind was blowing southwards the local wind, deflected downwards and back by Olympus and nearby mountains, would blow towards the north. The phenomenon is still noticed, not at Edessa, which is in any case too far from Olympus, but just south of the Haliakmon river. Finally, the details of an account of the attempt by a pretender to Philip's throne in 359 to raise Aigai in revolt make very little sense if Aigai is equated with Edessa, but accord perfectly with an identification in the area of the southernmost curve of the Haliakmon.[38]

For some decades at a site in that very region, on flat ground below the village of Vergina, archaeologists have explored a large number of iron age grave-tumuli dating from the early iron age onwards. Further up the hill, above Vergina, remains of a very big structure dating to the early third century had come to light.[39] Between the two sites there was a tomb of roughly the same date containing a marble chair or throne. Was this the grave of a king? One scholar came to think so, and then others.[40] The pieces of the jigsaw, though worn at the edges, nonetheless seemed to fit. Now the question is settled by the magnificent remains (described elsewhere in this volume) just unearthed from beneath the Great Tumulus at Vergina: certainly royal tombs, one of them very probably Philip's. The large building further up the slopes, some 104 metres by 88, may now be seen very probably, as some had earlier thought, as a palace or part of the palace-complex, perhaps built soon after damage wrought at Aigai by the Gallic mercenaries employed by Pyrrhos in 274.[41] Its ground-plan is now in most parts clear. The entrance on the eastern side gives, through a series of three *propylaia,* onto a large central courtyard surrounded by many rooms. At least the western end was two-storied. Built of poros stone coated with a fine plaster, higher up the walls were of sun-dried mud-brick. The palace contains the remains of some fine floor-mosaics; its plastered walls probably once bore frescoes. It post-dates Philip's reign, of course, by a generation or more, but its size and apparent splendour reflects the Macedonia that he built.[42]

Now that Aigai's location is certainly known, exploration of the surrounding area should increase, and no doubt much else, beyond the tombs already coming to light, will emerge. The theatre, in the entrance of which Philip was murdered, should not be far away, no doubt with other buildings from the classical period.[43]

Pella was adopted as the new Macedonian capital, certainly by Archelaos, for strategic reasons. During the fifth century the kingdom had continued to expand towards the east and by about 410 extended as far as the Strymon river. Aigai was now far from central and problems of communication and administration, matters given much attention by Archelaos, must have grown increasingly severe on account of its peripheral position. Thus the move was made to the existing town of Pella near the head of Thermaic Gulf on what was then a lake on the lower Loudias river. Surrounded mostly by low-lying, marshy terrain it was for that reason not particularly vulnerable from the sea, though it could evidently be reached from the gulf; and the combination of these swamps and its fortifications, centred upon the island of Phakos rising from the marshes and the nearby hill to its north and north-west, gave it an easily defensible outlook by land.[44]

Archelaos lavished much wealth on the development of his new city, so that it was said, with some sarcasm, that while no visitors came to see Archelaos they came from all over the world to see his palace. It grew rapidly; by about 380 it was the largest city in the land. Later, during the Hellenistic period, it was much expanded, and it is unfortunate for the study of Philip that, so far, most of what has been located and excavated is of that later time. Very impressive is the large public building which spans the modern Thessalonike-Giannitsa road and contains a now famous group of pebble-mosaics. But there is one extremely imposing building of the fourth century, the huge *tholos* 30.5 metres in diameter with three small *tholoi* attached on its circumference.[45] There are some signs in it of provision for cult-rituals, including animal-sacrifice, and there is reason for seeing in this circular building the influence of a similar sanctuary on the island of Thasos associated with Herakles' worship. But the extreme size of the building leads to the suggestion that it was also here that the king's nobles could be called into advisory session, that this was Macedonia's equivalent of a *bouleuterion,* or council-house.

Among the smaller remains there are some very fine artefacts, the best ones so far Hellenistic. But here too there are expressions of the theme we have already noticed in other connections: even in Macedonian society in its Hellenistic phase there was a curious and invigorating amalgam of the very old and the very new. It is seen clearly in a group of ash-grey ceramic cups (*kylikes*), in their fabric and their technique and style recalling wares of prehistoric, early Mycenaean, times. Their handles, however, are very plainly classical and they were found in association with perfectly typical Hellenistic pieces.[46]

Pella's great days — those when the city was at its largest — were those that followed the reigns of Philip and Alexander and it may be that the bulk of what will be found there in future may continue to be Hellenistic. But its first growth as capital, during the first three quarters of the fourth century B.C. , must have left its traces and the excavations to come hold much promise for Pella, as for Aigai. In particular, we might speculate, the great expansion in national wealth and morale effected by Philip II's kingship must have found expression — as it had in Athens a century before — in the buildings and adornments of the capital, and this largely still awaits our discovery. The importance of such work cannot be stated too strongly, for those who wrote of the Macedonians in the ancient world were interested almost wholly in their military exploits and very rarely with social or institutional matters, so that the balance that might be provided by the archaeological is of paramount importance. This remains an exciting prospect, we may hope, for the quite near future.

THE END OF PHILIP

It is impossible to understand the circumstances of Philip's death in 336 without taking into account the conditions of the Macedonian monarchy. By that date the royal house, the Temenids, had reigned for three and a half centuries. The founder, Perdikkas, had come from Peloponnesian Argos. He was a member of the Temenids who ruled there as descendants of Herakles, son of Zeus, and in the words of later oracles he founded his capital "by the waters of the Haliakmon" and called it Aigeai (Goat-town) after the "gleaming-horned, snowy-white goats" which lay there asleep. The site is at Vergina. There the kings were buried under a tumulus, as the Temenids, it seems, were buried at Argos, and the saying was that so long as the kings were buried there the Temenids would rule Macedonia. The break happened after Philip. The Macedonians to whom Perdikkas came were primitive pastoral people who grazed their flocks on the uplands of Olympus and Pieria in the summer and on the coastal lowlands in the winter. They owed their subsequent prosperity and power to their Temenid kings, for whom they had the deepest affection and veneration. Thus Philip was at the same time a Greek of the highest lineage and a Macedonian monarch.

The relationship between the monarch and the Macedonians was primarily military. The king was elected by the Makedones under arms; they beat their spears on their shields and their leaders donned their cuirasses to show that they would fight for their king. Since the lives of the Macedonians were dominated by wars with their neighbours, they gave the king almost absolute powers of command in war and in peace. Ceremonies of state were conducted under arms. So too trials for treason: the king prosecuted, the assembly judged, and anyone found guilty was killed usually by the weapons of the armed assembly. As the life of the king was vital to the life of the state, the punishment for treason was death not only of the traitor but of his family.

It was probably in the interest of military efficiency that the tribes of the pastoral stage, among which the Argeadai were the royal tribe, were replaced by a city-organisation for settled communities in most of Macedonia. Men-under-arms were "Makedones from Pella" or from other places; other persons were simply "Pellaioi" or "Aloritai", citizens of Pella or Aloros, etc. The "Makedones", i.e. the citizens of the Macedonian state, were the military élite. From them the king chose his commanders and his courtiers; they advised, fought and feasted as his "Friends" and "Companions", and their sons were educated together with the sons of the royal house as "Pages", waiting upon the king at table, joining him in the royal hunt and being flogged by the king for any misconduct. The king led his Companions into battle. His special guards were seven "Bodyguards" of high rank, the older Pages and an élite group of either Companion Cavalry or, in Philip's time, "Foot-Companions", as occasion demanded.

In order to provide heirs the kings were polygamous; Philip perhaps more than most in having seven or eight wives, and among them an Illyrian, a Molossian, two Thessalians, a Getic and probably a Scythian. The children of these marriages, and no doubt the wives themselves, were held in equal honour, and this was important not only for the succession but also for international diplomacy. They bore Philip several sons, but death by disease and in action reduced them to two by 337: the incompetent Arrhidaios, and the very capable but younger Alexander, who had led the cavalry charge at Chaironeia. Good sense, as well as inclination, led Philip at the age of forty-five to take another wife, Kleopatra, the ward of a leading Macedonian commander called Attalos, and to hope she would bear him sons. By then, 337, the mothers of Arrhidaios and Alexander were past child-bearing.

Polygamy had its dangers. The queens quarrelled, especially over the succession, each wanting her own son to succeed, and also in jealousy of one another. Thus Olympias, a woman of tempestuous temperament, the mother of Alexander, was angry with Philip for marrying Kleopatra. She became estranged from him. More serious were quarrels between half-brothers, which might pass from generation to generation and split the country. When Alexandros I died c. 452, he left at least five sons — Alketas, Philippos, Perdikkas, Menelaos and Amyntas —, and they and their sons too became contenders for the throne. By 399 it seems that the lines of the first two had come to an end in the struggle, but the next seven years saw kings descended from the other three: Orestes, Aeropos, Pausanias and Argaios from Perdikkas, Amyntas the Little from Menelaos and Amyntas from Amyntas. This last won the day as Amyntas III and the rest of the Temenid kings were descended from him. When Philip became regent and then king, he had to contend not only with Pausanias and Argaios of Perdikkas' line but also with three half-brothers, Archelaos, Arrhidaios and Menelaos. He survived as king only by eliminating all five of them. At the time of Philip's death those in the Amyntas line were in order of age Amyntas, son of Perdikkas III (a child king in 359 and now married to Kynna, a daughter of Philip), Arrhidaios and Alexander. But there were also descendants of the other branches which stemmed from Aeropos, Argaios and Amyntas the Little, kings in the 390s; among them were Leonnatos and Perdikkas (both bodyguards of Philip) and, as we shall see, "the sons of Aeropos". A reigning king gave high offices to all loyal princes (the treaty of Perdikkas II with Athens illustrates this), but he did what he could to designate a successor and a reserve. Thus Philip made Alexander his deputy in Macedonia, gave him command of the Companion Cavalry at Chaironeia and sent him as ambassador to Athens. At the same time he used Amyntas as an ambassador in 337.

The goings-on at the Macedonian court were ridiculed by the sophisticated Greeks of the south, who lived in republican city-states and regarded any king as a despot, and their attitude was inherited and shared by the Roman writers who provide much of our evidence. For example, Greek and Roman writers chose to regard one wife as "queen" and the others as "concubines" (slave-women in a Greek household) and rated the Pages as slaves. So they portrayed Menelaos as a bastard, Archelaos as a slave-woman's son, and Amyntas the Little as a slave-boy waiting on Aeropos (three of these four being kings in the 390s). The mother of Philip, Eurydike, was fair game. She was described as "an illiterate Illyrian" and she was said to have married her daughter to her own lover, Ptolemaios; plotted to kill Amyntas and replace him on the throne with Ptolemaios; killed her son Alexandros and replaced him with Ptolemaios; and then killed her second son, Perdikkas, without a pang for her little grandson, Amyntas. Such malicious fabrications, to which royal personages are still exposed, had a wide circulation in the Greek and Roman world. So too with Philip's court. He was represented as having one queen, Olympias, and like Hypereides, an Athenian orator, many mistresses. When Olympias withdrew to the court in Molossia, some time after the marriage of Philip and Kleopatra, this was blown up into a royal "divorce". And when Alexander showed his sympathy for Olympias and fell out with his father, this was magnified into the "banishment" of Alexander by Philip.

The truth was different. During the estrangement some friends of Alexander were exiled by Philip, but not Alexander. As the designated successor, Alexander had been given experience in Thrace, on the Danube campaign, on the Greek campaign and at Athens; now he served in some role in Illyria. On the day of Philip's death Alexander was to have walked beside him in the procession. There may well have been a quarrel between Alexander and Attalos at the time of Philip's marriage with Kleopatra, but the lurid details which Plutarch gave have all the marks of journalistic sensationalism. Again Plutarch's story about Pixodaros' daughter is unhistorical as it stands; for it repesents Arrhidaios as a "bastard" and has Philip mocking Pixodaros as a "barbarian slave to a barbarian". The suggestion that Alexander wanted to marry at this point is itself suspect, since as king he delayed his marriage for so long. Whatever quarrels there may have been between Philip and Alexander, we cannot know them, and the setting of the scene on the day of Philip's assassination shows that Philip ranked Alexander next to himself.

The assassination occurred during the celebration of a state wedding between Kleopatra, daughter of Philip and Olympias and so full sister of Alexander, and Alexandros, brother of Olympias, the reigning king of Molossia. It was a great event for both royal houses, and the two Alexanders were good friends. It was also unprecedented, in that the celebrations were attended by envoys from the Greek states, delegates from the Balkan dependencies and friends from abroad, as well as by leading Macedonians. The theatre at Aigeai was packed with these distinguished guests at dawn, when the first procession entered from the *parodos*: twelve magnificent statues of the Twelve Gods and with them a thirteenth statue "fit for a god", that of Philip (suggesting, if not claiming, that he was a god). It had been intended that Philip, flanked by the two Alexanders, bridegroom and heir, should then enter; but at the last moment, while they were waiting in the *parodos*, Philip sent the Alexanders and his own Friends ahead. They entered and took the seats reserved for them by Philip's throne in the front row facing the stage.

Meanwhile Philip was telling his select Foot

91. The death of Philip, during the celebration of the wedding of his daughter Kleopatra to Alexandros king of the Molossians, marked a turning point in the history of the kingdom of Macedonia. Philip had established Greek unity on a firm basis and had dispatched an advance-force under Parmenion and Attalos with instructions to liberate the Greek cities of Asia Minor; he was preparing to follow in person at the head of the main expeditionary force when at the height of his career and only 46 years old he was assassinated. The illustration shows a portrait of Philip from a medallion dating from the Roman period. Paris, Bibliothèque Nationale.

Companions to stand far aside, and when they entered they duly fanned out to focus attention for the king. In came Philip wearing a white cloak, to the huzzahs and congratulations of the assembled company; for he was at the pinnacle of success. At that moment, all unexpectedly, death struck. "One of the seven Bodyguards, Pausanias, seeing the king isolated, ran from behind, struck him dead, and rushed out towards the gates and the horses which had been prepared for the get-away. Some of the Bodyguards ran to the king; the others — among them Leonnatos, Perdikkas and Attalos — ran after the assassin. Pausanias was well ahead. He would have leapt onto his horse and got away, had he not caught his foot in a vine and fallen, so that Perdikkas and the others caught him as he was rising from the ground, speared him and killed him."

On that day or the next the Macedonians of Aigeai and of the neighbouring regions were summoned to an assembly under arms. They met to elect a king. Their choice was Alexander, and some leading Macedonians donned their cuirasses and escorted him to the nearby palace. Alexander's first task was to enquire into the assassination. Why had there been more than one horse prepared? Since no assassin provides the means of pursuit, Alexander must have assumed that more than one person had intended to kill and probably to kill more than one victim. Perhaps to end Philip's line in effect by killing Philip and Alexander at his side. Not of course at the moment of entry when closely guarded, but during the play when they were sitting as spectators. As it happened, Philip's last moment change of plan gave Pausanias the chance. He alone struck, anticipating and aborting the full plot. Who, then, might have been Pausanias' accomplices? Perhaps those who killed him and so prevented interrogation; perhaps some of the guards or some of the Friends; or others near the throne; and behind them perhaps a foreign power, such as Athens or Persia, or/and a coterie of Macedonians anxious to put someone other than Alexander on the throne. Such thoughts must have sprung to everyone's mind at the time.

Aristotle reported the personal motive of Pausanias, resentment that Philip had allowed him to be outraged "by those with Attalos", and Diodoros supplied an unsavoury homosexual background, as follows. Pausanias, having been supplanted in Philip's favours by another man, taunted the latter, who showed his courage in battle by defending the king and losing his life very gallantly in 337. Those who knew censured Pausanias, and in particular Attalos invited Pausanias to dinner, made him drunk and had him sexually assaulted by his grooms. Pausanias appealed to Philip but got no redress. Whether Diodoros' details are true is undiscoverable. Aristotle's assertion that Pausanias had a personal motive connected with Attalos for killing the king should be accepted as correct; for he knew the court and wrote for contemporaries of the event. It does not, of course, dispense with the probability of a wider plot and a political motivation.

Enquiries into the movements and contacts of Pausanias and all who came under suspicion must have taken some weeks. When they were complete, the trial was held by the assembly of Macedonians. A fragment of papyrus, found at Oxyrhynchus in Egypt, preserves a Hellenistic historian's account of the trial, at least as provisionally restored. "They (the Macedonians) acquitted those with him (Philip) in the theatre and his escorts and those round the throne. He (Alexander) handed the diviner over to attendants to bury … and by the burial …" In this trial, in autumn 336, the immediate entourage and the guards were acquitted. The diviner, having pronounced the omens favourable that day, paid the price of his profession. We know from other sources that three sons of Aeropos were accused. Two were found guilty of complicity, by name Heromenes and Arrhabaios; the third, Alexandros, was acquitted through the influence — at least in part — of the young king, whom he had been one of the first to acclaim by donning his cuirass. This Alexandros was certainly a member of the royal house. For when the leaders of the revolt at

Thebes said that the king was dead, they asserted that this Alexandros was in command, that is as his successor. Again, in winter 334-3, the Persian plan according to a Persian agent was to assassinate the king and put this Alexandros on the throne. The father of these three, Aeropos, was then either the grandson of the king Aeropos of the 390s or a descendant of Menelaos. The epithet "Lynkestes" which was applied in our sources to distinguish this Alexandros from the king Alexander is an indication not of racial descent but of residence. He was a resident of Lynkos, just as Ptolemaios had been called "Alorites", a resident of Aloros. At the time of the trial the king treasured the adherence of this prominent member of the royal house.

"Alexander took every possible care for the funeral of his father", said Diodoros and the recent discoveries at Vergina may bear him out. Now Justin gave a very strange account of that funeral. His aim was to incriminate Olympias, and he (or his source) put his own interpretation on the traditional facts. If we keep to his facts, we may see what was done in the funeral at Aigeai. The king's remains were under a tumulus; those found guilty of complicity were executed "at the tumulus"; the corpse of the assassin was hung, crucified, over the remains of the king and was later taken down and burnt. Another source adds that the sons of the assassins were executed too. Finally, an annual sacrifice was instituted at the tumulus — not to the assassin, as Justin said, but to the dead king, who was thus in some sense deified. We know from other sources that two Macedonian kings were worshipped as gods, Amyntas III at Pydna and Philip at Amphipolis, no doubt after death. The thirteenth statue in the procession had been symbolic of what happened so soon afterwards.

Though Philip was dead and buried, there were further repercussions. Two of the Bodyguards who had killed the assassin, Leonnatos and Perdikkas, were not made Bodyguards of Alexander until they won that honour by acts of valour. The third, Attalos, remained under suspicion. His conspicuous courage and genial manner made him extremely popular with the Macedonians, his ward's marriage to Philip had raised his prestige and perhaps his ambitions, and he now held high command in the army in Asia Minor. Diodoros reports as facts what may have been merely suspicions at the time, namely that Attalos was negotiating with Athens and corresponded with Demosthenes with a view to the Greek states rising and overthrowing Alexander. When Alexander thought he had grounds for bringing Attalos to trial, he sent a trusted officer with troops to Asia Minor. His orders were to bring back Attalos alive, but if that proved impossible to kill him as quickly as he could. Had he been brought back alive, he would have been tried for treason. In fact he was killed. No doubt he was condemned posthumously as a traitor by the assembly, and his family were executed under the law of treason; among the relatives were Kleopatra and her baby, a son born to Philip just before the assassination. That was probably in early 335.

In the same year Amyntas, son of Perdikkas, the child king of 359, was arraigned for treason. He was found guilty and executed. Plutarch made the comment that discontented Macedonians looked to Amyntas and the sons of Aeropos, i.e. as leaders of rising and as possible successors to the throne. He may have been thinking of the two sons of Aeropos who had been executed in 336; but if he meant to associate Amyntas with "the sons of Aeropos", he must have been using the term in the wider sense of "the descendants of Aeropos". Who were the discontented Macedonians? One was certainly Amyntas, son of Antiochos, a close friend of the executed Amyntas. He now fled and entered Persian service. Later, according to Arrian, he established a means of communication between the Persian king and Alexandros Lynkestes, and a Persian agent was sent to offer the throne of Macedonia to Alexandros Lynkestes if he should kill Alexander. The Persian agent was captured. Alexander put the facts before his staff of Friends. They advised him to remove Alexandros Lynkestes from the command of the

Thessalian cavalry, a very powerful force, and put him "out of the way". This was done. Arrested in 334-3, Alexandros Lynkestes was brought to trial only in 330; then the Macedonians in assembly found him guilty of treason and executed him with their spears.

When we look back over the whole affair from the antecedents in the royal house down to the execution of Alexandros Lynkestes in 330, we must note that constitutional procedures were being followed. These were based probably on precedent and "the unwritten law" and not on recorded statutes; but that made their authority, if anything, greater. The assembly of Macedonians had the right both of electing a king and of deposing a king (as they deposed Amyntas III in 393-2 and Amyntas IV *c.* 358), but by precedent they elected only a member of the Temenid house. The assembly had the right of judging cases of treason. Though the king prosecuted, it was no foregone conclusion. In 399 the killing of Archelaos during a royal hunt by Krateuas, a Page, did not lead to a verdict of guilty. In 336 Alexandros Lynkestes and other suspects were acquitted, and later in Asia several persons were accused of treason but acquitted. By the Greek standards of the time, indeed by some modern standards, trial by popular jury was considered the most equitable, and there are no grounds for making the assembly of the Macedonians an exception. The king had the right to arrest suspects. Sometimes a suspect was killed or killed himself in the course of arrest; but that happens even today. It is therefore incorrect to speak of Alexander killing Attalos or Amyntas.

The findings of the Macedonian assembly have the first claim on our credence. They were that the assassin Pausanias had been in league with two sons of Aeropos, members of the royal family, and on *prima facie* evidence that they had conspired also with Attalos. Quite separately they found Amyntas, son of Perdikkas II, and probably others unnamed in in our sources guilty of conspiring against Alexander. They carried out the unwritten law that the family of

those found guilty of treason were executed, this including Kleopatra and her infant child. Next, we have the indications in Diodoros that Demosthenes and probably other Athenians were aware of the plot to kill Philip, and the suspicion of Alexander, which Arrian reports, that Persia had also played a part in organising the conspiracy. All we can say is that these were likely hypotheses. Demosthenes was certainly fanatical enough in his hatred of Philip and Macedonia, and Persia may well have planned to kill Philip and his heir in 336, as she planned later to kill Alexander by the hand or agency of Alexandros Lynkestes.

If the findings of the Macedonian assembly are accepted as correct, there was considerable opposition within Macedonia to Philip's policies. There is one sign of it in the advice given to Alexander not to pursue Philip's forceful policy in Greece; and in Macedonia the transplantation of populations, the constant military training and operations and the unrelenting ambition and demands of Philip must have caused much resentment in some circles. By 336 it must have become clear that Philip's son and designated successor was no less ambitious and would make no less rigorous demands. If Philip's policies were to be arrested, it was necessary to remove both Philip and Alexander by assassination. The succession to the throne or the regency would then fall not on the half-witted Arrhidaios but on a descendant of Aeropos or on Amyntas, son of Perdikkas, whichever was the more likely to prove a capable king and commander. In the opinion of the Theban leaders, it was likely to be Alexandros, son of Aeropos,

92. Philip's wife Olympias, the daughter of Neoptolemos king of the Molossians, had a forceful personality and a mystic nature that often led her to violent, irrational actions. Her role in the murder of Philip has always been the subject of fierce controversy, renewed after the recent discoveries at Vergina. Her portrait is preserved on a medallion from the Roman period. Thessalonike, Archaeological Museum.

173

so-called Lynkestes. A conspiracy on these lines and with these aims has at least the merits of probability within the circumstances of the royal house and the Macedonian state.

The speculations of later writers begin by dismissing the findings of the Macedonian assembly as incorrect. They do so without having access to the evidence at the time, and usually without an understanding of the constitutional procedures. From this arbitrary assumption they pin the blame on Olympias as the arch-planner, who let assassins loose on the very day when her daughter was being married to her brother and when her son Alexander was an easy victim too. Then Justin, excerpting an Augustan writer called Pompeius Trogus, describes Olympias, enraged by her "divorce", planning, but failing, to drive her brother Alexandros, king of Molossia, into a war of revenge against Macedonia, and then instigating Pausanias to murder Philip and preparing the horses for his get-away. The deed done, she ran (?from Molossia over high Pindos) to attend the obsequies of Philip; at night she crowned the crucified Pausanias with a gold crown; later, she cremated Pausanias' corpse, had a tumulus built over it, and persuaded the people on grounds of "superstition" to make an annual sacrifice to the assassin. Next, she killed the baby at Kleopatra's breast and compelled Kleopatra to hang herself; and she dedicated the assassin's sword to Apollo. "All this", says Justin, "was done so openly, that she seems to have been afraid that it would not be realised she had committed the crime herself". What a story! It is in the class of bad detective novels or television plays. But in real life, not in a jungle but in a civilised state with constitutional procedures, it is fantastic to suppose that an estranged queen could have acted thus and imposed her will on the Macedonians. Plutarch, writing later than Pompeius Trogus, watered the story down to almost nothing and made Olympias the instigator. Finally, Pausanias either found in another source or himself invented a final horror: Olympias killed the baby and Kleopatra by dragging them across the top of a burning cauldron.

The next step for the sensational writer was to incriminate Alexander himself. Justin begins by saying that Alexander was "not unaware" of his mother's plan and of her part in the killing of his father; then after the assassination he makes Alexander organise the killing of Kleopatra's baby and follow this up by killing those relations of Kleopatra who were in prominent positions. Plutarch joins Justin but cautiously: Alexander, he says, was suspected, but he was away when Olympias killed Kleopatra so cruelly and he was angry with her. Justin assumes a society in which a king kills whom he pleases or organises the killings behind the scene, as in the worst days of the Roman Emperors. It is absurd to suppose that Alexander would have staged an assassination on the very occasion when he was himself exposed to the dagger, that he would have chosen to have the king murdered in the presence of envoys from the whole of Macedonia's orbit of influence, and that the assassin would not have realised that Alexander's first duty would be to prosecute the assassin and have him killed by the Macedonian assembly. If we keep a historical perspective, the complicity of Alexander is as incredible as the alleged actions of Olympias.

The real interest of Philip's end is that it reveals a considerable opposition to his policies among some leading Macedonians. It warned Alexander as successor to those policies that he would encounter opposition and might himself become the target of conspiracies among the leading Macedonians. What seems to have broken down in Philip's case was the ability of the king to win and maintain the support of the leading Macedonians, among whom the members of the royal house and the Bodyguards and Friends held a prominent position. Alexander in his turn was threatened by conspiracies of the same origin.

The assassination of Philip has always been seen as a critical event in world history. If Philip had lived to an old age, he would probably have held the Greek states to the terms of the Greek League and obtained more co-operation from them, and he might have restricted his conquests to Asia Minor or to the Euphrates line, in order to give Macedonia a central position in his sphere of domination. As it was, the assassin's steel put the power of Macedonia at the disposal of a young king, who showed less patience than Philip in dealing with the Greek states and who had an imperious urge to win glory by conquest.

PHILIP'S PERSONALITY

No author in antiquity has left us a genuine portrait of Philip. It is all the harder to gauge his personality because there is a manifest contradiction between the traits so finely etched in the speeches of his eternal enemy, the Athenian Demosthenes, and those presented by later writers, who saw in him, *post eventum,* the creator of a Macedonia powerful enough to dominate Greece, and the father of Alexander, who conquered the Persian Empire.

The account given by Demosthenes of his redoubtable foe is clear: he was a barbarian and therefore the born enemy of the Greeks, and particularly of the Athenians and their democracy. Here he is, for example, surrounded by his companions in ignominy, in the *Second Olynthiac:*[1]

"if there is anyone among them who can be described as experienced in war and battle, I was told that Philip from jealousy keeps all such in the background, because he wants to have the credit himself of every action, among his many faults being an insatiable ambition. Any fairly decent or honest man, who cannot stomach the licentiousness of his daily life, the drunkenness and the lewd dancing, is pushed aside as of no account. All the rest about his court, he said, are robbers and toadies, men capable of getting drunk and performing such dances as I hesitate to name to you here... low comedians, men who compose ribald songs to raise a laugh against boon companions — these are the men he welcomes and loves about him".

Even a historian like Theopompos, an admirer of the sovereign, lays stress on his debauches which constituted a danger to the Macedonian dynasty. The court intrigues, the turbulent atmosphere fostered by the royal polygamy, the quarrels that broke out with Alexander and his mother, Olympias, complete the picture of a barbarian governed by his disorderly instincts and violent temperament.

It is evident that life in the palace of the Macedonian kings was shaken by strange convulsions. Political assassination was a common event in the current exercise of power, and amorous intrigues had in half a century resulted in the deaths of two kings; Ar-

chelaos, killed by his favourite, and Alexandros II, killed on the orders of his mother Eurydike's lover. Wild tumultuous carousals and amours were part of the convivial life of the king and his companions, rough mountaineers with simple pleasures. This way of life, so close to that of ancient times, could not but appear barbarous to an urban society, notably that of Athens, where Middle Comedy (particularly when compared to the works of Aristophanes) and the Attic orators were displaying a new refinement in manners that certainly would have been unknown to the contemporaries of Perikles. It should be realised that this same way of life was also widespread in certain regions of Greece, for example in Thessaly; even in Athens not all the symposia had the high intellectual tone of the one depicted by Plato, while the private law court speeches disclose the ambiguous milieu of the *hetairai*, and pederasty played a determinative role in social relations.

This difference in manners accounts for the severity of the judgements passed on Philip and his retinue. However, an anecdote related by Diodoros Siculus shows clearly that the king did not allow himself to be completely carried away by his drinking:[2]

"in the drinking after dinner Philip downed a large amount of unmixed wine and forming with his friends a comus in celebration of the victory (of Chaironeia) paraded through the midst of his captives, jeering all the time at the misfortunes of the luckless men. Now Demades, the orator, who was then one of the captives spoke out boldly and made a remark able to curb the king's disgusting exhibition. He is said to have remarked: "O King, when Fortune has cast you in the role of Agamemnon, are you not ashamed to act the part of Thersites? Stung by this well-aimed shaft of rebuke, Philip altered his whole demeanour completely. He cast off his garland, brushed aside the symbols of pride that marked the comus, expressed admiration for the man who dared to speak so plainly, freed him from captivity and gave him a place in his own company with every mark of honour."

Intemperance, drunkenness and unbridled violence also form part of the traditional image of Alexander, and there is therefore ground for supposing that this is a *topos* (common standpoint) concerning the Argead sovereigns, which does not mean to say that there was no truth behind it.

As regards Philip's barbarism, which was the theme underlying Demosthenes' orations, it is evident that this was only a polemical argument without real historical value. Ethnically, the Macedonians were Greek; this is shown particularly by their dialect, which was closely related to Dorian speech. There had certainly been for centuries a marked difference in levels of culture between the kingdoms of northern Greece, Macedonia and Epeiros, and those of southern Greece, which had been exposed to two remarkable successive cultural impulses: the Mycenean kingdoms and the rise of the city-states. But this gap between the north and the south tended to diminish after the fifth century: Macedonia made considerable economic progress; production and trade increased. In particular, there was more intensive exploitation of her mineral resources; the power of the State was strengthened; and within this framework an acculturation of a Hellenic type developed among the dominant social strata, as is evident from the warm welcome given by the court to Pindar, Herodotos, Agathon and Euripides, to name only the more illustrious guests of the sovereigns.

As for Philip himself, there is little direct evidence to assess the degree of his personal culture. However, on the subject of his three years residence in Thebes as a hostage, when he was about fifteen years old, Diodoros wrote:[3]

"the Illyrians, who had taken Philip, the youngest son of Amyntas, as a hostage, placed him in the care of the Thebans. They in turn entrusted the lad to the father of Epameinondas and directed him both to keep careful watch over his ward and to superintend his upbringing and education. Since Epameinondas had as his instructor a philosopher of the Pythagorean school, Philip, who was reared along with him, acquired a wide acquaintance with the Pythagorean Philosophy. Inasmuch as both students showed natural ability and diligence they

177

proved to be superior in deeds of valour.''

Although this testimony is not altogether unambigous, especially in its chronology, it is apparent that his stay in Thebes left its stamp on Philip's development. It is equally apparent that he was acquainted with Greeks at the court of Pella before his accession to power and that he subsequently surrounded himself with Greeks. He attached so much importance to Greek culture, at least as a tool for political actions that he engaged Aristotle as tutor for his son, Alexander, although the former had not yet reached the peak of his fame. It is, in fact, as a Greek prince that we see Philip in action, having a surprising knowledge of the society of the cities and a extraordinary diplomatic ability, which was acknowledged even by his worst enemies. It was as a Greek prince that he conceived the administration of Thrace, which he had just conquered and where he proceeded to found cities, pursuing a bold policy of internal colonisation that was later to be readopted in Asia by Alexander.

The myths about the origins of Macedonian kingship fabricated at court contained the ideological element necessary to sustain and justify royal authority. The Argead dynasty traced its lineage back to the Herakleids of Argos, and thus ultimately back to Zeus, the supreme God of the Greek Pantheon. They were certainly no less fantastic than all the other myths about the return of the Herakleides, and in any case, Philip's personality could only enhance this plausibility.

If there is one human quality necessary for action in the Greek world, it is eloquence, and an abundance of evidence points to a remarkable oratorical talent in Philip. He knew how to speak to his men and rally their courage; we shall see how he took the Macedonian army in hand after its severe defeat by the Illyrians, in which king Perdikkas had perished with 4,000 of his men. And, what is undoubtedly even more difficult, he had an amazing knack of persuading and convincing in negotiations with the envoys of the Greek cities: in 346, in particular, he displayed such affability, courtesy and skill in argument before the Athenian ambassadors that on the journey home Demosthenes himself was forced to admit, at least according to Aischines' account, that Philip "was the most gifted of men".

Finally, there is one constant element in the picture of Philip given by his contemporaries, and that is his bravery. He fought in the front ranks, took the greatest of risks and received terrible wounds; his friend, the Athenian Isokrates, learning that he had been severely wounded in the campaign against the Illyrians, reproached him with having been "more reckless in assuming risks than is becoming to a king.''[4]

Even if this bravery, which was acknowledged by his worst enemies, completes the picture of a Barbarian, a man who followed his basic instincts rather than his reason, there was undoubtedly a measure of admiration, even on Demosthenes' part, for a hero with his endurance, animated by an unequalled *élan vital,* and in love with glory, while the Athenians were proving thenselves fickle in their endeavours, alternating between hope and despair, and incapable of upholding the great reputation their exploits had earned them in earlier times. The great Athenian orator himself, before describing the sufferings of the king's entourage and the degradation into which he dragged them, declaims in the *Second Olynthiac:*[5]

"No: glory is his sole object and ambition; in action and in danger he has elected to suffer whatever may befall him, putting before a life of safety the distinction of achieving what no other king of Macedonia ever achieved.''

What basically troubled the Greeks, more or less consciously, was the fact that Philip was an absolute monarch who could assert himself without fear and exercise his power without being accountable to anyone. Philip was not only a dangerous man, dangerous because of the very force of his singular personality, but above all he was a king. We must turn again to Demosthenes on this question. In one of the most powerful passages in his speech *On the Crown* he wrote:[6]

"In the first place, he (Philip) was the despotic commander of his adherents: and in war that is

93. Bust of a bearded man wearing a diadem, decorating the bottom of a hellenistic vase. Some scholars believe it to be a portrait of Philip. Athens, Goulandris Collection.

the most important of all advantages... Then he was well provided with money: he did whatever he chose, without giving notice by publishing decrees or deliberating in public, without fear of persecution by informers or indictment for illegal measures. He was responsible to nobody: he was the absolute autocrat, commander, and master of everybody and everything. And I, his chosen adversary... of what was I master? Of nothing at all! Public speaking was my only privilege: and that you permitted to Philip's hired servants on the same terms as to me."

It seems to us essential to get away from the traditional controversy about Philip's personality, which belongs more to the field of biography or portaiture of great men than to history. The most important aspect of the man is his well-developed political instinct, his ability to analyse the balance of power in Macedonia and the territories of his Greek and barbarian neighbours, and to take action on the basis of his analyses to try to use the distribution of power to his own advantage.

It is most instructive from this point of view to examine the actions he took to assert the royal authority in Macedonia. It seems clear to us nowadays,[7] after much uncertainty in the past, that Macedonian institutions remained tribal in kind for a long time, certainly until the end of the fifth century. Organised under a traditional and therefore unwritten *nomos,* they called for a king bearing the title King of the Macedonians (and thus a national king, according to Aymard's famous distinction), a council of noble chieftains and an assembly of the people, which in times of war was transformed into an assembly of soldiers, and whose actual power extended little beyond proclaiming the new king and judging capital cases. It is equally clear that the rapid development of Macedonia after the fifth century had strengthened the authority of the king, which had hitherto been limited by that of the nobles, many of whom themselves boasted the title of king, and that this had created new conditions for a further increase in royal power. The traditional king of the *nomos* had been little more than a *primus inter pares;* the office was

now being transformed into an absolute monarchy, the king alone being competent to make decisions.

This evolution was sufficiently advanced at the time of Philip's accession for him to be able to take advantage of it in many ways. The reduction of the power of the nobles was a dominant factor in his policy. It operated on several levels. First was the annexation of the four small mountain kingdoms of Upper Macedonia, which had preserved their independence in the upper Haliakmon valley and carried on a diplomacy that was a danger to Macedonia because of their contacts with the neighbouring Epeirotes or Illyrians. Their subjugation was effected either by military means or by princely marriages that were made possible by the royal practice of polygamy, accepted as legitimate; this practice will be observed again later on under certain of Alexander's immediate successors. It would be wrong, therefore to attribute to Philip's lecherous proclivities what was in fact the outcome of a strategic policy of dynastic marriage-making. The results were clear: not only was the kingdom considerably expanded, but the king was able to draw extensively on a source of first-rate foot-soldiers from a vast region that was apparently more populated than Lower Macedonia.

At the same time Philip was working to speed up the transformation of the structure of the landed nobility. He increased the number of his *hetairoi,* companions who surrounded the king at court and in the army - rather as in the Homeric Epics - who had previously been recruited only from the highest ranks of the aristocracy. He did not hesitate to introduce into this *corps* eminent foreigners who had entered his service, Greeks and even Persians; since ownership of large estates formed the tangible power basis of the *hetairoi,* he also granted them land. His purpose was to limit the power of the great families, jealous of their authority, whose chiefs perhaps found some consolation in being the only ones admitted to the new body of the *somatophylakes;* in addition he aimed to build up the social basis of his power among the rural nobility.

The institution of the *basilikoi paides* vividly illustrates Philip's political acumen. The attendants who mounted guard on the king's door, ate with him and accompanied him into battle were recruited among the young noblemen. As Quintus Curtius Rufus puts it:[8]

"this troupe among the Macedonians was a kind of training-school for generals and governors of Provinces; from these also their posterity had the kings from whose stock after many ages the Romans took away all power."

These children constituted hostages to the king for the great families, but they were also educated in the context of a monarchy that Philip wanted to make more and more centralised at the expense of a regionalism that still remained strong, to accomplish important tasks in the service of the king as officers, administrators and diplomats.

Philip's aim is clear, evolved from a lucid analysis of his needs and possibilities for change. It was to establish an absolute monarchy by transforming a naturally independent landed aristocracy into a court nobility at the service of the Macedonian state, which became more and more embodied in his own person. Such a transformation was only possible because the nobles, with the possible exception of one of most powerful families, found evident advantages in a policy of expansion that took them out of the closed milieu of traditional Macedonia, that offered them new sources of activity and power, and that, of course, brought them wealth. It is evident that as a whole the Macedonian nobles willingly collaborated with a sovereign whose policy could only be carried out with their support: whatever assistance he received from foreigners, it was the strong nationalistic sentiment of the Macedonian nobility, combined with the dictates of security which supplied the upper and middle levels of military leadership in a kingdom that was developing at an ever accelerating pace.

It is much harder to analyse Philip's policy in regard to the people. The relatively recent creation of a *phalanx* of heavy infantry was certainly a comparatively democratising factor, and gave the well-to-do peasants who composed it an importance entirely new, because until then the brunt of the responsibility for defence had rested on the aristocratic cavalry. It was a new source of support for the king, a check on the landed nobility on whom the peasantry was necessarily dependent in a more or less institutionalised fashion that is not easy to define.

In his capacity as supreme army commander, and as a commander, furthermore, who risked his life in battle alongside his men, Philip was popular with these soldier-citizens who constituted the majority of the people's assembly. It is enough to see the way in which he acted at the moment of extreme difficulty in which he found himself on the death of his brother Perdikkas, defeated and slain by the Illyrians with 4,000 of his men. Diodoros Siculus wrote:[9]

"the Macedonians because of the disaster sustained in the battle and the magnitude of the dangers pressing upon them were in the greatest perplexity. Yet even so, with such fears and dangers threatening them, Philip was not panic-stricken by the magnitude of the expected perils, but, bringing together the Macedonians in a series of assemblies and exhorting them with eloquent speeches to be men, he built up their morale... He was courteous in his intercourse with men and sought to win over the multitudes by his gifts and his promises to the fullest loyalty."

What Philip achieved, therefore, in the wake of the kings who had gone before, was the speeding up of the transformation of the power of the State and the establishment of new social relationships, rendered necessary by the development of the country. It was through the support of a state and social structure that preserved the traditional forms of prestige but afforded him greatly superior means of action, that the king was able to follow a general policy of expansion which was at the same time very determined but also prudent and progressive, cleverly combining a subtle oblique progression with great audacious strokes, that threw his adversaries into confusion. We do not need to analyse this policy here, but only to single out the methods he employed, because they reveal the personality of its promoter.

Philip took full account of the importance of the religious side, so intermingled in the politics of the Greek world. His intervention in the Third Sacred

War against the Phokians, who had sacked the sanctuary of Apollo at Delphi, was of an exemplary character. It is true that the first two Sacred Wars had been political operations conducted under the veil of religion, but this time the stake was much higher: it was over the definitive recognition of Philip's Greek status, of the moral supremacy of a prince who was able to put all his power at the disposal of the most renowned of all the Panhellenic sanctuaries. He emerged from the conflict with his position considerably enhanced, controlling two delegates in the college of the *hieromnemones* that administered the sanctuary, heaped with titles and honours, and even gratified by a gilded statue of himself. He could thus pose as the master of the Pythian Sanctuary, the common centre of the Hellenes, and already — in imagination if not yet in reality by force of arms — the master of Greece.

The capital that Philip built up in terms of confidence and trust among Greek men of thought, who could certainly not be accused of being his paid agents, is very significant. He profited both from the general aspiration for a strong monarchy, very apparent in Xenophon, and from the Panhellenic movement, which had at the beginning of the century been given expression by Gorgias and Lysias, but which was presented in its most developed form by Isokrates. The latter had been constantly seeking a reconciliation between the Greek cities that would allow them to take the offensive against Persia in a campaign which would be patriotic and religious as well as military; after many hopes and expectations had been proved false by events, he came round to the view that the Macedonian should be the leader of this crusade. After the peace of 346 he wrote the *Philippos*, a pamphlet urging reconciliation among the Greeks under the aegis of the king, the only man with the power to impose such a reconciliation, and urging a war of conquest against their hereditary enemy, the Great King. Even after the resumption of the conflict between Philip and Athens, he took up the same line again in the *Epistles*. On the very day after his country's final defeat at Chaironeia, he sent the king a final letter, very pressing, in which he rejoiced at the victory, showing himself in this to be more Greek than Athenian, and begging him to march against Persia now that he had subjugated Greece.

Philip made clever use of these new currents of opinion, born of a profound yearning after a true "common peace", and for a strong power that would unite the Greeks, even in spite of themselves. Here again religion came to the aid of politics, and Philip, who was very skilful at following the direction of the new demands of Hellenic consciousness, strengthened and justified his power by appealing to the supernatural element: he had his statue carried in a procession behind those of the twelve gods, and he commissioned Leochares to make a gold and ivory group representing him with his family, which he considered dedicating for worship in a *tholos* at Olympia, a veritable monument of a hero cult, and the beginning of a dynastic cult.

Thus Philip knew very well how to turn to his account ideological factors, the traditional respect accorded to the Panhellenic sanctuaries of Delphi and Olympia, the aspirations of a political thought that was in the process of transformation and no longer satisfied the city-state ideal. He also knew how to make use of other weapons for his propaganda, especially the corruptibility of his enemies, barbarian and Greek; the reorganisation of his kingdom's finances opened up vast possibilities in this field. This was nothing new in the diplomatic life of the Greek world: for almost a century the Great King had distributed his gold widely around Greece to buy consciences and to dominate without fighting. However, if Demosthenes is to be believed, there was a vast enterprise in Athens devoted to corrupting those orators who could effectively sway the assembly of

94. Ancient and modern historians alike pass contradictory judgements on Philip's personality. The bleak picture of him painted by his relentless enemy Demosthenes has been disputed by later historians who have seen in him the creator of Macedonian power and the pragmatic politician who finally achieved Greek unity. The mounted figure wearing the broad-brimmed hat (Kausia) on this silver tetradrachm of Philip has been identified with the Macedonian monarch. Athens, Numismatic Museum.

the people, financed by Philip. Nevertheless, it should be said the philo-Macedonian party which operated there in his favour, even if it were not certainly disinterested, was able to appear in the eyes of certain sections of opinion to be pursuing a realistic and even progressive objective for a city wrapped in contradictions in a Greece no less wrapped in the same contradictions.

Buying consciences was only one method among others of pursuing a realistic policy based on a perceptive analysis of the distribution of power. Philip also used all the resources of a tortuous, efficacious diplomacy, lulling his adversaries or misleading them with false promises. It is clear that behind all his diplomatic actions lay an objective reality which afforded him the means to act without scruples: the incomparable might of the Macedonian army, which he had reorganised and reinforced with the Thessalian army after he had made himself master of prosperous Thessaly by skilful intrigues in which bribery played a full part.

The goal he was pursuing by all these methods was obviously to ensure his domination over Greece. He still had to find an institutional framework that would assure him of a certain acquiescence on the part of the subjugated cities. A study of the creation of the League of Corinth is especially significant to the extent to which it reveals, perhaps more than any other in a long career, his clarity of thought and breadth of vision. After Chaironeia and even before the gathering at Corinth of the delegates from nearly all the cities, he had organised a great propaganda campaign, using the tried and trusted theme of the struggle against Persia. Diodoros wrote:[10]

"he spread the word that he wanted to make war on the Persians on the Greeks' behalf and to punish them for the profanation of the temples, and this won him the loyal support of the Greeks."

He was able then to propose and impose a common confederate structure based on perpetual peace and the prohibition of subversion of the existing order which would unite the Greeks into a league directed by a *synedrion*, of which he was the *strategos autokrator*. The traditional and thus non-traumatic

elements are evident: respect for the cities and confederations and for their institutions; revival of the *symmachia*, the defensive and offensive alliances that had played such an important role in the international relations of the Greeks ever since the 6th century. Thus he bent public opinion to his own ends, but in such a roundabout way that he had unanimous consent. Even Athens, treated with generosity by her victor in war, could not but play along: she accepted co-operation, honoured Philip with her citizenship and set up a statue of him in the Agora. It is very clear that by cleverly manipulating all the contingencies he put a final end to the secular regime of the *polis*, the sovereign city-state, and that he established over Greece a protectorate in which force of arms and a degree of popular acquiescence in practice assured him of an autocratic authority. The whole affair was dressed up in an ideology of common peace, security and stability, and paradoxically, of a crusade — revenge against the Persians —, an ideology that was effective after a century and a half in which wars and humiliations before the Great King had acquired an endemic status. This alliance between all the Greeks and the Macedonian king is a masterpiece of ingenuity: it crowns and consecrates an imperialist enterprise vigorously pursued over more than two decades, and all with the consent of those who were being dominated, because they could legitimately see in it hopes of improving the long-troubled condition of Hellas, and even of distant conquests that would cancel out a past of subjugation to the Great King, and would open up new vistas of wealth.

The coherence of Philip's imperialist project — the main drive of all his policies — is well illustrated by the Asian expedition that took place soon after the

95. The dazzling story of Alexander and the dissemination of Greek culture in the East usually overshadow the personality and achievements of his father. The foundations of the power of the Macedonian kingdom, however, in both the military and the political sphere were unquestionably laid by Philip. The illustration shows the Azzara herm, a copy of the famous portrait of Alexander executed by Lysippos. Paris, Louvre.

formation of the League of Corinth. His precise purpose has been and will always be a matter for debate: was it to conquer the northwestern corner of Anatolia in order to cut the Persians off from the Thracians and the Greeks? To conquer Anatolia from Sinope on the Black Sea down to Cilicia, as Isokrates suggested? To conquer the entire Persian Empire? No cause existed that need have confined his ambitions narrowly to the first alternative: neither the isolation of Sparta, nor a certain restlessness prevailing at Athens constituted a threat to him; on the contrary, it was by involving the League of Corinth in the project that he was able to give coherence and solidarity to the alliance. On the other hand, it is equally clear that to attack the Great King was no small enterprise, whatever the state of disintegration existing in the Persian Empire. By sending Parmenion into Asia at the head of a contingent of 10,000 men Philip was taking on a great responsibility, one that had already matured in his mind. It found a natural place in the carefully elaborated scheme that he had in mind: to extend his power and consolidate his dominion over Greece compelling the Greeks to act in concert and under his leadership, and, to open up new zones of expansion that would relieve a Greece whose commerce was on the decline, as Rostowtzeff has magisterially shown, with all the risks of social explosion that it would entail. Isokrates' exhortations in the *Panegyrikos* to go and conquer fertile lands from the Persians shows clearly that this latter motive cannot be excluded, when we remember that the king had displayed such concern for the economic development of his kingdom and such an interest in the interior colonisation of Thrace after its conquest: it was, in the final analysis, the resumption of the policy of expansion followed by the cities of Archaic Greece, with the double motive of conquering new land for exploitation and giving an impetus to trade and commerce, in other words, of holding out prospects that could unite a great following around himself.

We believe it is possible to look beyond the traditional judgements on Philip's moral character. His "vices and virtues" — terms inspired directly by the biographical and moralising propensities of the ancient historians — are best put an one side; the Macedonian is better characterised in terms of his determination. Starting from a complex situation that he had subjected to cold analysis, he allowed neither difficulties nor temporary setbacks nor scruples to hinder him from carrying out an autocratic imperialist project. In this respect his son Alexander resembled him, though his project was on a different scale; but it would not have been possible without Philip's successes. The *pleonexia,* so often used of both of them, is really a translation into moral terms of the concept of imperialism.

The judgements of the ancients on Philip all lay stress on his exploits and achievements, but with differences of emphasis which it is interesting to consider. As early as the fourth century the historian Theopompos[11] declared that never had Europe possessed a statesman to compare with him. Diodoros gives a fuller portrait of him, which is only seemingly paradoxical, and which above all recognises Philip's skilfulness in managing to win a large consensus of agreement:[12]

"Philip... had made himself the greatest of the kings in Europe in his time, and because of the extent of his kingdom had made himself a throned companion of the twelve gods. He is known to fame as one who with but the slenderest resources to support his claim to a throne won for himself the greatest empire in the Greek world, while the growth of his position was not due so much to his prowess in arms as to his adroitness and cordiality in diplomacy. Philip himself is said to have been prouder of his grasp of strategy and his diplomatic successes than of his valour in actual battle. Every member of his army shared in the successes which were won in the field but he alone got credit for victories won through negotiation."

Pausanias again[13] introduced a different version stressing his moral deficiencies:

"Philip may be supposed to have accomplished exploits greater than those of any Macedonian king who reigned either before or after. But nobody of sound mind would call him a good general, for no man has so sinned by continually trampling on oaths to heaven, and by breaking treaties and dishonouring his word on every occasion."

Modern writers are almost all unanimous in their admiration for the man and his achievements. J. G. Droysen, the romantic initiator of studies of the Macedonian's conquests, shows that "he established once and for all the supremacy of the monarchy both in Macedonia and in Greece as a whole, where the precision of his designs, his promptness in executing them, and the mastery and reflection which governed his conduct, enabled him to crush all resistance."[14] The importance of his work as the unifier of Greece has above all been emphasised by the German scholars, who have seen it from the viewpoint of the unification of Germany; looked at from this angle it is quite natural for E. Kornemann to have compared him to Bismarck. Apart from these more specific reactions, he is everywhere hailed as the creator of a modern State, structured, and effective because of the huge dimensions he gave it: and the resounding success of his son Alexander only added further to the glory of the father, without whose energetic action the conquest of the East could not have been accomplished, and who, furthermore, took the decisive intitiative of sending an army into Asia Minor against the Persians.

This general judgement admits of many nuances. On the one hand Philip created a vast autocratic state at the expense of the freedom of the Greek cities, hence the widely differing viewpoints, which vary according to the particular historian's attachment to the city-state and its democratic forms, and according to the degree of his mistrust of absolute power. On the other hand Philip's "moral" failings are weighed to a greater or lesser degree in the judgement of the authors, whether it be over his taste for drink and women, or his unscrupulous policy: G. Glotz and R. Cohen[15] conclude that "if it is true that the end justifies the means, posterity can only endorse the judgement of Theopompos" who proclaimed him greatest statesman Europe had ever produced.

These assesments bear the stamp of an old-fashioned historiography in which the historian set himself up as a judge of the past. They must in every case be regarded in the light of two considerations. First, the cities, fiercely attached to their own liberty, did not respect that of others, and the whole history of classical Greece is one of harsh hegemonies established over their rivals by the most powerful city-states among them: Athens, Sparta and Thebes. Philip was following in the footsteps of their policies of domination. Second, the realism of his actions, his ruses and tricks, and the massacres he perpetrated are no less in keeping with the strategic methods employed by the cities, who subsequently justified as best they could what their superior force had allowed them to obtain, and it is enough to reread Thucydides to be convinced of this. One may be surprised at the final conclusions of P. Cloché about the Macedonian: "Philip left a kingdom armed with a material might that was without doubt impressive and renowned, but always devoid — or very nearly so — of those eminent human values with which his principal enemies were so richly provided."[16]

In fact, the real problem for the historian is a much greater one than simply that of Philip's personality. It is the problem of the new balance of power that was introduced as a result of the newly acquired dynamism of Macedonia and the disintegration of the *poleis*. This is not the place to attempt to explain this double evolution, whose causes were very clearly as much socio-economic as political. But in the conjunction of these two events Philip played a leading part, contributing to speeding up the transformation of obsolete social relationships in Macedonia, and to building a state that was more suited to the development of productive forces, production and circulation, and using his indomitable practical energies to hasten the disintegration of the *poleis* in Greece.

THE ROYAL TOMBS AT AIGAI (VERGINA)

After his murder in 336, Philip was buried at Aigai in conformity with an ancient custom prescribing that all Macedonian kings should be interred there. No matter where they met their death, the bodies of the kings were brought for burial to the original capital of the kingdom, even after Archelaos (413-399) had made Pella the new capital. If, therefore, we knew the site of Aigai, the royal tombs should be found in the surrounding area; conversely, if the royal tombs were discovered, this would establish definitively the site of Aigai. For many years, the identification of modern Edessa with ancient Aigai met with general acceptance. To my knowledge, attention was first drawn to the insurmountable difficulties involved in this identification by Fanoula Papazoglou in 1957, though she did not discuss the problem exhaustively.[1] Ten years later N.G.L. Hammond combined all the archaeological and literary evidence at our disposal in an imaginative but thoroughly sound fashion and propounded the theory that Aigai should be located at Vergina; this was a site that had yielded the magnificent palace dating from the last years of the fourth century, and two Macedonian tombs, one of which contained a marble throne. His arguments were set forth in great detail in the first volume of "*A History of Macedonia*".[2] The excavations of the present writer at this site, which are still in progress, have in his opinion produced conclusive evidence in favour of this thesis. We may now claim with almost complete certainty that the heartland of the Macedonian kingdom was the region on the northern fringes of Pieria, south of the river Haliakmon,[3] and that the capital, Aigai, was in the area of modern Vergina.[4]

In the light of this hypothesis, the archaeological finds from the area acquire special importance. The unique cemetery extending underneath the palace between the villages of Palatitsia and Vergina becomes an invaluable source of historical evidence:[5] for it may now be called the cemetery of Aigai.

The cemetery of Aigai is without parallel, not only in Macedonia, but throughout the whole of the

Greek world. It consists of a large number of tumuli covering a wide area of the plain stretching immediately to the north of the hills on which we should probably place the site of the city of Aigai. The tumuli have an average diameter of c. 20 m. and their height ranges from 0.50 to 3.00 m. Excavation has so far yielded a wealth of material especially from the first phase of the cemetery, which dates to the early Iron Age (1000-700). In every tumulus dating from this period there were numbers of burials, male, female and infant, and each tumulus, therefore, clearly belonged to a single family. The dead were laid in simple graves (cremation is exceedingly rare) and clay pots, usually two in number, were placed next to the bodies. In the case of male burials, the deceased's iron weapons were buried with him; they consisted mainly of swords and, more rarely, spearheads, arrowheads and daggers. It should be noted that some of the swords are the largest ever found in Greece in geometric tombs. The male burials, however, are austere in comparison with the female, in which rich jewellery of bronze, and occasionally gold, was found. The jewellery was designed to adorn the head, the arms and hands and the clothes: there are large numbers of rings and spiral 'syringes' worn in the hair, spiral bracelets, rings for the fingers, brooches used to fasten the dress at the shoulders and disc-shaped belt clasps. A number of graves contained triple double-axes which must either have been the symbol of some priestly authority or have denoted social rank. In one grave an object was found that could be described as a crown; it is unique as far as I know. One of the main features of its decoration is a centrally located circle with a cross — a motif known to symbolize the sun. Perhaps this is a distant ancestor of the radiate symbol of the sun found on Macedonian coins and shields, and also decorating the two golden larnakes in the royal tomb discussed below.

The latest finds in these early tumuli date from the beginning of the seventh century. Many of the other tumuli excavated so far belong to later periods, beginning in the fourth century and continuing down to the end of the Hellenistic period. The finds associated with these burials are of no great interest, since the burials themselves were not particularly rich. The richer tombs, of course, have been the target of grave-robbers since antiquity, and in fact all the built tombs of these periods that have so far been excavated were found to have been plundered. The dimensions of the tombs, their mode of construction, and the scanty remains of the booty left behind are all strong indications that the robbers carried off a very valuable haul. The most important of this group is a small vaulted tomb, of Macedonian type, dating from the middle of the second century. Despite the fact that it was robbed, it produced a large number of ceramic and other objects that, along with the monument itself, attest the fact that its occupant was a man of considerable wealth.[6]

Curiously, none of the tombs hitherto discovered belong to the sixth or fifth centuries. The obvious hypothesis that the area was not inhabited during these centuries might have constituted the most serious argument against identification of this city with Aigai. Those scholars who have recently cast doubt on Hammond's thesis, which I personally support, could easily have pointed to this gap in the evidence; that they have failed to do so results, I imagine, from their having observed that although no tombs from this period have yet been found, there have been a number of chance discoveries of Corinthian *kotylai* and black-glazed Attic vases that cover the sixth century at least.[7] During the most recent excavations, in 1978, the fill of the Great Tumulus produced the first funerary monument from the fifth century (see below) and we may now claim that the use of the cemetery and hence the life of the settlement commenced about the year 1000 and continued without interruption at least until the end of the Hellenistic period, and in all probability into the early Roman period.

Funerary monuments of some note, however, have been discovered in the area of Vergina outside

96. Vergina has three sites of archaeological interest: the cemetery of the tumuli, dating from the Geometric period, the magnificent Hellenistic palace shown here in an aerial photograph; and the royal tombs in the middle of the modern village. The landscape surrounding the archaeological sites — the tree-clad slopes of the Pierian mountains and the endless plain stretching out in front of them — is very impressive.

the boundaries of the cemetery comprising these tumuli. The French archaeologist Léon Heuzey was the first to draw attention to the region and undertook the first excavations there in 1861. The main objective of these excavations was the imposing palace, but at the same time he excavated a Macedonian vaulted tomb at a site near Palatitsia. This tomb is today buried beneath a deposit of soil, following the collapse of the vault; but along with the tomb at Pydna uncovered at the same time by Heuzey, it was the first of its type known to archaeologists. Though plundered, it had a simple, imposing facade, and dates probably from the fourth century.

In 1937, after a considerable interval of time, excavation was resumed at Vergina by Konstantinos A. Romaios, Professor of Archaeology at the University of Thessalonike. He continued to excavate the palace and discovered a third Macedonian tomb *c*. 500 m. to the north of it. Interestingly, this tomb was discovered on the last of the terraces facing the plain, over which the Hellenistic city at least must have extended, and in a position which neither lay within the bounds of the cemetery, nor formed part of a private country estate. The tomb had been robbed, but the deposits of earth that covered part of the interior contained the broken marble leaves of the two doorways and the fragments of a magnificent marble throne, which was restored and set in its original position in the north-east corner of the chamber. The ante-chamber and the frieze on the facade both had painted borders decorated with multi-coloured plant motifs. Colour was also preserved on the Ionic capitals of the half-columns beneath its gabled facade. This tomb is distinguished from all the other known Macedonian tombs by its architecture, the care taken in its construction and its size. The dating of it to the third century may be regarded as certain,[8] though it may not be from the beginning of that century as Romaios believed.

Heuzey grasped the significance of his first finds and although he identified the site with the almost unknown Macedonian city of Balla, he also observed that it was clearly a very important Macedonian centre of Greek culture. Heuzey also believed that the mounds in the cemetery probably concealed other monuments like the one he had uncovered. He was impressed above all by an exceptionally large mound that rose on the edge of the cemetery containing the smaller mounds. Its huge size made it unique — it was 110 m. in diameter and had an average height of 12 m. — and it was certainly an imposing structure to which the epithet τηλεφανής, (conspicuous), used by Homer of the burial mounds of his heroes, could well be applied. Heuzey believed that the Great Tumulus, as it was called by the local inhabitants, probably concealed a large Macedonian tomb, but he himself did not have time to investigate it. His belief was shared by Romaios, who continued his excavations from 1937 to 1940 and 1954 to 1956, concentrating on the palace.

My own excavations since 1951 have been focussed on the Great Tumulus and the cemetery of the mounds; I anticipate that work in this area will continue for many years to come. The results of the excavation of the cemetery have been known for some years and, as I have already observed, furnish a wealth of evidence for the first phase both of the cemetery itself and the settlement it served. The results of the excavations of the Great Tumulus,

97-99. The cemetery at Aigai covers a considerable area and consists of a great number of small tumuli in which burials of both men and women were found. Most of the jewellery was of bronze and was found in female burials. The most common objects are the "spectacle" (eight-shaped) fibulae used to fasten the dress at the shoulder (97) and the coiled armbands (98). In a number of tombs triple double axes were found (99); they were possibly a symbol of priestly authority or of high social status. Thessalonike, Archaeological Museum.

100. Bronze diadem from a tumulus at Vergina. The central panel has an embossed cross inscribed in a circle, the well-known motif symbolizing the sun's disc. Thessalonike, Archaeological Museum.

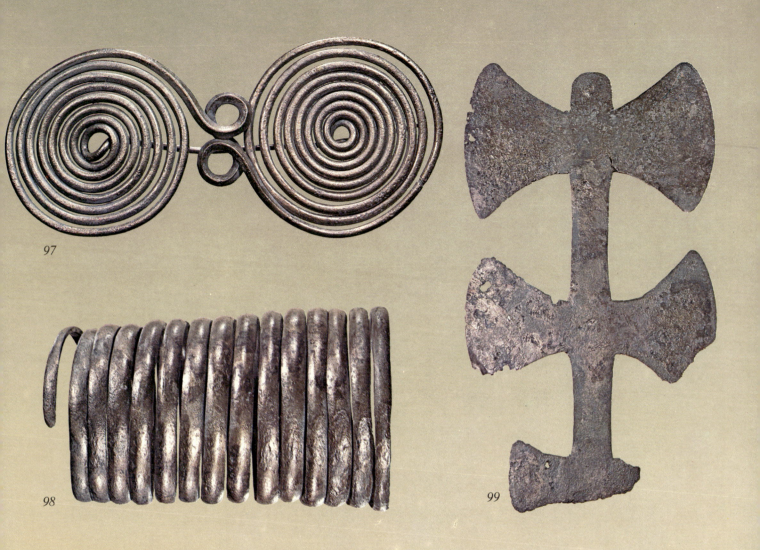

97

98

99

100

especially the most recent, were made public immediately in general terms, the first account of them appearing in the journal of the Archaeological Service.[9] The final publication must wait, however, since the excavation work has not yet been completed and the study of the finds has scarcely begun. I shall confine myself, therefore, to a generalised, interim presentation of those discoveries that offer some sound evidence about the cemetery of Aigai and contribute to an understanding of its history and its importance.

Up to the present (February 1979) three tombs and the foundations of a building that stood above ground level have been discovered beneath the fill of the Great Tumulus. The excavation of the mound, however, has yielded much finer and much more important discoveries than these buildings. The first finds precede the beginning of archaeological excavation. In 1948, a military unit digging trenches in the mound found ten fragments of a grave stele with a relief scene and an epigram, and the upper part of a second that simply bore the name of the deceased man.[10] They were dated to *c*. 350 and demonstrated that the cemetery at Vergina contained some excellent fourth century funerary monuments, comparable typologically and morphologically with those from the rest of Greece. The flawless pair of elegiac couplets, the earliest from central Macedonia to my knowledge, constitute invaluable historical evidence about the reign of Philip.

The existence of fragments of funerary monuments in the fill of the Great Tumulus had posed a number of questions which were to become more pressing with the commencement of systematic excavation in the years that followed. The excavations of 1952, 1962, 1963 and 1976 were very productive, despite the fact that they did not uncover the tombs concealed beneath the Great Tumulus. The deep

101. Aerial photograph of the Great Tumulus at Vergina after its excavation by M. Andronikos. The three royal tombs have been roofed over for protection.

102. Reconstruction drawing of the large tomb at Vergina. It was vaulted and consisted of a main chamber and an antechamber, with a Doric facade and large marble doors, preserved intact and in situ. The tomb was covered by a mound. At a later date, possibly the beginning of the 3rd century, massive deposits of earth and stone were heaped above the smaller mound to form the Great Tumulus.

trenches sunk in the enormous earth deposits revealed that in order to construct the mound, incredible quantities of material had been transported from the surrounding area; it consisted of a mixture of reddish soil, gravel, sand and unworked stones, amongst them a large number of broken grave stelai, most of which had been dumped there as useless material along with the unworked stone. The obvious conclusion to be drawn from this unexpected harvest was that the cemetery that was the source of all these funerary monuments had been violently destroyed at some date. The latest of the stelai were dated to the beginning of the third century, and the destruction probably occurred, therefore, some time after 300 and before 250. The attempt to establish who was responsible for it led to some particularly important and interesting conclusions. Starting from the hypothesis propounded by Hammond that Vergina was the site of Aigai, I attributed the destruction of the cemetery to the Galatian mercenaries left by Pyrrhos as a garrison at Aigai in 274/3, when he captured the old Macedonian capital along with some other cities. This theory was based on Plutarch's statement that the Galatian mercenaries plundered the royal tombs at Aigai;[11] it seemed to me that this act of sacrilege would naturally extend to the entire cemetery. The ramifications of the statement in Plutarch are much greater, however: if my interpretation was accepted it followed (1) that the identification of Aigai with the site at Vergina was correct; (2) that the royal Macedonian tombs lay somewhere in this area; (3) that the unusually large Great Tumulus probably concealed these royal tombs, or at least some of them.[12] These hypotheses, as we shall

103. An exciting spectacle awaited the first to enter the unplundered tomb: a variety of weapons and vessels lay against the walls and on the floor, which was covered by a layer of decomposed organic matter, mainly wood. The large bronze circular object in the illustration is the protective cover of a large gold and ivory shield.

see, were corroborated by the results of the 1977 and 1978 excavations and may now be regarded as virtually certain.

As the work of excavation continued, the number of fragments of grave monuments yielded by the mound increased enormously and they now constitute a very important body of material awaiting study.[13] Without wishing in any way to anticipate the conclusions of my colleague responsible for this study, I shall attempt to deduce from the material certain evidence of importance for the history of the cemetery and the population of the surrounding area. The fragments from the mound so far (1978) belong to at least 40 different funerary monuments. The majority are marble stelai, but there are also some stelai of poros and some marble *loutrophoroi* and *lekythoi*. Most of the stelai are simply inscribed with the name of the dead persons while a few have traces of paint, demonstrating that although only the inscription is now preserved, they were once decorated with painted scenes. In addition to the stele first mentioned there is a second carved in relief, with an excellent portrayal of an athlete, and bearing an epigram;[14] this is the largest stele of all, though not all the pieces of it have been found, at least to date. In a number of cases the painted decoration is in a good state of preservation, and was clearly the work of competent artists; it enables us to form an accurate impression of the level of attainment achieved in painting in northern Greece during the fourth century.[15] An important relief grave stele was discovered in 1978. The dead man is portrayed wearing a petasos and a short chiton; he is holding a bird in one

105

106

104-106. In the ante-chamber and the chamber of the large tomb two marble sarcophagi were found (104 and 105). Each contained a gold larnax with the characteristic Macedonian star. In the smaller larnax, found in the ante-chamber, (105), were laid the bones of a young woman wrapped in a gold and purple cloth (106). Its border has a design of spiral meanders while the main field is covered with plant motifs.

107. *The ante-chamber of the large tomb contained a magnificent gorytos (combined bow-case and quiver) covered with gold, bearing relief scenes. A number of bronze arrows were found inside it. Behind the pair of greaves can be seen the large marble door to the main chamber.*

108. *Silver vessels, lying as they were found in the great tomb.*

hand and two spears in the other and his sword hangs at his side. The figure is very reminiscent of those on fifth century Thessalian grave stelai, and especially no. 741 in the National Archaeological Museum at Athens. The stele should accordingly be dated about the middle of the fifth century; it belongs, in other words, to the period when Aigai was still the capital of the Macedonian kingdom, and is the earliest funerary monument from the cemetery. We are thus in a position to form a clear picture of the grave monuments that stood in the cemetery of Aigai from the fifth century until at least the beginning of the third. These monuments were probably erected over the small mounds that concealed family tombs. Relief or painted stelai, marble funerary vases, other, simpler stelai probably coated with plaster and painted — all these grave monuments, judging by their size, marked the graves of ordinary Macedonians, and did not belong to the tombs of the wealthy, distinguished nobility: the famous *hetairoi* of the king. The prosopography that can be compiled from the names on the stelai dating from the fourth century is particularly valuable in the light of the fact that we are dealing with Aigai, the ancient capital of the Macedonian kingdom. It is my own view that the controversy surrounding the nationality of the ancient Macedonians is meaningless in that it deals with a non-problem; however, the 75 names of ordinary Macedonians known so far from the stelai found in the Great Tumulus make a crucial, indeed definitive, contribution to the debate. It is of particular significance that the list is preserved by chance and is therefore entirely random. I limit myself to a few of the typical names: *Alketas, Hermon, Theokritos, Theodoros, Theophanes, Kleitomachos, Laandros, Peukolaos, Philotas, Bernika, Kleio.* A cursory comparison with Thracian names not only of the fourth and third centuries but also from the Roman period suffices to make the distinction between the two groups clear. The names from Vergina have unequivocally pure Greek roots with manifestly Macedonian traits that betray a centuries old indigen-

ous tradition; they thus constitute a convincing rebuttal of the theories that the Macedonians were in fact hellenized barbarians, for personal names are handed on from generation to generation over a long period of time and are not easily eradicated by foreign influences.[16]

The results of the most recent excavations, which uncovered the magnificent royal tombs, have demonstrated that the Macedonian kings must have been buried in this cemetery, possibly in an area specially set aside for the purpose. I noted earlier that the excavation of the Great Tumulus is not yet complete, and I should add at this point that even the tombs found so far have not been fully uncovered and investigated. The mound almost certainly conceals more tombs, the evidence from which will make a decisive contribution to a correct understanding and interpretation of the area. What follows, therefore, is merely the first preliminary report and is offered with great reservation as a description of the finds, and a provisional interpretation of their significance.

The three tombs that have so far come to light are located on the southwest edge of the large mound. They were originally concealed by a smaller mound of earlier date which was covered by the larger mound after what must have been a considerable period of time. The reasons for the construction of the large mound remain problematic; the view I expressed earlier, that it was erected at the behest of Antigonos Gonatas in order to conceal his own tomb along with the other royal tombs, has not yet been verified. The excavation of the centre of the mound, where one would have expected to find this tomb, did not yield positive results. Outside the area of the earlier mound, though still within the large mound, the foundations were found of a small rectangular building measuring 8 × 9.60 m. A few marble fragments of the superstructure have survived, the craftsmanship of which is of a very high order. The use of marble is also significant, for we have no other instance of it at this time from this region. The existence of this building next to the mound containing the tombs is susceptible of only one interpretation: it must have been a *Heroön* connected with the dead. This very fact in itself suggests that the tombs close by could not have been those of ordinary men and offers strong support to the conclusion emerging from the finds discovered in the tombs themselves: that they were in fact royal tombs. A second, external circumstance that reinforces the theory is the fact that three sumptuous and imposing tombs lay beneath the same mound — a phenomenon unparalleled in the rest of Macedonia.

The smallest of the three, on the southern fringe of the mound, consists of a rectangular chamber with internal dimensions of 2.09 × 3.50 m. and a depth (or height) of 3 m., covered with long narrow slabs of poros laid horizontally. It was plundered in antiquity, the robbers breaking one of the covering slabs to create a small opening through which they gained access to the chamber. They also smashed and removed one of the stones in the west wall, but apparently encountered some obstacle barring their way into the interior and were obliged to abandon their efforts at this point. The tomb was pillaged in a thorough-going fashion. A few sherds from black-glazed vases were found in the earth that had fallen in through the openings, and a large number of bones were discovered, disturbed by the robbers. The most valuable item in the tomb could not be carried off, however: the frescoes. With the exception of the narrow west wall, which probably held a shelf, the upper part of all the others were decorated with painted scenes, separated by a band of decorative griffins and flowers from a red dado.

The main and certainly the most impressive fresco, is the one on the north wall. The subject is the rape of Persephone by Pluto. The god is standing in his four-horsed chariot, holding the reins and his sceptre in his right hand; his left encircles the waist of Kore who is stretching backwards, her arms outstretched in a gesture of despair. Hermes is running in front of the chariot leading the way, while a friend of the young goddess (Kyane?) is kneeling behind it in an attitude of astonishment and anguish. The entire scene is marked by great sensitivity, unusually powerful lines, an admirable grasp of composition, an awareness of perspective, and above all, the mature skill of a great artist. The brush-strokes are applied confidently and surely and attest the quickness of hand of an experienced painter. The range of colour is limited but deployed in a most expressive manner, the main emphasis being on the warm tones (yellow, red, violet, mid-brown). There can be no doubt that this was the work of a master. Pliny claims that Nikomachos, the famous fourth century painter who was renowned for the speed with which he executed his compositions, once painted the exceedingly rare scene of the rape of Persephone; it is tempting to suggest that the Vergina fresco was also his work.

The narrow east wall is decorated with a seated female figure, rendered entirely in outline without the use of colour. Here too, the lines are exceptionally well drawn and the figure is flawless. It may represent Demeter, for the other long wall is also decorated with figures taken from mythology, and to the left of it is something rather like a rock, which may depict the ἀγέλαστος πέτρα (mirthless stone).

The long wall to the south is occupied by three seated female figures. They are not so well preserved as the scenes on the other walls and the work of cleaning them has not yet been completed; the lines and the colours cannot therefore be distinguished clearly, though the latter seem to have been limited in range. It seemed probable from the very beginning that the figures were the three Moirai (Fates) and this now seems to have been confirmed: one of them appears to be holding the distaff, in which case she is Klotho and the other two Lachesis and Atropos. The magnificence of the decoration of the tomb, together with the fact that the robbers left nothing behind — an indication that all its contents were valuable — both strongly reinforce the original thesis that these were not the tombs of common men.

Any lingering doubt on this point is dispelled in my opinion by the large vaulted tomb a few metres to

109-110. The majority of the grave stelai found in the Great Tumulus at Vergina are dated to the second half of the 4th century B.C. with a number of them belonging to the 3rd. Many of the names inscribed on them are typically Macedonian and clearly Greek. The implication that ordinary Macedonians in the period 400-350 B.C. had Greek names is decisive supporting evidence that the Macedonians were Greeks and neither Illyrian nor Thracian in origin.

the northwest of the smaller one. The facade of this tomb has not yet been excavated down to the original ground level and we do not yet now how it was decorated, or what stands on the floor. Neither has the ante-chamber, been properly investigated and the material from the main chamber is still being cleaned and restored. It is nonetheless possible to form a clear picture of the architecture of the tomb and the burials it contained.

The tomb has a Doric facade; the colours used on both the *tainiai* and the cornices and on the architectural members are preserved. The crowning member is not a pediment but a horizontal cornice above which there is a painted frieze surmounted in turn by a second cornice. The frieze is 1.16 m. wide and 5.56 m. long, and is decorated with a hunting scene that occupies its entire length. Three men on horse-back and seven on foot, wild animals (a deer, a lion and wild boars), hunting dogs, trees, rocks and a stele are arranged in a masterful design, the composition of which is matched by the powerful drawing. The range of colours attests a sensibility and control that is equalled by the grasp of perspective, though the latter does not go beyond the bounds of the classical tradition which had not yet broken free from the old conventions. The main emphasis in the composition is concentrated on the area immediately to the right of centre. The central position itself is occupied by a youthful mounted figure whose posture recalls that of Alexander in the Naples mosaic. Just to his right two men on foot and a horseman are hitting a lion, the main quarry of the hunt. The horseman is on higher plane than all the other figures and is riding forwards, moving out of the background; he is the only mature man in the entire scene and, in my opinion, the figure is probably a portrait. The frieze is a superb creation and has many features in common with the Alexander mosaic in the Naples Museum, in terms both of the overall composition and of many points of detail. It is tempting to suggest that it was the work of the painter responsible for the original on which the mosaic was modelled, or at

least to his workshop, since this original is thought to have dated from *c*. 320.

"The rape of Persephone" and "The lion and boar hunt" in these two tombs are the only surviving examples of large-scale Greek painting. For the first time we are in a position to evaluate the famous works of the fourth century painters, known hitherto only from the pale reflections of them in the Roman imitations buried and preserved by the lava of Vesuvius. We can now understand the admiration in which these painters were held by both Greeks and Romans and expressed in brief references by contemporary and later writers. Over and above their contribution to our knowledge of ancient Greek painting, however, these two scenes make clear the importance of the tombs they adorn in comparison with the other Macedonian tombs uncovered so far. All of these, of course, had been robbed and we do not know what they contained. The majority are fairly well preserved, however, and their architectural features and decoration have survived. The most important of them from this point of view is the tomb at Lefkadia with the two-storey facade.[17] On it there are four separate painted figures, each of them well-drawn, which were previously the best surviving examples of early Greek painting. A cursory comparison is enough to reveal the difference in quality between these figures and the Vergina compositions. Whereas the Lefkadia painter was a skilled craftsman, the painters of Vergina were creative artists possessed of a boldness of imagination and

111. Detail of the "rape of Persephone" which decorated the small tomb at Vergina. Pluto, holding his sceptre and the reins in his right hand, has seized Persephone around the waist with his left. With his right foot he steps into the chariot while his left is still on the ground; the flowers that Persephone and her companions were gathering can also be seen. The excavator believes that the painter of this composition may have been the great 4th century artist Nikomachos.

112-113. A hunting scene adorns the upper part of the facade of the large tomb. Men, mounted and on foot, are set in a landscape with trees, rocks and a tall stele. The sure grasp of composition, the control of perspective, the sensitivity of line and colour and the feeling for mass and architectural balance all attest to its being the work of a great fourth century painter; it may have been by the same artist that produced the mosaic of Alexander in the Naples Museum. Below: a detail of the fresco showing a horseman. Right: provisional restoration drawing of this detail.

112

originality that went beyond the conventions of the day.

Enough of the facade of the tomb has been uncovered to make it clear that the two-leaf marble door has survived unbroken *in situ*. This is thus the first Macedonian tomb to be found unviolated and the first ancient door to be discovered in its original position. This highly satisfying circumstance obliged us to change the strategy of the excavation; we decided to uncover the vault so as to be able to enter the tomb from the rear.

The excavation of the vault revealed a number of hitherto unknown features. The first was that its entire length was covered with a thick layer of plaster, which is unparalleled to my knowledge, in any other Macedonian tomb. Secondly, it was discovered that the vault is not a single structure but is divided above the partition wall separating the main chamber from the ante-chamber. The vault over the ante-chamber must therefore have been constructed at a second stage — a conclusion supported by the evidence from inside the two chambers.

The most important new feature, however, was found at the west end of the vault, on the roof of the main chamber. At this point a large number of square mud bricks were found; they presumably belonged to a square or rectangular structure, erected on top of the vault which must have collapsed later under the weight of the deposits of earth.

Some of the bricks bore traces of plaster, demonstrating that the interior of the structure at least had been coated with this material. Clear traces of fire reveal that this structure served sacrificial purposes; it was probably a kind of altar. The most important find of all, however, was a group of two iron swords, a spear head and a large number of other iron pieces from horse trappings, all of which showed signs of intense fire. Other finds included a bronze *oinochoe* and a few gold acorns which it later transpired must have formed part of the gold wreath belonging to the man buried in the main chamber. These discoveries suggest that horses had probably been sacrificed at the funerary pyre — a custom recalling the funeral of Patroklos in the Iliad and typical of the burial practices associated with heroes in the Homeric poems. Even before we became aware of its contents, then, it was clear that we were dealing with a unique tomb and that sacrifices of an unusual nature, recalling ancient Homeric practices, had been carried out at the funeral of its occupant.

The thesis was reinforced and the picture completed by the contents of the tomb. A marble sarcophagus, almost rectangular in shape and covered with a horizontal marble slab, was found very close to the centre of the west wall of the tomb. Bronze and iron vessels and weapons were discovered in the southwest corner of the main chamber. Near the north wall was a group of vases, most of them of silver and few of them of clay. The remains of a wooden piece of furniture richly decorated with ivory ornamentation lay on the floor in front of the sarcophagus, covering the area roughly to the centre of the chamber. The cleaning and study of this material has not yet been completed, but it is my view that it came from a wooden bed; beds are usually found in Macedonian tombs, though in the later ones they are made of stone. Although very few pieces have been preserved, it is nevertheless abundantly clear that the process of decay has deprived us of the most impressive and valuable object within the tomb; had it survived, it would have been evidence enough of the exceptionally high rank of the dead man. Finally, an iron cuirass was found on the floor, where it had fallen, a short distance away from where the bed had stood, towards the partitioned wall.

The walls of the chamber stand in stark contrast

114. Gold larnax found in the main chamber of the large tomb. It contained the bones of the dead king, wrapped in a purple cloth, and a gold oak wreath. The lid bears a star — the emblem of the Macedonian dynasty. The sides are decorated with rich plant motifs highlighted by inlaid blue glass-paste. Thessalonike, Archaeological Museum.

115-119. *The miniature ivory heads which decorated the bed are amongst the most important finds from the tomb. One (118) is a portrait of the youthful Alexander; a second portrays a mature woman who may have been Olympias (117). The most interesting of them shows a mature, bearded man (119), most probably Philip. Thessalonike, Archaeological Museum.*

120. *The gilded silver diadem belonging to the deceased. Its diameter could be adjusted by means of a separate cylinder which was decorated in relief with a "knot of Herakles". It was probably a royal diadem. Thessalonike, Archaeological Museum.*

121. *The gold oak wreath found on top of the bones of the deceased man in the larnax in the large tomb. It is the most impressive ancient wreath discovered to date. Thessalonike, Archaeological Museum.*

with the wealth and artistic quality of the objects found therein. I know of no other large-scale Macedonian tomb in which the plaster is so poor and so roughly applied. Not only is there nowhere any trace of painted decoration — the walls were not even coated with a single colour — but the fine plaster used in other Macedonian structures as the final coat that constituted the visible surface of the walls was never applied. A large area was covered only with the first layer of rough plaster; in some places the second, finer, coat can be found, but there is nowhere any trace of the third coat. One is thus left with the impression that the walls were plastered with considerable haste.

The finds in the chamber may be divided into the following broad categories:
1. The weapons of the dead man.
2. Large vessels used mainly for storing, heating and drawing water.
3. Silver vases, mainly for wine.
4. Clay pottery.

In addition to these there was a unique object made of silver and gold, which I believe to be the royal diadem; a bronze tripod, probably an old family heirloom; a lantern (a bronze vessel pierced with holes in which a ceramic lamp stood); a torch; and a sponge. Almost all these objects were obviously the personal belongings of the deceased and had been used by him during his lifetime (only the ceramic vases seem to be unused). We may claim, then, that despite the sumptuous nature of these finds, as a group of funerary offerings they in no way overstep the measure of greek taste; the impression conveyed, as I have written elsewhere, is one of frugal luxury.

One of the features to make the most immediate impact, not only on the archaeologist but also on the

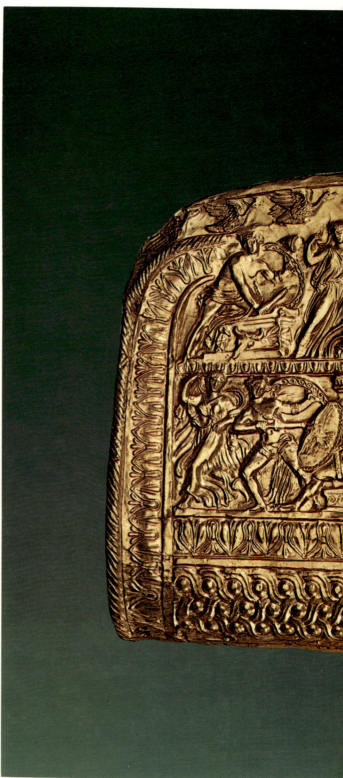

122. Gold plate that was used to decorate the gorytos, showing scenes of a battle during the capture of a city. Similar objects have been recovered from the Scythian tombs in South Russia. Thessalonike, Archaeological Museum.

layman, is the strikingly high quality of all the finds. Bronze and silver vessels alike are flawlessly worked and sensitively decorated, and the forms are conceived and executed with an artistry that sets them apart from all others of their kind. They are, in short, superb artistic creations, and splendid examples of the achievements of Greek metal-working and sculpture. Not only were these objects of exceptionally high quality; many of them are unique. The torch, for instance, is the first surviving example of its kind to my knowledge. The weapons merit a separate description.

For the first time we have before us the complete panoply of a distinguished warrior. The complete range of defensive and offensive weapons is represented, in some cases by more than one example (spear heads and swords). The items of defence (greaves, cuirass, shield and helmet) are naturally the most splendid pieces. It would hardly be an exaggeration to claim that almost all the weapons found in the Vergina tomb are the most magnificent examples of their kind surviving from the ancient world and in some cases — the cuirass, helmet and shield — are quite unique. The cuirass was made of very fine sheets of iron covered with leather and cloth. The iron plates are hinged, four to the body and two on each shoulder, so that the wearer could move swiftly and easily. In form, it is almost identical with the one worn by Alexander in the famous Naples mosaic. All its edges are adorned with gold *kymatia* and there are broader horizontal bands of gold on both the front and the back. The breast was decorated with six lions' heads and rings and there were apparently two more like them on the left side, where it was fastened. Another small plate of gold decorated with a representation of Athena wearing full armour adorned one of the sides, probably the right. Finally, the flaps at the bottom consisted of gold leaves with a relief decoration of anthemia. The cuirass is not only a magnificent work of art but also a marvellous technological achievement for the fourth century. This same level of technological attainment can be seen in the iron Macedonian helmet which has a high crest and cheek-pieces and is decorated with a head of Athena in the middle of the forehead. It is the first Macedonian helmet ever discovered.

The most splendid find of all, however, was the shield, which was unfortunately not intact; the frame appears to have been made of wood and leather which have completely rotted away. Although the shield had disintegrated, the surviving pieces made it clear from the start that it was a true masterpiece, and I expressed the hope that even if it were not feasible to reconstitute it in its original form it might nevertheless prove possible to restore it to the point where we could say with confidence what that original form was. Work on it is still in the initial stages, but it is already far enough advanced to indicate that my hopes will not be disappointed. At this point in time, we can detect that the outer rim (*antyx*) was covered with ivory decorated with a spiral meander design in which the interstices between the spirals were inlaid with pieces of glass covered by fine gold leaf. This enclosed a second circle of gold and silver. The boss of the shield was gilded, with two ivory figures attached to the gold background, depicting a youth seizing a young girl. These two statuettes are unfortunately very badly preserved. On the inside the shield had four bands of gold decorated with relief representations of flying Nikai (Victories) and terminating in anthemia. They were probably arranged in the form of a cross around a central, broad plaque of gold decorated with two pairs of heraldic lions. This plaque was the attachment for the handle, which was probably made of leather. This shield is an unparalleled archaeological find but does not fit any of the descriptions in the literary sources, unless we may make so bold as to cite the mythical shield made

123. *Detail from the battle scenes of the gorytos. The upper band shows a warrior and women who are trying to escape. Below, a suppliant has taken refuge next to the "Palladion" in the temple; to the right is a wounded warrior. Thessalonike, Archaeological Museum.*

124. The excellent silver vessels from the 4th century B.C. discovered in the large tomb are among the most important finds. The reliefs with which they are decorated (the head illustrated here is a Silenos) are masterpieces of Greek craftsmanship.

125. This lantern consists of a bronze vessel pierced with holes. An iron support in the bottom held a terracotta lamp in position. Thessalonike, Archaeological Museum.

126. *Hilt of the iron sword belonging to the dead man, exquisitely decorated with gold. Thessalonike, Archaeological Museum.*

127. *The craftsmanship of the iron cuirass shows both advanced technical skill and artistic sensitivity. It is adorned with gold bands and borders, and with miniature lions' heads at front and back. Thessalonike, Archaeological Museum.*

126

by Hephaestos for Achilles. It seems unlikely that it was intended for use in battle; it was more probably a "ceremonial" shield. The restoration of this fragile, precious shield has lent support to my original theory that a bronze, shield-shaped object found above the shields was probably its protective cover.

A further unexpected detail is added to the picture emerging from the finds described above by the "ossuary" discovered inside the marble sarcophagus. It consists of a valuable gold larnax, the sides and lid of which are exquisitely decorated. The predominant motif is the large radiate star familiar from Macedonian coins and shields, which was probably the royal emblem. The bones were laid inside the larnax with great care; they had obviously been carefully retrieved from the pyre, washed and then wrapped in a purple cloth, the colour of which had stained many of the bones and the bottom of the larnax. Once again one is reminded of Homeric burial practices. A precious gold wreath, consisting of oak-leaves and acorns, had been laid (crushed) on top of the bones; it is the most impressive ancient Greek wreath I know.

All the evidence at our disposal suggests that this was a royal burial. The conclusion is reinforced by yet another unique discovery: a gold and silver hoop consisting of a hollow tube, circular in section, the ends of which fit into a separate cylinder, thus making it possible to adjust the size. The outer surface of this latter piece is decorated with a knot with the ends of a band at either side. I believe this to have been a royal diadem. A provisional comparison shows that it is similar to the ones found in portraits of some of the kings — Antigonos, for example, Attalos III (?) and Antiochos III — and also in a number of portraits of Alexander; it must, therefore, have been a royal diadem. If this conclusion is correct, it necessarily follows that the deceased was a king.

Reference was made earlier to the decomposed remains of a wooden bed with ivory decoration found in front of the sarcophagus. All that can be said about

128. *Pair of gilded bronze greaves of unequal height. Thessalonike, Archaeological Museum.*

129. *This iron Macedonian helmet is unique. It has an impressive crest, decorated cheek-pieces, and the head of Athena over the forehead. Thessalonike, Archaeological Museum.*

it at this stage is that it must have been a very impressive item. It was decorated with gold and adorned with ivory reliefs, amongst them a group rendered in bas relief and a second consisting of figures carved almost in the round both of which were probably attached to a decorative frieze of the bed. We cannot yet say with certainty whether both groups belonged to the same frieze. A number of legs and arms and eight small heads have so far been recovered from the second group. Five of the heads were discovered during the first few days of the investigation of the chamber and three of these are of special importance. One of them is a portrait of Alexander at a very young age: apart from the fact that it bears a close resemblance to the portraits of him already known, its features fit the descriptions of him in the literary sources with astonishing accuracy. The head next to it had very similar features, but is that of a mature woman; it is not impossible, in my opinion, that it is a portrait of Olympias, though this cannot be established beyond doubt at this stage. The third head is that of a mature, bearded man; the artist clearly attempted to differentiate the right eye from the left, skilfully indicating that the former was blind, without marring the beauty of the face. This feature, together with the resemblance of the head to the portrait of Philip on the Tarsos medallion is convincing evidence that this is in fact another portrait of Philip. This interpretation is the more convincing because of the discovery in the chamber of a head of Alexander, the identification of which can hardly be called into question.

The finds in the ante-chamber were totally unexpected. The evidence deriving from other Macedonian tombs — albeit plundered — pointed to the conclusion that the ante-chamber was not likely to contain many important objects, and we certainly did not expect to find a second burial. What we found on entering it, however, was totally different from anything we had anticipated. Firstly, the walls were very carefully plastered with a white dado surmounted by a red colour and a band of rosettes defining the springing of the vault. Near the south wall, to the left of the entrance to the thomb, there was a second marble sarcophagus slightly larger than the one in the main chamber. On the ground in front of it were found the decomposed remains of a wooden piece of furniture, possibly a bed, with gold plating and ivory decoration. A gold wreath lay on the ground next to the sarcophagus; it was very delicately worked and consisted of myrtle leaves and flowers. The remains of what may have been a painted wooden shelf were discovered near the north wall, with a gilded pectoral next to it, decorated with relief horsemen and rosettes. A number of objects were found on the threshold of the door connecting the two chambers. A gold plate was found standing in the corner of the doorway which had once adorned the *gorytos* (combined bow case and quiver) that exactly resembled those found in the Scythian tombs of South Russia. Behind it were the bronze arrows that the *gorytos* had contained, and a pair of bronze, gilded greaves were found next to it. These were noticeably different in length (the left is 3.5 cm. shorter than the right) and in the formation of the tibia. A large number of *alabastra* lay scattered over the floor at this point, along with a "Cypriote" amphora typical of the middle of the fourth century.

The most precious object in the ante-chamber, as in the main chamber, was found inside the sarcophagus. The sarcophagus itself contained a second gold larnax, smaller than that in the main chamber and less lavishly decorated, but with the same radiate star on the lid. When we opened it we were astonished to find a superb gold and purple cloth with a fringe of spiral meanders covering the cremated bones. At the present time, the work of conservation has progressed to the point where we can confidently claim that this is one of the finest pieces of ancient Greek cloth discovered anywhere. Crushed against the narrow side of the larnax was a woman's diadem consisting of an arrangement of flowers and leaves on slender stalks and stems. Once it had been restored to its original form, it was clear that it was not simply a masterpiece of ancient Greek gold work, but in fact the finest piece of ancient jewellery known. The consummate skill of its creator went hand in hand with his artistic creativity, and the sensitivity of the workmanship is matched by the extreme elegance of the motifs, in which the sensuous vegetation is masterfully combined with a spiritual abstraction of form.

These, in brief, are the discoveries yielded by the large Macedonian tomb uncovered in 1977. The first, and most crucial, problem connected with it is the question of its date. The sherds discovered above it are securely dated to the third quarter of the fourth century (350-325). The three pots found in the main chamber (a lamp, a red-figure *askos* and a black-glazed *oinochoe*) also date from this period, and the same date may be assigned to the silver vases, especially those decorated with relief heads of Silenus, Herakles and Pan. It would be possible to make out a case for dating all the finds to *c.* 340. The architecture of the tomb suits this date well and it is further reinforced by the painting on the large frieze on the facade, as far as one can judge from a preliminary examination of the technique.

The second problem concerns the identity of the dead man, or rather persons, interred in the tomb. All the finds point to the conclusion that it was a royal tomb. The hoop which, as we have seen, was probably a "royal diadem" suggests that the man buried in the main chamber was a king. If this interpretation and the date suggested for the tomb are both correct, this must have been the tomb of Philip, since no other king died in Macedonia in the period from 350 to 325.

I am well aware that this hypothesis will be met with scepticism, and also that it has significant implications in the fields of both archaeology and history. I therefore feel it incumbent upon me to re-state that it is based on an interpretation of the archaeological probabilities consonant with, and indeed imposed by, the demands of rigorous scholarship. The conclusion I have reached is provisional, but by no means arbit-rary. If we assume that the main chamber contained the remains of Philip, we are faced with the question of the identity of the man, or rather the woman, interred in the ante-chamber. In this case there is more than one possible answer to the question; it could be Philip's last wife, Kleopatra, or (excepting only Olympias) one of his earlier wives who died at unknown dates and under unknown circumstances.

In concluding my discussion of this phase of the excavation, I would like to emphasize that its greatest importance lies in the finds themselves, particularly the frescoes. Through these we can form some acquaintance with and study in some detail a large number of cultural and other features of the Macedonian aspect of Greek civilisation, and assess accurately the position it occupied in the world of the fourth century.

The excavations of 1978 revealed a smaller, unplundered Macedonian tomb which completed the picture we had formed from the first two and lent support to the theory that they were royal burials. The third tomb is a few metres to the northwest of the large tomb. Its facade has approximately the same architectural form as the latter, with the familiar painted frieze at the top. Unfortunately, the composition adorning the frieze was painted on an applied surface of some organic material (probably leather on a wooden panel) which has completely decomposed, leaving only a very few traces on the plaster. Internally, the tomb comprises a chamber and an ante-chamber. One of the leaves of the door connecting the two collapsed into the main chamber at some point and was found shattered, covering part of the floor; it has probably crushed a number of objects beneath it. Against the west wall, in the position usually occupied by the sarcophagus, there was a built altar, cuboid in shape. This had a hollow in the centre, in which stood the silver hydria containing the bones. A gold wreath of oak-leaves and acorns had been placed on the shoulder of the hydria. The floor was almost completely covered with the decomposed remains of wooden furniture and perhaps of a number of leather covers. It is fairly certain that the remains are those of a wooden bed with ivory decoration; a piece of the latter, which was attached to the upper part of one of the legs of the bed, has been successfully restored. These three ivory figures alone (Pan and a Dionysiac couple) are enough to demonstrate that the lost bed was a master-piece of ancient furniture. The three plastic figures are powerfully yet sensitively sculpted, their flesh is delicate yet compact and the rendering of the folds of their garments has a charming quality of its own; it is clearly an outstanding piece of miniature sculpture, from about the middle of the fourth century, and is a further reminder of what we have lost from that creative period of Greek art of which we have only a distorted idea through the sickly sweet copies of the Roman period.

The northwest corner of the chamber contained two large bronze vessels, silver plated on both the outside and inside, with a tall, silver-plated iron lamp-stand next to them. The clay lamp was found nearby, where it had fallen.

In the southwest corner there were a large number of silver vases, amongst them a fine *oinochoe*, two *kadiskoi* and a *patera*, the handle of which terminated in a superbly worked plastic ram's head. A few more silver vessels were found on top of the remains of the bed. So far, a total of 27 of these silver vessels have been restored; together with the 20 discovered in the large tomb they constitute the most valuable and the most representative collection of silver vases known from the fourth century.

Another notable discovery was a pair of gilded greaves with a band of anthemia decorating the lower edge.

On the floor of the north part of the ante-chamber were found traces of a folded gold decorated garment. It had probably been placed on a piece of wooden furniture or on a wooden shelf which has decomposed. It may have been made of leather, which has rotted to a paste-like consistency. Thanks to the humidity, however, the outline of the garment has been preserved at a number of points.

The south part of the ante-chamber also bore traces of the decomposed remains of organic matter, with bronze and iron curry-combs amongst them. Next to these was the iron tip and the butt and lower part of a spear of which the wooden shaft was covered by gold; the wood has decomposed, leaving only the gold.

The most interesting feature of the ante-chamber, however, was the painted border encircling the four walls. This narrow band was decorated with a chariot race for *synorides* (two-horse chariots). The nature and dimensions of the space available did not lend themselves to a work of great inspiration, but limited the artist to a purely decorative scene. He has nonetheless achieved a notable composition, evidencing his experience, his mastery of his craft and his sensitivity. The large number of chariots are not merely monotonous, mechanical repetitions of each other but form a dynamic composition in which each of them has its own movement and individual character, with the horses pulling it and the ground over which it moves rendered in a distinctive manner. It is a significant example of fourth century painting and, though inferior to the inspired compositions in the other two tombs, is nonetheless superior to any other hitherto discovered.

The evidence at our disposal suggests that this too, must have been a royal tomb — not only because it formed part of the same group as the first two but because some of the finds (the gold spear and greaves etc.) are unique and the quality and wealth of the silver vases and the silver plated bronze vessels show clearly that the deceased was of high social status. There is not yet enough chronological evidence to permit a secure dating; my first impression is that the tomb should be assigned to roughly the middle of the fourth century and certainly cannot be later than the third quarter of that century.

This dazzling picture of the cemetery at Aigai is based on the finds of archaeological excavation over the last twenty-five years. The most recent discoveries lend strong support to the hypotheses and conclusions propounded after the uncovering of the first two tombs. It is my belief that the three tombs were almost certainly royal, and Hammond's theory that Vergina is to be identified with ancient Aigai now replaces the traditional view that located the first capital city of the Macedonians at Edessa. The reason for the construction of the Great Tumulus remains unknown, however. Our investigations in the centre of the mound did not produce positive results and we must await further excavation before attempting to answer this question. What is certain is that it was constructed at a date much later than the period of the tombs excavated, since its fill contained broken fragments of inscribed funerary stelai dating very probably from the third century. The area of it that remains uninvestigated probably conceals other tombs, and as the work of excavation proceeds it will hopefully yield more valuable finds and more evidence bearing on the problems that remain unsolved.

CHRONOLOGICAL TABLE

359	**Spring**	Defeat and death of Perdikkas III in battle against the Illyrians in Upper Macedonia. Philip assumes power. Defeat of the pretender Argaios. Peace treaty between Philip and Athens.
359-358		Organisation and training of the Macedonian army.
358	**Spring**	Philip's invasion of Paionia; defeat of Lyppeios.
	Summer	Philip campaigns in Illyria, defeats Bardylis and regains control of Upper Macedonia.
	Autumn - Winter	Philip's first invasion of Thessaly.
357	**Spring - Summer**	*Outbreak of the Athenian "War of the Allies".* Philip attacks Amphipolis.
	Autumn - Winter	Capture of Amphipolis. Philip's marriage with Olympias.
356	**Winter**	Seizure of Pydna.
	Spring	Macedonian - Chalkidian alliance.
	Summer	Occupation of Krenides, foundation of Philippi. Coalition of Thracians, Illyrians and Paionians against Philip; Athens joins the anti-Macedonian coalition. *The Phokians seize Delphi.* Birth of Alexander. Parmenion's victory over the Illyrians. Philip's race horse wins at Olympia. Philip captures Potidaia, which he hands over to the Chalkidian League. Capture of Apollonia, Galepsos and Oisyme.
355	**Spring - Summer**	*Conclusion of the Athenian war against her Allies.* Philip in Thessaly.
	Autumn - Winter	*Declaration of the Third Sacred War against the Phokians.* Philip invests Methone.
354	**Spring**	Capture of Methone.
	Summer - Autumn	Philip advances on Thrace, captures Abdera and Maroneia.
353	**Summer**	Philip enters Thessaly; victory over Phayllos and the Pheraian-Phokian allies.
	Autumn	Philip, defeated by the Phokian general Onomarchos, withdraws to Macedonia.
352	**Spring - Summer**	Philip returns to Thessaly; he is elected *archon* of the Thessalians for life. Defeat of the Phokians under Onomarchos on Crocus Plain. Capture of Pherai and Pagasai. Foundation of a Macedonian colony at Gonnoi.
	Summer	Philip's chariot wins in the Olympic Games. Philip threatens Thermopylai but is obliged to withdraw.
	Winter	Chalkidian-Athenian alliance. Philip advances in Thrace; he is taken ill.
351		Warning campaign in Chalkidike. Demosthenes delivers the *First Philippic.*

350		Philip in Epeiros: Arybbas becomes regent; Alexandros the Molossian comes to Pella.
349	**Summer**	Philip invades Chalkidike; captures Stageira.
	Autumn	First Athenian reinforcements sent to Olynthos. Philip intervenes again in Thessaly.
348		*Defection of Euboia from Athens.*
	Spring	Second Athenian reinforcements sent to Olynthos. Philip invests and captures Olynthos.
	Summer - Autumn	Peace proposals brought to Athens.
347		Philip intervenes in Central Greece; beginning of the siege of Halos. Athenian efforts for the formation of a panhellenic coalition against Philip.
346	**Winter**	First Athenian embassy to Pella. Philip campaigns in Thrace against Kersebleptes.
	April	Athenian Assembly votes for peace with Philip. Defeat of Kersebleptes.
	May	Second Athenian embassy to Pella. Philip returns to his capital.
	July	Philip at Thermopylai. Confirmation of the Peace of Philokrates. The Phokians surrender to Philip. Convocation of the Amphictyonic Council.
	Summer-Autumn	Philip presides over the Pythian Games at Delphi.
345	**Spring**	Philip campaigns against Pleuratos, king of the Illyrians. Isokrates' second *Epistle* to Philip. Megalopolitans and Messenians join the Amphictyonic League.
344	**Spring**	Philip enters Thessaly, reintroduces *tetrarchies*. Demosthenes heads embassy to Peloponnese.
	Autumn	Macedonian embassy to Athens. Demosthenes delivers his *Second Philippic*.
343		Philip supports pro-Macedonian parties in Central and Southern Greece.
342	**Winter**	Philip in Epeiros; he removes Arybbas and installs Alexandros on the Molossian throne.
	Spring	Aristotle settles in Macedonia as Alexander's tutor. Philip campaigns in Thrace.
341	**Winter**	Philip supports Kardia against Athens.
	Spring	Athenian raids in the Gulf of Pagasai and against the Aegean coast of Thrace. Demosthenes delivers his *Chersonesos* oration and his *Third* and *Fourth Philippic*.
	Summer	Philip defeats and deposes the Thracian kings Teres and Kersebleptes. Alliance with Kothelas, king of the Getai, and marriage with his daughter Meda. Foundation of Philippoupolis, Veroia and other Macedonian colonies in Thrace.
	Autumn	Athenian embassies visit cities of Eastern Thrace, Chios, Rhodes and Persia. Philip campaigns in Scythia Minor.
341/40	**Winter**	Demosthenes and Kallias in Peloponnese and Western Greece working for the formation of an anti-Macedonian coalition.

340		Philip's alliance with Ataias, king of the Scythians.
	Spring	Philip in Eastern Thrace. Siege of Perinthos.
	Summer	Siege of Selymbria.
	Autumn	Philip attacks Byzantion; captures the Athenian corn fleet.
		Athens declares war on Philip.
		Alexander defeats the Maidoi; founding of Alexandropolis.
339	**Winter**	*The Amphictyonic League declares Sacred War on Amphissa.*
		Philip abandons the siege of Byzantion.
	Summer	Campaign against the Scythians.
		Thebes seizes Nikaia.
		Philip returns to Macedonia.
	Autumn	The Amphictyonic League appoints Philip *hegemon* for the war against Amphissa.
		Philip occupies Elateia.
		Athenian-Theban alliance.
338	**Spring**	Parmenion advances on Central and Western Greece.
	Aug. 22	Battle of Chaironeia.
		Philip signs peace with Athens and Thebes.
		Isokrates' third *Epistle* to Philip.
	Autumn	Philip enters Peloponnese.
337		*Common Peace* established at Corinth. Declaration of panhellenic campaign against Persia.
		Philip appointed *strategos autokrator* of the Hellenes.
	Summer	Philip returns to Macedonia; marries Kleopatra.
336	**Spring**	Philip campaigns in Illyria against Pleurias(?). Advance force under Parmenion crosses to Asia Minor.
		Marriage of Alexandros, king of the Molossians, to Philip's daughter Kleopatra at Aigai.
		Assassination of Philip.

BIBLIOGRAPHY

Abel	Abel, O., *Makedonien vor König Philipp*, Leipzig, 1847.
Andronicos, *Vergina*	Ἀνδρόνικος, Μ., Βεργίνα, v. I. *Τό νεκροταφεῖο τῶν τύμβων*, Athens, 1969.
Beloch	Beloch, K.J., *Griechische Geschichte*², v. III Berlin and Leipzig, 1922-23.
Bengtson	Bengtson, H., *Griechische Geschichte*², Munich, 1960.
Berve	Berve, H., *Das Alexanderreich auf prosopographischer Grundlage*, vols. I-II. Munich, 1926.
CAH VI	*Cambridge Ancient History*, vol. VI, Cambridge, 1927.
Cawkwell	Cawkwell, G., *Philip of Macedon*, London, 1978.
Cloché	Cloché, P., *Un Fondateur d'empire: Philippe II roi de Macédoine*, Saint-Etienne, 1956.
Ellis, *Philip II*	Ellis, J.R., *Philip II and Macedonian Imperialism*, London, 1976.
Gaebler	Gaebler, H., *Die antiken Münzen Nord-Griechenlands 3, Makedonia und Paionia 2*. Berlin, 1935.
Geyer	Geyer, F., *Makedonien bis zur Thronbesteigung Philipps II*, Munich and Berlin, 1930.
Glotz-Cohen	Glotz, G. and Cohen, R., *Histoire grecque*, vol. III, Paris, 1936.
Griffith, *Mercenaries*	Griffith, G.T., *The Mercenaries of the Hellenistic World*, Cambridge, 1935.
Hammond, *Epirus*	Hammond, N.G.L., *Epirus*, Oxford, 1976.
Hammond, *Macedonia I*	Hammond, N.G.L., *A History of Macedonia*, vol. I, Oxford 1972.
Hammond-Griffith, *Macedonia II*	Hammond, N.G.L., and Griffith, G.T., *A History of Macedonia*, vol. II, Oxford, 1978.
Hampl	Hampl, F., *Der König der Makedonen*, Weida, Leipzig, 1934.
Hoffmann	Hoffmann, O., *Die Makedonen, ihre Sprache und Volkstum*, Göttingen, 1906.
Jacoby, *Fragmente*	Jacoby, F., *Die Fragmente der griechischen Historiker*, Berlin, 1923-30, Leiden, 1940-58.
Kalléris	Kalléris, J.N., *Les Anciens Macédoniens*, vol. I-II, Athens 1954 and 1976.
Momigliano	Momigliano, A., *Filippo il Macedone*, Florence, 1934.
Sylloge³	Dittenberger, W., *Sylloge Inscriptionum Graecarum*³, Leipzig, 1915.
Tarn	Tarn, W.W., *Alexander the Great*, v. I-II, Cambridge, 1948.
Tod	Tod, M.N., *Greek Historical Inscriptions*, vol.I-II Oxford 1946-48.
West	West, A.B., *The History of the Chalcidic League*, Madison, Wisconsin, 1918.
Westlake	Westlake, H.O., *Thessaly in the Fourth Century B.C.* London, 1935.
Wüst	Wüst, F.R., *Philipp II von Makedonien und Griechenland 346-338*, Munich, 1938.

SELECT BIBLIOGRAPHY AND NOTES

EARLY MACEDONIA

Bibliography

Edson (1947) = Edson, C., Notes on the Thracian Phoros, *Classical Philology* 42 (1947), 85-105.

Edson (1951) = Edson, C., The Location of Celiae and the Route of the Via Egnatia in Western Macedonia, *Classical Philology* 46 (1951), 1-16.

Edson (1955) = Edson, C., Strepsa (Thucydides **1**.61.4), *Classical Philology* 50 (1955), 169-190.

Kahrstedt = Kahrstedt, U., Städte in Makedonien, *Hermes* 81 (1953), 85-111.

Kanatsoulis (1953) = Κανατσούλης, Δ., Ποῦ ἔκειτο ἡ ἀρχαία πόλις Ἐλίμεια, *Μακεδονικά* 2 (1953), 179-192.

Kanatsoulis (1956) = Κανατσούλης, Δ., Τό κοινόν τῶν Μακεδόνων, *Μακεδονικά* 3 (1956), 27-102.

Kanatsoulis (1958) = Κανατσούλης, Δ., Ἡ δυτική Μακεδονία κατά τούς ἀρχαίους χρόνους, Thessalonike 1958.

Kanatsoulis (1960) = Κανατσούλης, Δ., Ἡ μακεδονική πόλις, *Μακεδονικά* 4 (1960), 232-314.

Kanatsoulis (1976) = Κανατσούλης, Δ., Ἡ Μακεδονία ἀπό ἀρχαιοτάτων χρόνων μέχρι τῆς ἀνόδου τοῦ Φιλίππου Β´, v. II Ἐσωτερική Ἱστορία, Thessalonike, 1976.

Merker = Merker, I.L., The Ancient Kingdom of Paionia, *Balkan Studies* 6 (1956), 35-54.

Notes

This essay is a concise revision of a lecture delivered at the international symposium on pre-Byzantine Macedonia held at Thessalonike in August 1968 under the auspices of the Society for Macedonian Studies and the Institute for Balkan Studies. It was published in the volume Ἀρχαία Μακεδονία (Ancient Macedonia), Thessalonike 1970, 17-44. For full documentation reference is made to that publication.

1. Herodotus **1**.56.3 and in particular **8**.48: Δωρικόν τε καί Μακεδνόν ἔθνος.
2. Proclus in his Chrestomathia [Allen] 109, lines 8-16, states that the cyclic poet Eugammon in his "Telegonia" made Odysseus come to the aid of the queen of the Thesprotoi in her war against the Thracian Brygoi. The Greek chronographical tradition (Diodorus **7**.15 and Syncellus [Dindorf], I, 373 and 498-99) has Karanos the first Macedonian King come to the aid of the Orestai in their war with the Eordoi. These two passages surely reflect the movement of peoples from southwest to northeast across the crest of the Pindos.
3. The "Epirotic" tribes along the western slopes of the Pindos gave their own names to the territories they inhabited: Aithikes - Aithikia, Athamanes - Athama̅nia, Atintanes - Atintania, Chaones - Chaonia, Kassopes - Kassopeia, Molossoi-Molossis, Thesprotoi-Thesprotia. But the "Macedonian" tribes along the eastern slopes of the Pindos took their names from landscapes or physical features: Elimeia-hence Elimiotai, Lynkos-hence Lynkestai (the stem Lynko-plus the suffix-estes), *oros* ("mountain") hence Orestai (the stem ore/o plus - estes), Parauaioi - those "beside" the Auos (Aoös) river, mount Tymphe - hence Tymphaioi. The Pelagones in Pelagonia, the northern portion of the central basin of the Erigon river seem to be an exception, but they in fact take their name from *pelagos* one of whose meanings is "flooded-plain" (LSJ s.v. 3) a term accurately descriptive of the upper basin of the Erigon.
   In Stephanus Byzantius the Parauaioi are called "a thesprotian *ethnos*" and Mount Tymbe appears as "a Thesprotian mountain". Hecataeus of Miletus (**Jacoby, Fragmente** no. 1, F107) calls the Orestai a "Molossian ethnos".
4. Appian, *Syriake* 63.
5. Hesiod [West-Merkelbach] F. 3, the earliest source to mention the Macedonians, associates them with Pieria. Thucydides (**2**.99.3) asserts that Pieria was the first conquest of the Argeadai.
6. Cf. **Edson, (1947)** 91.
7. There exists as yet no adequate study of the institution of Kingship in Macedonia. F. Hampl's Leipzig dissertation, *Der König der Makedonen* (Weida, 1934) has not illuminated the subject. Note, however, A. Aymard, Βασιλεύς Μακεδόνων (Mélanges de Visscher), *Revue Internationale des droits de l'antiquité*, 4 (1950) 61-97.
8. F. Granier, Die Makedonische Heersversammlung *Münchener Beiträge*, 13 (Münich, 1931); A. Aymard, "Sur l'assemblée macédonienne", *Revue des Etudes Anciennes* 52 (1950) 115-35.
9. M.P. Nilson, *Homer and Mycenae*, London, 1933, Ch. VI, 212-47.
10. Athenaeus, 13. 572d. Compare Herakles Κυναγίδας. This patronymic epithet is sufficiently attested in Macedonian inscriptions.
11. Curtius **6**.11.20.Cf. Diodorus **19**.51.1 and 5.
12. *Politica* 1324b.
13. Curtius **8**.4.27. See M. Renard and J. Servais, A Propos du mariage d'Alexandre et Roxane, *L'Antiquite Classique*, 24 (1955) 29-50.
14. **Kalleris,** I, 237-38 with references there cited.
15. Ch. Edson, Oxford Classical Dictionary, 526.
16. Herodotus **6**.45. The ancient chronographical tradition as preserved in Syncellus, op. cit. (above n. 2), I, 469, remembered that Alexandros I "gave earth and water to the Persians".
17. Herodotus, **7**.185.2.
18. Demosthenes, **23**.200 (whence **13**.24). The

phrase employed, τέλειον ἀτύχημα, is very strong indeed. The orator wrongly attributes this achievement to Perdikkas (II), but this is a mere lapse.

19. Thucydides, **2**.99.4: Strabo **7**. Frs. 10 and 20. I follow Thucydides· listing of the Argead conquests which he largely arranges in chronological order.

20. From Thucydides (**2**.99.5) it appears that at sometime before thè outbreak of the Peloponnesian War the Argeadai had decimated the Eordoi and expelled the survivors from "what is now called Eordoia". But Herodotus (**7**.185.2) specifically lists the Eordoi among the peoples who followed Xerxes to Greece. It follows that the Argead subjugation of Eordaia must be placed between Xerxes' invasion and the Peloponnesian War. Alexandros I is the obvious candidate. I have associated the conquest of Almopia with that of Eordaia because Thucydides (**2**.99.5) does so, and it is my belief, which must be justified at greater length elsewhere, that the historian lists the Argead conquests in approximately the correct chronological sequence. For the location of Eordaia see **Edson (1951),** 8 with nn. 55 and 56.

21. Thucydides **2**.99.2. The treaty between Athens and Perdikkas II (Inscriptiones Graecae I² 71; Supplementum Epigraphicum Graecum X, 86) calls these rulers "the kings with (μετά) Perdikkas". The phrase clearly implies that there were other kings who were not "with" Perdikkas, and those kings can only be the rulers of the Makedian tribes on the western slopes of the Pindos.

22. Because according to Herodotus **8**.116 the king of the Bisaltai also ruled over the Crestonians. Crestonia's location is given with the utmost clarity by Herodotus, **7**.124.

23. Thucydides **2**.99.6. For Anthemous see **Edson (1955)**, 171-72.

24. Herodotus, who completed his history not long after the beginning of the Peloponnesian War is the first author to use the term "Macedonia".

25. D. Raymond, *Macedonia Royal Coinage to 413 B.C.*, Numismatic Notes and Monographs, No. 126 (New York, 1953).

26. Thucydides **2**.96-97.

27. See **Merker** 35-54.

28. Arrian, *Anabasis* **1**.5.7.

29. Jacoby, *Fragmente* no. 72, F4.

30. Curtius **6**.8.25.

31. Note Thucydides' remarks (**4**.108.1) on the importance of Amphipolis to Athens.

32. Schol. Aeschines **2**.31.

33. Herodotus **9**.75; Thucydides **1**.100.3, **4**.102.3.

34. Plutarch, *Cimon* 14.3.

35. Plutarch, *Pericles* 11.5.

36. **Edson (1947)** 91.

37. **Edson (1955)** 169-90.

38. E.g. Thucydides **5**.83.4.

39. Thucydides **1**.57.3.

40. B.D. Meritt, H.T. Wade-Gery and M.F. McGregor, *The Athenian Tribute Lists* (Harvard, 1939-1953), v. III, 313, n. 61.

41. Thucydides **1**.57.3.

42. Thucydides **2**.95.3.

43. Thucydides **2**.100.3-5.

44. Supplementum Epigraphicum Graecum X, 88.

45. Thucydides **4**.125.1.

46. Curtius **6**.11.26 Cf. Ch. Edson review of D. Raymond (op. cit. above n. 25) *Classical Philology* 52 (1957) 280, n. 6.

47. D. Raymond op. cit., above n. 25.

48. Thucydides **1**.57.2.

49. According to Pydna is unknown. According to Plutarch (*Moralia* 293 A-B) Methone was an Eretrian colony. I am quite unable to accept **Kahrstedt's** suggestion that these two cities were not really southern Greek colonies at all but communities of his supposed "Greek" element in the Macedonian area.

50. Thucydides **6**.7.3.

51. For this route see **Edson (1955)**, 173-82.

52. Supplementum Epigraphicum Graecum X 86, line 23.

53. See the monograph by D. Kanatsoulis, Ὁ Ἀρχέλαος καί αἱ μεταρρυθμίσεις του ἐν Μακεδονίᾳ, (Thessalonike, 1948), for a collection and discussion of the evidence.

54. Andocides **2**.11.

55. Thucydides **2**.100.2.

56. See Kanatsoulis, op. cit. (above n. 53), 77-82.

57. **Edson (1955)**, 188, n. 5.

58. Aristotle, *Politica* 1311b.

59. Andocides (**2**.11) calls Archelaos his *xenos patrikos*. In 426/5 Andocides' father Leogoras appears as the leader of an Athenian embassy to Perdikkas II: op. cit. above n. 40, II, D. 4, line 50 (p. 49).

60. See **Hoffman** and **Kalleris** I. From Curtius (**6**.11.4) it appears that some ordinary Macedonians did not understand (Attic?) Greek but needed interpreters. But this need mean no more than that Macedonian was a highly dialectical form of Greek. Note also Curtius **6**.10.23 (from the speech of Philotas): "iam pridem nativus ille sermo commercio aliarum gentium exolevit."

61. Note that the area to which the Koiné was extended coincides almost precisely with the area of Alexander's conquests. See **Beloch** IV, 2, the last map at the end of the volume entitled "Das griechische Sprachgebiet um 220 v. Chr.". Regions immediately contiguous to Attica such as

Boiotia and Megara maintained their local dialects throughout the Hellenistic period, admittedly with increasing evidence of Koiné influence.

62. Herodotus **5**.22.

63. **Edson (1947)**, 97.

64. Note the Argead royal cult of Herakles *Propator:* Arrian, *Anabasis* **6**.3.2.

65. See above, note 5.

66. If we are to take Speusippus' citation of Damastes of Sigeum (**Jacoby,** *Fragmente* no. 5, F 4) at its face value, Herakleion was already in existence as early as 480 B.C.

67. Pausanias **7**.25.6.

68. **Jacoby,** *Fragmente*, no. 115, F.387 (Theopompus). See L. Robert, *Etudes de numismatique grècque* (Paris, 1951), 179-216.

69. Thucydides **4**.124.1.

70. Pindar, Frs. 120, 121 [Snell].

71. Bacchylides, F 20 B [Snell].

72. D. Raymond op. cit. (above n. 25), 164; **Gaebler** II, 155, no. 12.

73. **Gaebler** II, 156 nos. 8-10.

74. The Suda (s. nomm) states that Hippocrates the physician and the dithyrambic poet Melanippides were at Perdikkas' court. Plutach (Moralia 1095 D) seems to associate Melanippides with Archelaos.

75. Dio Chrysostomus 13.30: - πολλὰ εἰδώς καί πολλοῖς συγγεγονώς τῶν σοφῶν...

76. Aelian, *Varia Historia* 14.17.

77. Athenaeus **8**.345d.

78. Plutarch, *Moralia* 117 B F 24 [Page].

79. Aelian, *Varia Historia* 2.21; 13.4.

80. Seneca, *De beneficiis* **5**.6.6.: Diogenes Laertius 2.95; Dio Chrysostomus 13.30.

81. W. Baege, *De Macedonum sacris*, (Halle, 1913), 10-12.

82. The Macedonian poet Adaeus in his epitaph on Euripides (Anthologia Palatina 7.51, line 4) speaks of the poet as "honored by the companionship" - ἑταιρείη - "of Archelaos". Note also Aelian, *Varia Historia* 13.4.

83. The plot of the play is preserved in Hyginus, *Fabulae*, CCXIX [Rose] 143-44. Cf. Dio Chrysostomus **4**.70-72. Note the new fragment of the prologue published by E. Siegmann in B. Snell *Griechische Papyri der Hamburger Staats und Universitäts Bibliothek* (Hamburg, 1954), 1-14.

84. Frs. [Nauck] 232, 233, 236, 237, 238, 239, 240, 242, 243, 244 and 246.

85. Itinerarium Burdigalense 604. 6-7 [Cuntz]; Ammianus Marcellinus **27**.4.8.

86. Gellius, *Noctes Atticae* 15.20.9.

87. [Aristotle], *Problemata* 954b.

88. Aristotle, *Politica* 1311b.

89. The evidence for this period is conveniently assembled by Geyer, ch. 5, 105-39.

90. Arrian, *Anabasis* **5**.26.6 and **7**.9.2.

91. See **Merker.**

THE UNIFICATION OF MACEDONIA

Bibliography and Notes

1. Thucydides **2**.99.2.
2. **Hammond**, *Macedonia I*, 156ff.
3. **Abel** 153ff, **Geyer** 45f.
4. Schol. Thuc. **1**.57.3.
5. Athenaeus **13**.557.
6. Thucydides **1**.57.3 and **1**.59.
7. Athenaeus **13**.557, **10**.436c.
8. Strabo **7**.326.
9. Inscriptiones Graecae 11² 71.75ff.
10. Aristotle, *Politica* 5.1311b; cf. Thucydides **4**.79, 83f. and 124ff.
11. Inscriptiones Graecae 11² no. 110 (= **Tod** II no. 143 Sylloge I no 188 (=**Tod** II no 148), Demosthenes **4**.27.
12. Strabo **7**.326, Plutarch, *Moralia* 14, Suda s.v. *'Karanos'*, Libanius, *Vita Demosthenes*, 296 [Westermann].
13. J.R. Ellis, Population Transplants under Philip II, Μακεδονικὰ 9 (1969) 1ff. with references.
14. **Ellis**, *Philip II*, 47f.
15. Diodorus **16**.2.5ff.
16. Athenaeus **13**.557 and 560a.
17. Isocrates **5**.46: H.J. Dell, The Western Frontier of the Macedonian Monarchy, Ἀρχαία Μακεδονία I (Thessalonike 1970), 115ff.
18. Diodorus **16**.3. and 4.1.
19. Diodorus **16**.3.1f.
20. Diodorus **16**.4.
21. Diodorus **16**.4.3.
22. Diodorus **16**.35.4f.
23. Diodorus **16**.74.5.
24. Diodorus **16**.85.5.
25. Diodorus **17**.17.
26. On the military reforms in general see the chapter "Philip as a general" of this volume; also, principally, U. Wilcken, *Alexander the Great* (Engl. trans.), chapter 2, **Tarn** II, 138ff., **Ellis**, *Philip II*, 52ff, **Cawkwell**, 30ff.
27. A.B. Bosworth, Ἀσθέταιροι, *Classical Quarterly* 23 (1973) 245-252.
28. Arrian 6.9.3 and 7.23.3 with Inscriptiones Graecae II² no. 239 (= **Tod** II, 184), on which see **Berve** I 193ff, **Griffith**, *Mercenaries* 299 n.1.
29. Theopompus F224 (**Jacoby**, *Fragmente* no. 115).
30. Ibid.
31. Diodorus **16**.34.5, G.T. Griffith, The Macedonian Background, *Greece and Rome* 12 (1965) 136f.
32. Athenaeus **13**.557.
33. On the transplanting of population-groups see J.R. Ellis (op. cit. above n. 13) 9ff.
34. Polyaenus **4**.2.12.
35. Justin **8**.5.7ff.
36. Arrian **7**.9.
37. Strabo **7**.320 (with Demosthenes **8**.44, Ptolemaeus, *Geographia* 3.11), Theopompus F110, Pliny, *Naturalis Historia* 4.18, Stephanus Byzantius s. *'Philippou polis'*, Frontinus, *Strategemata* 1.3.13.
38. B. Helly, *Gonnoi I*, Amsterdam, 1973, 81ff.
39. Plutarch, *Alexander* 9.1.
40. Perhaps Thessalian Gomphoi, for example: Stephanus Byzantius s. *'Philippoi'*, **Westlake** 178 n. 5, M. Sordi, *La lega tessala fino ad Alessandro Magno*. Rome, 1958, 258.
41. N. Machiavelli, **Discourses** 1.26.
42. Arrian 2.9.3, **1**.2.5 with **3**.11.8.
43. Plutarch, *Pelopidas* 26f.
44. Arrian, *Anabasis* **4**.13.1; see also Aelian, *Varia Historia* **14**.48, Curtius **8**.6.2ff.
45. Plutarch, *Alexander* 10, Arrian, *Anabasis* **3**.6.6.
46. Curtius **8**.6.6. and **5**.1.42.
47. For references and discussion see W. S. Tarn, *Antigonus Gonatas*, 185, F.W. Walbank, *Philip V of Macedon*, 163, 183 and **Hammond**, *Epirus* 620.
48. Plutarch, *Moralia* 327C. J.R. Ellis, The Security of the Macedonian throne under Philip II, Ἀρχαία Μακεδονία I (Thessalonike 1970), 68ff, and Amyntas Perdikka, Philip II and Alexander the Great, *Journal of Hellenic Studies* 91 (1971), 15ff.

THE COINAGE OF PHILIP AND THE PANGAION MINES

Bibliography

Casson = Casson, S., *Macedonia, Thrace and Illyria,* Oxford, 1926.
Collart, *Philippes* = Collart, P., *Philippes, ville de Macédoine*, Paris, 1937.
Le Rider (1975) = Le Rider, G., Contremarques et surfrappés dans l'antiquité grecque. "Numismatique Antique. Problèmes et Méthodes", *Annales de l'Est* (1975), 46-56.
Le Rider, *Philip II* = Le Rider. G., *Le monnayage d'argent et d'or de Philippe II frappé en Macédoine de 359 à 294*, Paris, 1977.
Newell = Newell, E.T., *Alexander Hoards*, Demanhur 1905. Numismatic Notes and Monographs 19 (1923) 69-70.

Seltman = Seltman, C.T., *Greek Coins*, London, 1955.

Notes

1. Perdiccas III, killed in a battle against the Illyrians (Diodorus **16**. 2. 4.) or murdered by his mother, Eurydike (Justin **6**. 5. 6-8), left behind a young son, Amyntas, still only a child. It has often been thought that Amyntas was proclaimed king in 359, and that Philip II remained for a time his guardian, his *epitropos*. In fact it seems likely that Philip II took the title of king at the time of his brother's death, or at least in the weeks following this event. I have set out the circumstances of the matter in *Le monnayage d'argent et d'or de Philippe II frappé en Macédoine de 359 à 294*, Paris 1977, 386-7.
2. Philip II in 359 wished to avoid any trouble with Athens and so to remain free to eliminate his rivals and avert the Illyrian danger.
3. A table of the natural resources of gold and silver in Macedonia is given by **Casson**, 59-63. The Mount Bermion and Dysoron regions, which belonged to Philip II, contained deposits of precious metal, but it is not known whether they were exploited at this period. The waters of the river Echeidorus (which also runs into the Thermaic Gulf) were reputed to be rich in gold dust.
4. See the judicious comments of Henri Seyring, Revue Numismatique (1963), 28

and n. 3, who refers to the questions raised by Edward Will, notably in his article *"Limites, possibilités et tâches de l'histoire économique et sociale du monde grec antique"*, Etudes Archéologiques. *École Pratique des Hautes Etudes-VI, Section Centre de Recherches Historiques, Archéologie et Civilisation I*, (Paris 1963), 154, n. 1.

5. Cf. **Le Rider**, (1975), 46-56.
6. **Le Rider**, *Philippe II*, 387. The silver currency of Philip II consisted above all of tetradrachms; some didrachms, drachms and hemidrachms are also known; of ibid., pl. l.ff; the standard chosen by Philip II is the Thraco-Macedonian standard; cf. ibid., 354-6.
7. I am only dealing with silver and gold coins in this paper. It can be taken as certain that Philip II also struck bronze coins from the time of his accession, but that does not interest us here.
8. **Collart**, *Philippes*, 47-55. For the mines, see also **Casson**, 63-66. Collart and Casson are not in complete agreement over the exact locality of the mines. Casson, further, indicates that gold should equally be found in the torrents and streams that have their sources in the mountain.

9. **Collart**, *Philippes*, 49; see the general references given ibid, 58, n. 3.
10. Diodorus **16**. 8. 5-6.
11. **Le Rider**, *Philippe II*, 428.
12. Ibid., 432-3.
13. Ibid., 435-6.
14. Ibid., 339 and 438-9, cf. pl. 93, 1-2.
15. This is Seltman's point of view; he supposes that during those years Philip II would only have struck gold coins of small size; cf. **Le Rider**, *Philippe II*, 428.
16. Cf. **Le Rider** *Philippe II*, 438-9.
17. Ibid., 339.
18. Demosthenes 19.139: "Philip... kept offering them presents beginning with captives and the like and ending with gold and silver goblets". In this oration, given in 343, Demosthenes continually speaks of gifts being offered by Philip to Aeschines and various politicians: δῶρα, χρήματα. Among these δῶρα figured not only slaves and precious objects, but also, probably, metal ingots.
19. Cf. **Le Rider**, *Philippe II*, 325-339.
20. Ibid., 339-349; on the measures taken by

Philip in regard to Amphipolis and on the statute granted to the city cf. ibid., 338.
21. **Le Rider**, *Philippe II* 390, 393, 400.
22. Ibid., 400.
23. Ibid., 385.
24. Ibid., 428-433.
25. Ibid., 435.
26. Ibid., 439-441.
27. See above note.
28. In *Philippe II*, 435, I also show that this decision could have been influenced by an ambition to create a coin that would rival the daric of the Great King.
29. If it is accepted that the first staters were struck in 342-340, then only 29 obverse dies out of 376 were engraved during the king's lifetime; see **Le Rider**, *Philippe II*, 435-6.
30. According to the same chronology, out of 29 stater obverse dies, 28 were used at Pella, only one at Amphipolis.
31. Cf. **Le Rider**, *Philippe II*, 433-4.
32. Ibid., 442.
33. Amphipolis became the foremost mint for striking coins in the empire; see **Newell**, 69-70.

PHILIP AS A GENERAL AND THE MACEDONIAN ARMY

Bibliography

Anderson = Anderson J.K., *Military Theory and Practice in the age of Xenophon*, Berkeley and Los Angeles, 1970.
Andronicos, *Sarissa* = Andronicos, M. Sarissa, *Bulletin de Correspondence Hellénique* 94 (1970), 91ff.
Best = Best, J.G.P., *Thracian Peltasts and their Influence on Greek Warfare*, (Groningen, 1969).
Bosworth = Bosworth, A.B., 'Ασθέταιροι, *Classical Quarterly* 23 (1973), 245ff.
Brunt = Brunt, P.A., *Arrian, History of Alexander and Indica*, I Introduction, lxix ff., in Loeb Classical Library (1976).
Lammert = Lammert, F., Sarisse, in Pauly-Wissowa-Kroll, Realenzyklopädie der Artertumswissenschaft 2.1A (1920), 215ff.
Markle (1977) = Markle, Minor, M, The Macedonian Sarissa, Spear, and related Armor, *American Journal of Archaeology*, 81 (1977), 323-39.
Markle (1978) = Markle, Minor, M., Use of the Sarissa by Philip and Alexander of Macedon, *American Journal of Archaeology* 82 (1978), 483-97.
Marsden = Marsden, E.W., Macedonian Military Machinery and its Designers under Philip and Alexander, 'Αρχαία Μακεδονία II (Thessalonike, 1977), 211-23.
Milns = Milns, R.D, 'The army of Alexander the Great' Entretiens Fondation Hardt, 22, Geneva, 1976, 89ff.
Snodgrass = Snodgrass A.M., *Arms and Armour of the Greeks*. London, 1967, chap. 5.
Tarn = Tarn, W.W., *Alexander the Great, II. Sources and Studies*. Cambridge 1948, 135ff.

Notes

1. On "pezhetairoi" etc., especially **Jacoby**, *Fragmente* no. 115 (Theopompus), F 348; no. 72 (Anaximenes), F4, **Hammond-Griffith**, *Macedonia II* 426 ff., **Bosworth** 245 ff. and **Milns** 89ff.
2. Plutarch, *Pelopidas* 26.5-8; 27.3f., etc.; **Hammond-Griffith**, *Macedonia II*, 204ff.
3. Diodorus **16**.3.1f.; **16**.4.3-7.
4. Diodorus **16**.4.3; **17**.17.3ff.; also **Brunt** lxix ff.
5. **Andronikos**, *Sarissa* 96-107; **Lammert** 2515 ff.
6. **Markle** (1977) and (1978), especially (1978), 492f.
7. Polyaenus **4**.2.1; **4**.2.3; **4**.2.10; Frontinus **4**.1.6.
8. Polyaenus **4**.2.2; **4**.2.7; (and see Arrian, *Anabasis* **1**.6.2f.).
9. **Bosworth** 245ff.; Robin Lane Fox, *Alexander the Great*, London 1973, 512; **Hammond-Griffith**, *Macedonia II* 426 ff., 709ff.; **Milns** 89ff.
10. Diodorus **16**.35.5.
11. Demosthenes **18**.235; and **9**.49f. for their variety.
12. Athenaeus Mechanicus [Wescher] **10**.5ff.;

Vitruvius **10**.13.3; **7** praef. 14; see **Marsden** especially 213 ff.

13. See now the interesting and valuable discussions of **Markle (1977)** and **(1978).**
14. Asklepiodotus Taktikus **7**.3; Aelian, *Taktika* **18**.4.
15. Diodorus **16**.4.4-7; **16**.35.4-6.
16. Diodorus **16**.4.5-6.
17. Xenophon, *Hellenica* **7**.5.23f.; **6**.4.10ff.; **Cawkwell** 159.
18. Diodorus **16**.35.5.
19. Polyaenus 4.2.2; **Hammond-Griffith,** *Macedonia II* 596 ff.
20. Polyaenus **2**.38.2.
21. Diodorus **16**.35.2.
22. Diodorus **16**.35.4-6; Justin **8**.3.2
23. See too Diodorus **16**.3.1 and 3.
24. Polyaenus **4**.2.6.

25. **Jacoby**, *Fragmente* no. 115, F 224.
26. Curtius Rufus **8**.1.24.
27. Demosthenes **18**.67; Didymus, *In Dem.* **12**.63-65; **13**.1-7.
28. Demosthenes **1**.4... καί πανταχοῦ αὐτόν παρεῖναι τῷ στρατεύματι...
29. Plutarch, *Moralia* 177C.2.
30. Demosthenes **1**.4; **18**.235.
31. Diodorus **16**.95.2-4.
32. Diodorus **16**.8.7; Demosthenes **19**.259ff. and 265ff.; **18**.295; Cicero, *ad Atticum* **1**.16.12 etc.
33. Diodorus **16**.3.3; Polyaenus **4**.2.17.
34. Diodorus **16**.8.3-6.
35. See **Hammond-Griffith**, *Macedonia II* 324ff. and 375ff. for some discussion, in relation to Chalkidike especially.
36. For Lyppeios (Lykkeios), see **Hammond-**

Griffith, *Macedonia II* 666 and 669.
37. Ibid. 218ff., 267ff.
38. Ibid. 278ff.
39. Diodorus **16**.38.1-2.
40. Demosthenes **23**.107-9; **4**.17.; **Hammond-Griffith**, *Macedonia II* 296ff.
41. See **Hammond-Griffith**, *Macedonia II* 315ff.
42. Diodorus **16**.77.3.
43. Demosthenes **2**.18.
44. See **Hammond-Griffith**, *Macedonia II* 589ff. (Elateia): 603ff. (after Chaironeia): 616ff. (Sparta).
45. Aeschines **2**.12ff.
46. Isocrates **5**.86ff.
47. See **Hammond-Griffith**, *Macedonia II* 609-9.
48. Ibid 310ff.; 567ff.; 580.

PHILIP AND THE AMPHICTYONIC LEAGUE

Notes

1. [Herodes] Peri Politeias **6** and **33**, Diodorus **14**.92.3, Isocrates **5**.20
2. Justin **7**.5.1f.
3. Diodorus **16**.4.1-2, Justin **7**.6.7f., **Jacoby**, *Fragmente* no. 115 (Theopompus) F35.
4. Isocrates **15**.155 (Cf. Isocrates **8**.117f.).
5. Xenophon, *Hellenica* **6**.1.8. and Isocrates **8**.118.
6. Xenophon, *Hellenica* **5**.4.56 and **6**.1.11, Plutarch, *Moralia* 193E.
7. Xenophon, *Hellenica* **6**.1.5ff. and **19**, Diodorus **15**.57.2 and 60.2, Isocrates **5**.119.
8. Xenophon, *Hellenica* **6**.4.35f., **Tod**, no. 147 and schol. Aristides, *Panathen.* 179.6.
9. Diodorus **16**.35.1f. and Polybius **2**.38.2.
10. Justin **8**.2.1f., Demosthenes **1**.22, Diodorus **16**.35.4f., 37.3 and **38**.1, Strabo 433C.
11. Demosthenes **6**.22, **8**.62, **9**.26 Cf. Harpokra-

tion s.v.v. *dekadarchia, tetrarchia* and **Jacoby**, *Fragmente* no. 115 (Theopompus) F208.
12. Justin **8**.2.3.
13. Diodorus **16**.23, Justin **8**.15; Schol. Demosth. **19**.20.
14. Diodorus **16**.24.3, 25.1 and 25.3. (= 28.4).
15. Diodorus **16**.30.4.
16. Diodorus **16**.36. 1 and 37.2ff. Justin **8**.2.8-12, Diodorus **16**.38.2, Demosthenes **19**.84 and 319, **4**.17 and **18**.32.
17. Demosthenes **18**.19.
18. Diodorus **16**.56ff., Aeschines **2**.131.
19. Aeschines **2**.132ff., Diodorus **16**.59.1f., cf. Demosthenes **19**.154f.
20. Justin **8**.4 and Aeschines **2**.112 and 104; Demosthenes **19**.139ff., **9**.11 etc.
21. Justin **8**.4.4f. Demosthenes **19**.140f; Aeschines **2**.108-17 and 135; Demosthenes **9**.11.
22. Demosthenes **19**.158 and 163.

23. Demosthenes **19**.58.17f., Aeschines **3**.85, Demosthenes **8**.74 and 75.
24. Diodorus **16**.59.3.
25. Aeschines **2**.142. Cf. Diodorus **16**.61-64, Diodorus **16**.57 and 61 etc.; Justin **8**.2.5f., Pausanias **10**.2-6ff.
26. Diodorus **16**.59.4.
27. Demosthenes **19**.64f. and 81; Diodorus **16**.60; Justin **8**.5; Aeschines **2**.142ff. (Cf. Pausanias **10**.2 and 4) Demosthenes **5**.22; Demosthenes **19**.60 and 127.6-7.
28. Pausanias **10**.8.2 and **Sylloge³** no. 241B l. 76f., cf. l. 117 and C, l. 143; Demosthenes **19**.111 and **5**.22 and 24.
29. Diodorus **16**.60.4f.
30. Philochorus (**Jacoby**, *Fragmente* no. 328) F56b.
31. Demosthenes **18**.143ff.; Aeschines **3**.128ff.
32. Demosthenes **6**.14 and **19**.81, **Sylloge³** nos. 230 and 232.

PHILIP AND MACEDONIA'S NORTHERN NEIGHBORS

Bibliographical Note

There is no single work on Philip and his neighbors or on the frontier as a whole. It must be pieced together from the chance interest of the biographer or the specialized article of the scholar. Of particular interest is the fine biography of Philip: J. R. Ellis, *Philip II and Macedonian Imperialism*, and the masterful N.G.L. Hammond, *A History of* *Macedonia*, I, and volume II in collaboration with G. T. Griffith.

Other sources of information by area are the following:

For Illyria and Western Macedonia:

Dell, H. J., The Western Frontier of the Macedonian Monarchy. Ἀρχαία Μακεδονία I, Thessalonike 1970, 115-126.

Ellis, J.R., Population-transplants under Philip II, Μακεδονικά 9 (1969), 9-16.

Hammond, N.G.L., Alexander's Campaign in Illyria, *Journal of Hellenic Studies* 94 (1974), 66-87.

Hammond, N.G.L., The Campaign of Alexander against Cleitus and Glaucias, Ἀρχαία Μακεδονία II, Thessalonike 1977, 503-509.

Hammond N.G.L., Epirus, Oxford, 1967.

Hammond, N.G.L., The Kingdoms in Illyria, ca. 400-167 B.C., *Annual of the British School of Archaeology at Athens* 61 (1966), 239- 253.

Hammond, N.G.L., The Western Frontier of Macedonia in the Reign of Philip II (forthcoming). *Institute for Balkan Studies,* Thessalonike.

My own description of the frontiers established by Philip and of his policy owes much to the above article.

For Paionia and Axios:

Merker, I.L, The Ancient Kingdom of Paionia, *Balkan Studies* 6 (1965), 35-54.

Vulič, N., La nationalité des Péoniens, *Musée Belge* 30 (1926), 107-117.

For Thrace and the Scythians:

Ellis, J.R., Philip's Thracian Campaign of 352/351, *Classical Philology* 72 (1977), 32-39.

Ellis, J.R., Population-transplants under Philip II, Μακεδονικά 9 (1969), 9-16.

Gerov, B., Probleme der historischen Geographie Nordostmakedoniens, Ἀρχαία Μακεδονία II, Thessalonike, 1977, 45-52.

Mihailov, G., La Thrace aux IVe et IIIe siècles avant notre ère, *Athenaeum* 39 (1961), 33-44. .

Mihailov, G., La Thrace et la Macédoine jusqu'à l'invasion des Celtes, Ἀρχαία Μακεδονία I, Thessalonike, 1970, 76-85.

Pippidi, D.M., Les Macédoniens en Scythie Mineure de Philippe II à Lysimaque, Ἀρχαία Μακεδονία II, Thessalonike, 1977, 381- 396.

PHILIP AND ATHENS

Notes

1. Thucydides **4**.108.1 and Livy **45**.30.3.
2. Polybius **4**.2.17, Diodorus **16**.3.3 and 4.1; Demosthenes **23**.121 etc.
3. Diodorus **16**.34.3f., IG II² No. 1613, Demosthenes **23**.103 etc.
4. Demosthenes **6**.20, Diodorus **16**.8.3 (Cf. Demosthenes **2**.6 and 20) etc.; Demosthenes **9**.56 and **19**.265.
5. Demosthenes **23**.109, **3**.7 and **4**.43.
6. Demosthenes **9**.11.
7. Demosthenes **10**.37, Isocrates **8**.37 and Xenophon, *Poroi* 2.6.
8. Demosthenes **1**.19f, **3**.11f and 33, Aeschines **3**.25 etc.
9. Philochorus (**Jacoby**, *Fragmente* No. 328) F51, Suidas s.v. *Karanos*.
10. Demosthenes **21**.205-207, **19**.290 with schol.
11. Philochorus (**Jacoby**, *Fragmente* No. 328) F49-51, Diodorus **16**.52-53, Demosthenes **19**.192 etc.
12. Diodorus **16**.53.3 and 55, Aeschines **2**.156, Demosthenes **19**.193ff and 306; **9**.26.
13. Aeschines **2**.18 and 22.
14. Aeschines **3**.67, **2**.61, 65, 109ff. Demosthenes **18**.28 and **19**.144 etc.
15. Demosthenes **19**.158.
16. Demosthenes **19**.58.17ff. and 31 and **8**.74 and 75 etc.
17. Demosthenes **19**.19.51.
18. Hypothesis Demosthenes **6**; Demosthenes **18**.136, **7**.18ff, *Epistulae* 2.10.
19. Demosthenes **6**.34 and **7**.19ff.
20. Plutarch, *Demosthenes* 15.
21. Demosthenes **19**.260 and 294, **9**.27, **18**.295, **19**.87, 204, 295 etc.
22. Demosthenes **7**.32, 36f and **19**.204.
23. Demosthenes **23**.58.
24. Philochorus (**Jacoby**, *Fragmente* No. 328), F158; Aeschines **1**.63; Demosthenes **8**.6 and **9**.12.3.
25. Hypothesis Demosthenes **8**.
26. **Jacoby**, *Fragmente* 390 § 26ff. Demosthenes **18**.139, Diodorus **16**.74ff. and Plutarch, *Alexander* 70.5.
27. Demosthenes, *Epistulae* 53 and **18**.76.50.18ff Philochorus (see above) F54 and 162. Theopompus (see **Jacoby**, *Fragmente* Nr 115) F292, Arrian, *Anabasis* 2.14.4.
28. Demosthenes **2**.22, **4**.12, **8**.69. **11**. 15 ff. **18**.194 and 40, Polybius **18**.14.
29. Diodorus **16**.1.5 and Justin **9**.2, 1-3 and 3,3.
30. **Cawkwell** 133 ff.
31. Demosthenes **18**.169ff.
32. Diodorus **16**.85.5, Justin **9**.3.9.
33. Plutarch, *Alexander* 9.3.
34. Diodorus **16**.85.5 and 86.
35. Polyaenus 4.2-2.
36. Diodorus **16**.87.1-3, Pausanias **1**.25.3 and 34.1, Suidas s.v. *Demades, Demosthenes* **18**.285, Demades, *On the Twelve Years,* 9ff.,
37. Polybius **18**.14.

PHILIP AND THE SOUTHERN GREEKS

Notes

1. Xenophon, *Poroi,* Isocrates, **8**.
2. Demosthenes, **16**.
3. Demosthenes, **15**.
4. Demosthenes, **1**.7-9, 17, 23-25; **2**.2, 5f, 11-12; **3**.12, 35, 38f; **9**.16; **10**. 8-9.
5. Demosthenes, **1**.6, 9, 10, 14; **2**.4, 5, 11, 22-24, 27, 30-31; **3**.3, 4, 6-7, 14, 28, 33; **4**.2, 3, 6-7, 10, 11, 41, 43-44.
6. Demosthenes, **4**.35-36.
7. Demosthenes, **1**.19-20; **3**.10-12.

8. Demosthenes, **3**.29-31.
9. Demosthenes, **5**.5.
10. Demosthenes **19**. 10ff, 303ff.
11. Demosthenes **10**.37-38.
12. See above, p. 116.
13. Demosthenes **19**.84.
14. Demosthenes **4**.28.
15. See above, p. 40.
16. See above, pp. 40 and 58-77.

17. Demosthenes **2**.15; [Demosthenes]. 11.8.
18. Demosthenes, **2**.15; 9.52
19. Demosthenes **2**.17.
20. Demosthenes **4**.40, **9**.52.
21. Demosthenes **2**.16.17; **11**.9.
22. Demosthenes **2**.17.
23. Demosthenes **1**.22-23; **4**.8.
24. See below, p. 138.
25. Demosthenes **3**.22, Cf Isocrates **12**.12.

26. Demosthenes **2**.29-30.
28. See above p. 36 ff; See also, **Ellis,** *Philip II,*
    8 and **Cawkwell**, 23, 25-26.
29. See above, p. 74 ff.
30. Demosthenes **4**.47.
31. Demosthenes **2**.28.
32. Herodotus **5**.78.
33. Thucydides **1**.70.

PANHELLENISM: FROM CONCEPT TO POLICY

Notes

1. According to Diodoros **14**. 109, this happened in 388. Most scholars accept it. But G.B. Grote, *History of Greece,* 1888, v. iii, 72 n.2, v, ix, 31 n. 1, argues that this speech was delivered on the next occasion of the Games, i.e. 384. One, at least, of his arguments is telling: Lysias' phrase that a large area was in the possession of barbarians (see below, n. 2) is more easily understood with reference to the period after the King's Peace of 386 when the Persians re-gained possession of the Greek cities on the western shores of Asia Minor. Some scholars agree with Grote's opinion.
2. Lysias **23**, =Dionysius of Halicarnassus, *Lysias* 28-29.
3. Isocrates, **4**. 10, 15-17.
4. Cf. G. Mathieu and E. Brémond, in the edition of Isocrates in the series *Collections des Universités de France*, IV. 163ff.
5. Compare also the testimony of Speusippus, in his *Letter to Philip*, 13, R. Hercher, *Epistolographi Graeci*, Paris, 1873, 632 = E. Bickermann, J. Sykurtis, "Speusipps Brief an König Philip", Berichte über die Verhandlung der Sächsischen Academie der Wissenschaften, Philologisch-Historische Klasse, 80 Band, 3 Heft, Leipzig, 1928, II.
6. Isocrates, **4**. 131, 133, 136, 166, 167, 172, 173, 174, 184, 187; **5**. 120 122; **12**. 13-14; Epistulae **9**. 12-14, 19
7. Isocrates, **4**. 118-184; **5**. 9, 96, 120-123; Epistulae **9**. 9.
8. Isocrates **4**. 120-121, 137.
9. Isocrates Epistulae **9**. 8.
10. Isocrates **4**. 184; Epistulae **9**. 19.
11. Isocrates **4**. 132; Epistulae **9**. 19.
12. Isocrates **4**. 183, 184; **5**. 124-125.

13. Isocrates **5**. 125.
14. Isocrates **5**. 126.
15. Isocrates **5**. 137.
16. Isocrates **4**. 184.
17. Isocrates **5**. 132.
18. Isocrates **4**. 181.
19. Isocrates **5**. 124.
20. Isocrates **5**. 132.
21. Isocrates **4**. 131; **5**. 83, 86. Epistulae **9**. 12;
22. Isocrates, Epistulae **9**. 12-14; **5**. 83, 86-88. The Spartans and their allies mounted an expedition to Asia Minor in 399 to protect the Greek cities there from the Persians. Apart from being leader of this campaign from 396, Agesilaos, king of Sparta, was also its inspirer. Advocating its cause he compared it to the panhellenic campaign against the Trojans. After winning a series of victories he was recalled to Greece when Sparta faced a conspiracy of her enemies in 395.
23. Isocrates **4**. 173; **5**. 9, 83, 86.
24. G. Mathieu, *Les Idées Politiques d'Isocrate²*, Paris, 1966, 96-99, upholds the view that Isocrates thought first of the Athenian general, Timotheos, before he turned to foreign rulers.
25. For the ideas of Isocrates on the monarchy, see R. Pöhlmann, "Isokrates und das Problem der Demokratie", *Sitzungsberichte der Bayerischen Akademie der Wissenschaften*, 1913, 2ff; G. Mathieu (above, note 24) 96ff., 122-152; K. Bringmann, "Studien zu den politischen Ideen des Isokrates", Hypomnemata, no. 14, Göttingen 1965, 103-108.
26. Isocrates, Epistulae **1**. 7.
27. Isocrates, Epistulae **9**. 2ff., 18.
28. Isocrates **5**. 127, 132.
29. Isocrates **5**. 153.
30. Isocrates **5**. 41.
31. Isocrates **5**. 137.
32. Isocrates **5**. 127.

33. Isocrates **5**. 16, 30, 38, 41, 45, 50, 52, 57.
34. Isocrates **5**. 73-77.
35. Isocrates **5**. 16, 31.
36. Isocrates **5**. 106-107. Cf. G. Dobesch, "Der Panhellenistische Gedanke im 4 Jh. v. Chr. und der Philippos des Isokrates", *Österreichisches Archaologisches Institut*, Vienna, 1968, 95 ff.
37. Isocrates **5**. 123.
38. Isocrates **5**. 16, 97, 127.
39. Isocrates **5**. 32-33.
40. Isocrates **4**. 138-166.
41. Isocrates **4**. 166.
42. Isocrates **5**. 125.
43. Isocrates **5**. 132.
44. Isocrates **5**. 99-103.
45. Isocrates **5**. 96.
46. Isocrates **4**. 131.
47. Isocrates **4**. 154.
48. Isocrates **4**. 166-186.
49. Isocrates **5**. 120.
50. Isocrates **5**. 120, 123.
51. Isocrates **4**. 131.
52. Isocrates Epistulae **3**. 5 (of doubtful authenticity).
53. See Dobesch (above, note 36) 213 ff. where there are quotations and commentary.
54. Dobesch has more recently treated this theme, (above, note 36) 89ff., 213 ff.
55. See especially the interpretation of paragraphs 69-71 and 79-80 (Isocrates **5**). The text of § 69-71 is as follows: "For what good fortune could then surpass your own? Men of the highest renown will come as ambassadors from the greatest states to your court; you will advise with them about the general welfare, for which no other man will be found to have shown a like concern; you will see all Hellas on tiptoe with interest in whatever you happen to propose; and no one will be indifferent to the measures which are being decided in

your councils, but, on the contrary, some will seek news of how matters stand, some will pray that you will not be thwarted in your aims, and others will fear lest something befall you before your efforts are crowned with success. If all this should come to pass, would you not have good reason to be proud? Would you not rejoice throughout your life in the knowledge that you had been a leader in such great affairs?''

This passage has given rise to several problems (1) and conclusions, (2,3,4). Are we to interpret the *presbeis* as ambassadors or as delegates of the city-states to a *synedrion* like that summoned by Philip in 338/337? If the latter is the case, does Isocrates suggest the formation of such body of delegates to function only during the phase of unification of the Greeks, or does he intend it to be a permanent institution? 2) Only the major city-states would have had the right to send *presbeis* to Philip or to be represented at the *synedrion*. 3) The term *eudokimountes* (men of the highest renown) suggests the exclusion of the lower classes from the holding of public office, thereby favouring oligarchic rule in the Greek cities. 4) From the way in which the text continues, it becomes clear that Philip would give the orders, and that he would not tolerate the slightest change in his wishes: this interpretation, however, conflicts with other passages in the *Philippos*, where Isocrates counsels the Macedonian king to avoid force in any form, and always and everywhere to employ persuasion. But all the above are pseudo-problems and conclusions without foundation. The orator does not give Philip advice with a political content, but stresses the moral satisfaction that Philip would reap if he made up his mind to put the Panhellenic programme into practice. Note how the passage begins, and how it ends; in between Isocrates mentions those attentions that would give Philip cause for lasting felicity: he would receive ambassadors from the most famous city-states (it goes without saying that Philip might feel less flattered if the ambassadors came from less famous states); these ambassadors would be the most distinguished (it goes without saying that Philip would reap less satisfaction if the ambassadors came from the lower classes); the Greeks would be attentive to his wishes (were this not the case, Philip would simply have to forfeit some part of his satisfaction). This passage, moreover, contains other thoughts which in no way lend themselves to political interpretation, but which serve only to tempt Philip to realise the writer's vision: a) "you will see all Hellas on tiptoe with interest in what-ever you happen to propose…'' b) "some will pray that you will not be thwarted in your aims'' c) "and others will fear lest something befall you before your efforts are crowned with success.''

Paragraphs 79-80 run as follows: "when you have brought the Hellenes to feel toward you as you see the Lacedaemonians feel toward their kings, and as your companions feel toward yourself.''

Many unfounded conclusions about the political beliefs of Isocrates have sprung from this passage together with a non-existent problem. It has also given rise to this two-fold question: "how could Philip have with all the Greeks the relations that he had in Macedonia with the privileged companions alone? Must we therefore assume that Isocrates wished, and expected, Philip to favour class distinctions in each state?'' Yet the content of this paragraph is by no means political. It is interwoven with the preceding phrase from which it should not be severed: "…on the contrary, you ought then, and only then, to be satisfied that you enjoy a reputation which is good and great and worthy of yourself and of your forefathers and of the achievements of your line,…''

56. Isocrates **5**. 106-107.
57. Isocrates **5**. 79.
58. Isocrates **5**. 95.
59. Cf. Dobesch, (above, note 36), 95ff., 180, 184ff., 198, 203ff.
60. Isocrates **12**. 13-14. It should be noted, however, that Isocrates contradicts himself in this text. Here he appears to claim that he is the first to write in this spirit, while in the *Panegyrikos* (**4**. 15-17), he recognizes that he had forerunners.
61. *Tagos* was the chief magistrate of Thessaly and the supreme commander of the military forces. Once elected he held office for life. But it was not uncommon for the office to be left vacant for several years.
62. Xenophon, *Hellenika,* **6**. 1, 12; Isocrates **5**. 119.
63. See below, p. 136 ff.
64. See above, p. 102.
65. See below p. 88 ff.
66. See below, p. 145.
67. Plutarch *Moralia* 177C.
68. See below, p. 138
69. See below, p. 141
70. Cf. recent works: **Ellis,** *Philip II*, 233; **Cawkwell,**, 108ff.: **Hammond - Griffith,** *Macedonia II*, 460-461. It should be added that Ellis dates the interest of Philip in Asia from 349 though without any explanation; Griffith is of the opinion that Philip began to behave in a conciliatory fashion towards the Athenians from 348. **Momigliano,** 138, believes that Philip adopted the Asian part of Isocrates' programme as late as 338.
71. Views on Philip's motives and goals can be divided into three groups: I) Philip shaped and put into practice, from 346 at least, a policy which took into account the interests of the southern Greeks. Of those to express this opinion most recently, let us note **Momigliano,** 133ff., **Cloché,** 40-45 and *Histoire de la Macédonie*, Paris, 1960, 145ff., and **Wüst,** 20ff., 169 f, f. Momigliano stresses that from 346 onwards Philip attempted to gain the sympathy of the southern Greeks, to dispel the fears of those opposed to him, to conciliate Athens and in general to win the Greeks to his side without violence with the long term aim of uniting the Greeks under his sway and to offer them peace and concord even at the cost of some restriction of their liberties. This view is more fully developed by Cloché: Philip in the beginning pursued Macedonian interests; later Panhellenic and finally Asiatic. In the first years of his rule he could not afford to look further than the problems and the interests of Macedonia. Once he solved these, his other interests developed as natural and organic extensions of his Macedonian policy; but no new ambition supplanted the old; it enriched and extended it. P. Trèves, *Demostene e la Libertà Greca*, Bari, 1931, 29ff. places the turning point from Macedonian to Greek policy as late as 338, and hints at an intention of Philip to assimilate the Macedonians into the southern Greeks.
II) Philip was engaged in an exclusively Macedonian policy, that is to say that he attempted to bring under Macedonian rule Greece, the Balkan countries and parts of Asia. This general view has several variations. Thus E. Meyer, *Kleine Schriften zur Geschichts-theorie und zur wirtschaftlichen und politischen Geschicte des Altertums*, Halle, 1910, v. I, 245ff., 291 ff. supports the view that for Philip the conquest of a large part of the Balkan lands north of Greece had greater importance than the conquest of the Greek peninsula, while J. Kaerst, *Geschichte des hellenistichen Zeitalters*, Leipzig, 1901 VI, 201 ff. = *Geschichte de Hellenismus* Leipzig and Berlin 1927 v. I³, 268 ff, U. Wilcken, *Philip II von Macedonien und die panhellenische Idee*, Sitzungsbericht der Bayerischen Akademie der Wissenschaften, 1929, 290ff. and *Alexander der Grosse*, Leipzig, 1931, 25, 32 ff., and H. Triepel, *Die Hegemonie, Ein Buch von Führenden Staaten*, Stuttgart, 1938 and G.T. Griffith in **Hammond-Griffith,** *Macedonia, II*, 623-624 are all of the opinion that Philip first conceived the plan to lead a Panhellenic expedition to the East and that both his expansion north-

wards and his establishment of a Panhellenic peace were preliminary steps to this end: the former to secure his rear, the latter to enable him to draw on the manpower of the Greek states. But, if Philip had nothing else in mind than the expansion of Macedonia he would not have spared Greece south of Olympus.

The views of those authors who assert that Philip laid more stress on his expansion northwards and eastwards rather than southwards are belied by Philip's own behaviour on both the diplomatic and military levels: for Philip spared himself no effort to win supremacy over southern Greece and exhausted all his leniency in order to inflict as little damage to it as possible. E. Frolow, in the collection of essays entitled *Hellenische Poleis* (ed. E. Ch. Welskopf), Darmstadt, 1974 v. I, 450-451, supports the view of Kaerst and Wilcken with the addition that Philip had devised his expedition to Asia merely to justify in the eyes of southern Greeks his hegemony over them, and to channel their resentment over their lost independence into a war against the Great King.

III) The motives of Philip were entirely personal: he could not help pandering to an insatiable thirst for power and sovereignty. That he cared at all in establishing authority over the Greek people must be seen solely in the light of the immense prestige he would acquire by posing as their *hegemon*. Yet Philip's actions give the lie to this idea which was put forward by F. Hampl, *Die griechischen Staats-verträge des 4. Jahr. Geb.* Leipzig, 1938, 89ff. Certainly Philip was far from indifferent to power and authority. But these motives urge on all dominating personalities, even those who serve unselfish aims.

Diametrically opposed to the preceding views that seek to present whatever Philip achieved as a by-product of his obsession for self-assertion is Ellis' view, **op. cit**, 227, that interprets Philip's achievements as the outcome of the interplay of various tendencies in Macedonian society. This important approach to the interpretation of Philip's deeds has, unfortunately, been overlooked, but, on the other hand it must not be given undue stress. That success would have eluded Philip had he not been in tune with the tendencies of Macedonian society is certain. But it is equally certain that he alone decided both his tactics and his strategy, as well as the time and manner of their execution. Moreover, the fact that he did not annex the southern Greeks to his kingdom demonstrates his wish to keep them out of the interplay of Macedonian trends and to control them personally. More is said on this topic in the text.

72. See following chapter.
73. See for example, Tod, no, 111, 123, 136 = H. Bengtson, *Die Staatsverträge des Altertums*, v. II, *Die Verträge der griechischrömische Welt von 700 bis 338 v. Chr.*, Munich and Berlin, 1962, nos. 231, 257, 280.
74. See **Hammond-Griffith**, *Macedonia II*, 454. Cf. also Philip's refusal to hand over the fortress of Nicaia close to Thermopylae to the Thebans.
75. Demosthenes **12**. 18 ff.
76. Demosthenes **10**. 32, ff.
77. Diodorus **16**. 87. 2.
78. According to the most common opinion.
79. See H. Triepel, (above note 71), 399 and T.T.B. Ryder, *Koine Eirene*, London, 1965.
80. Two fragments from the Athenian copy of this text have survived. The information it contains can be supplemented from literary sources. All these texts are to be found together in the work of H. Bengtson, above n. 73 no. 403.
81. The re-classification of the treaty's terms and the order in which they are ennumerated here is the author's responsibility.
82. W. Schwahn, "Heeresmatrikel und Landfriede Philips II von Makedonien", *Klio*, Beiheft 21, 1930, 36-38; F. Hampl, (above n. 71), 52, **Ellis**, 199-206, C. Roebuck, "The Settlements of Philip II with the Greek States in 338 B.C.", *Classical Philology*, 46, (1948), 73 ff. believe that it goes without saying that Philip had separate treaties with each of the Greek states (according to Roebuck and Ellis these states must have been the ones that participated against Philip). But, in the text of any Greek treaty there was always a clause binding the contracting parties to respect its terms, this obligation not being the subject of a separate agreement. An exception to this rule were the terms of alliance between Athenians and other Greeks signed after the King's Peace, whose terms stressed explicitly that the agreement in no way ran counter to the King's Peace. But this clause was put there to avoid the combined reactions of the Spartans and of the Great King, that is to say of a third party. According to another opinion, Ryder, (above n. 79) 152 and **Hammond-Griffith**, *Macedonia II*, 627, this problematic term sums up the main body of the agreement which has not survived. Yet the only complete text of the treaty of which the main part and the oaths of the contracting parties have survived [Tod, no. 27 = Bengtson, (above n. 73) no. 263] shows us that the oaths repeated all the terms agreed in the main part; moreover, even the text of the oath in question mentioned many of the terms agreed upon; we must therefore assume that it is improbable not to have

mentioned each one in particular, but to label some of them as treaties in summary.
83. From the second part of the inscription, see above note 80.
84. Disagreeing with other scholars, Schwahn, (above n. 81), 4 ff. and **Cawkwell**, 172 believe that these figures do not denote the number of seats held by representatives, but that they relate to the apportionment of some military obligation.
85. Triepel, (above n. 71), 398, Ryder (above n. 79), 153.
86. Very often the term *hegemon* of the contract of "common peace" is confused with that of *strategos autokrator* of the Asian campaign, so much so that some historians reckon that the same contract also contained the agreements of alliance on the basis of which the expedition to Asia was decided. But, as we shall see below, everything connected with this military operation was laid down in a different text.
87. Agreements of this sort are not found in earlier pacts of "common peace". In some alliance-treaties [Bengston (above n. 73), no. 290, lines 25-35, no. 293, l. 18-19, 28] the contracting parties undertook to act in unison in quelling any attempt at constitutional change on the part of either contracting state's opposition, but not on the part of those in power as those of the text we are commenting on seems to suggest.
88. After their defeat at the Battle of Chaironeia, the Athenians decided they would resist Philip, if he tried to besiege Athens. To increase their manpower, they invited both their slaves and the metics to fight in their army with the promise of freedom for the slaves and citizenship for the metics.
89. Some historians referred to by Frolow, (above n. 71), 445, support the view that Philip first and foremost served the interest of the wealthier classes in southern Greece. Frolow rejects this view and maintains that Philip above all pursued political ends.
90. The conclusion that there were two separate agreements, one a pact of "common peace", the other a treaty of offensive alliance, is reached also by others: W. Schwahn (above n. 81), 81; F. Taeger, "Die Friede von 362/1", *Tubinger Beitrage zur Altertums wissenschaft*, 11, 1930, 60 ff., F. Schehl, "Zum Korinthischen Bund von Jahre 338/337 v. Chr." *Jahreshefte des Österreichischen Archäologischen Instituts*, 27, (1932), 115 ff., A. Momigliano, "La 'Koine Eirene' dal 386 al 338 A.C.", *Rivista di Filologia e d'Istruzione Classica*, 62, 1934, 498 ff. and *Filipo il Macedone*, 165, F. Geyer, RE XIX, 1938, lines 2299-2300, U. Wilcken, *Griechische Gesichte*, 5th ed. 1943, 178, 9th ed. 1962, 224, Chr. C. Pa-

244

tsavos, *The Unification of the Greeks under Macedonian Hegemony*, Athens, 1965, 94. The opinion that the pact of "common peace" was also a treaty of offensive alliance, or perhaps primarily a treaty of alliance and only secondarily an agreement of "common peace", is supported by the following scholars: U. Wilcken (above n. 71), 300, although he later adopted the view which we referred to above; A. W. Pickard in *Cambridge Ancient History*, vol. VI, (1927), 267, Triepel, (above n. 71), 407, H. Berve, *Gnomon*, 9, (1933), 309 ff., H. Bengtson, *Die Strategie in der hellenistischen Zeit*, Munich, vol. XI, 1937, 3-9, 45 ff., V. Ehrenberg, *Alexander and the Greeks*, Oxford, 1938, 12, *Der Staat der Griechen*, Leipzig, 1957-58, V. I-II, 137, J. A. O. Larsen, "Federation for Peace in Ancient Greece", *Classical Philology*, 39, (1944), 160, and *Representative Government in Greek and Roman History*, Berkeley and Los Angeles, 1955, 51 ff., H. Bengtson, *Griechische Geschichte*, Munich, 1950, 304-305, 4th ed. Munich, 1968, 326-327, K. Dienelt, "Der Korinthischer Bunde", *Jahreshefte des Österreichischen Archäologischen Instituts*, 43 (1956), p. 247 ff., E. Frolow, (above n. 71), 446-448, C.

Roebuck, "The Settlements of Philip II with the Greek States in 338 B.C.", *Classical Philology*, 43 (1948), 72-74, 89. Other historians believe that there was but one agreement — the pact of "common" peace: F. Hampl, (above n. 71), 34 ff., A. Heuss, "Antigonos Monophthalmos und die griechischen Städte", *Hermes* 73, (1938), 171 ff., Wüst (Critique of the work of F. Hampl, *Die griechischen Staatsvertrage...*) *Gnomon* 14, (1938), 371 ff., E. Meyer, *Zeitschrift der Savigny-Stiftung fur Rechtsgesichte*, T.T.B. Ryder, (above n. 79), 102 ff., 150 ff., and Griffith in **Hammond-Griffith**, *Macedonia II*, 624-630. Of these, Hampl asserts that there was no need for a separate alliance-treaty; Ryder and Griffith are of the opinion that a state of alliance, whether *de iure* or only *de facto*, was created by the decision of the *synedrion* to mount a campaign against the Persians.

Only one scholar, H. Raue, *Unterschungen zur Geschichte des griechischen Bundes*, 1932, advances the view that the agreement of 338/337 is a treaty of alliance between Philip and the southern Greek states.

91. See **Tod**, no. 121 = **Bengtson**, no. 256, 1. 5-6; **Tod**, no. 123, = **Bengtson,** no. 257,

l. 7-8, 15-19, 25-27, 32-33, 49, 57-58, 60, 78; **Tod**, no. 126 = **Bengtson**, no. 262, l. 9; **Tod**, no. 127 = Bengtson no. 263, l. 21-22, 32-33; **Tod**, no. 144 = **Bengtson**, no. 290, l. 13, 16-17, 18-19. See also Xenophon, *Hellenika* 6. 5.1.

92. So Philip would be in a position (1) to make use of all his allies as and when he wished, empowered thus by the decisions of the *synedrion* itself, which would have been imposed on it by him, whereas the allies would not have been able to make any decisions of that sort, for example concerning the Macedonian armed forces (**Momigliano**, 165); (2) to be the arbitrator in disputes arising between the allies instead of being himself amongst the parties involved; (3) to avoid drawing on himself the resentment of the allies by any measure taken since these would have been decided upon by the *synedrion* of the alliance of which he was not a member.

93. Isocrates' writings differ from Philip's settlements in that they contain, as we have seen, no suggestions of a legal nature, whereas the political settlements of the Macedonian king could not but have such a character.

94. Isocrates, Epistulae **3**. 3.

MACEDONIA UNDER PHILIP

Notes

1. On the language of the Macedonians see **Hoffmann, Kalleris** I and especially **Hammond-Griffith**, *Macedonia II*, 43ff.
2. Herodotus **5**.22, **8**.137.1, Thucydides 2.99.3, **5**.80.2.
3. Strabo **7**.326.
4. See, for example, Curtius 6.10.23.
5. **Hammond-Griffith**, *Macedonia II* (see above note 1).
6. Aeschines **2** and **3**, passim but esp. 2.41ff., 47; Demosthenes **18** and **19**, passim but esp. **19**.308.
7. Plutarch, *Alexander* 47.3; also Curtius 8.5.1ff.
8. Demosthenes **3**.16, 24, **9**.31.
9. Thucydides 2.80.5-7, 81.7f., **4**.124.1.
10. The evidence for Macedonian religion is collected in **Hammond-Griffith**, *Macedonia II*.
11. Diodorus 16.92ff.
12. For Alexander's reign see, for example, Arrian **3**.16.9, **5**.3.6, **6**.3.2, **7**.25.2f., Diodorus **17**.16.3, **18**.1, etc.
13. See **Ellis**, *Philip II* esp. 82, 120ff., 204, etc.
14. Diodorus **17**.16.2.
15. Arrian **4**.11.6, **3**.16.9.
16. Curtius **6**.8.25; **9**.2, Arrian 3.26.2, Diodorus **17**.79, Plutarch, *Alexander* 42, Polyainus 4.6.14, Polybius 5.27.5f., and 29.6.
17. Curtius **10**.6ff. (after Alexander's death); see F.W. Walbank, *Philip V of Macedon* (Cambridge 1940; reprint. 1967) 3f., 295ff. for the references to Antigonos Doson's regency; some such machinery is also entailed in Philip II's acclamation as king.
18. See, for example, Polybius **5**.27.5f.
19. Demosthenes **4**.40f.
20. Ph. M. Petsas, Pella, Literary Tradition and Archaeological Research, *Balkan Studies* 1 (1960) 113ff.
21. Diodorus **16**.92ff., **Ellis**, *Philip II* 219-223.
22. Demosthenes **5**.6, **19**.12, 315, Aeschines **2**.15, 19, 52, Plutarch, *Alexander* 10; also Theopompus F236 (**Jacoby**, *Fragmente* no. 115), Suda, s.v. 'Anaxandrides'.
23. Demosthenes **2**.17-19, Theopompus F224, F225, F236 (**Jacoby**, *Fragmente* no. 115).
24. Suda, s.v. 'Antipatros', Diogenes Laertius **5**.11, 27, Pausanias 6.4.8, Plutarch, *Alexander* 74.
25. Nearchus: **Jacoby**, *Fragmente* no. 133, Arrian, *Indica* **18**.10.4, Plutarch, *Alexander* 10; Eumenes: Plutarch, *Eumenes* 1, Nepos,

Eumenes 1.

26. **Ellis**, *Philip II* 160 and 281 n.4.
27. **Jacoby,** *Fragmente* no. 115, esp. F27 and F256.
28. Aeschines **2**.125 and schol., Isocrates **5**.19.
29. Isocrates, **5**, *Epistulae* 2 and 3.
30. **Cawkwell**, 54f.
31. W. Jaeger, *Aristotle* 111ff. (English transl.), A.H. Chroust, *Review of Politics* 34 (1972) 367f.
32. Dionysius Halicarnassus, *Ep. ad Ammaeus* 1.5, Strabo **13**.608 (with Didymus, *in Demosthenes* 6.15ff.), Diogenes Laertius **5**.10.
33. Leonidas: Plutarch, *Alexander* 5.4f., 22.5, 25.4f; Lysimachos: **Berne, II** no. 481, with references.
34. Plutarch, *Alexander* 8, 26, Strabo 69C.
35. Plutarch, *Alexander* 9.
36. Plutarch, *Alexander* 7, Arrian **4**.13.2, Pliny,

Naturalis Historia **31**.30, Didymus, *in Demosthenes* 6.49, Ph. M. Petsas, Πρακτικά τῆς ἐν ᾿Αθήναις ᾿Αρχαιολογικῆς ᾿Εταιρείας (1965) 36ff; (1968) 65ff.
37. Diodorus **7**.16, Hyginus, *Fabulae* 291, Justin **7**.1.7ff., Herodotus **8**.137-139, Isocrates **5**.105f.
38. Theophrastus, *de Ventis* 27, Diodorus **16**.2.6, 3.3ff., Justin **7**.1, 6, Demosthenes **23**.121.
39. M. Andronicos, Ch. Makaronas, N. Moutsopoulos, G. Bakalakis, Τό ἀνάκτορο τῆς Βεργίνας, Athens 1961, and **Andronicos,** *Vergina*, Ch. Makaronas, ᾿Ανασκαφαί Πέλλης, ᾿Αρχαιολογικόν Δελτίον 19 (1964) 340ff.
40. N.G.L. Hammond, The Archaeological Background to the Macedonian Kingdom, ᾿Αρχαία Μακεδονία, 1, Thessalonike 1970 65 n. 17, **Hammond**, *Macedonia 1* 156ff. R.L. Fox, *Alexander the Great*, London 1973, 19, 553,

Ellis, *Philip II* 35f, 50, 248 n.60, 251 n.25, M. Andronicos, ᾿Ανασκαφή στήν Μ. Τούμπα τῆς Βεργίνας, *Athens Annals of Archaeology* 9.2 (1976) 123ff.
41. Plutarch, *Pyrrhus* 26.11f.
42. See above n.39.
43. Diodorus **16**.92ff., Justin **9**.6.3.
44. For the history, the topography and the remains of Pella see especially Ph. M. Petsas (above n. 20) 113ff. and Pella, *Studies in Mediterranean Archaeology*, Lund XIV. (1964) 1ff.
45. T. H. Price, An Enigma in Pella: The Tholos and Herakles Phylakos, *American Journal of Archaeology* 77 (1973) 66ff.; also M. Andronicos, ᾿Αρχαιολογικόν Δελτίον 20 (1965) 414ff.
46. Petsas (see above n.20).

THE END OF PHILIP

Bibliography

Badian, E., The death of Philip II, *Phoenix 17* (1963) 244ff.

Bosworth, A.B., Philip II and Upper Macedonia, *Classical Quarterly* 21 (1971) 93ff.

Ellis, J.R., Amyntas Perdikka, Philip II and Alexander the Great, *Journal of Hellenic Studies* 91 (1971) 15ff.

Hammond, N.G.L., "Philip's Tomb" in Historical Context, *Greek, Roman and Byzantine Studies* 19 (1978) 331ff.

Kraft, K., Der rationale Alexander. Frankfurt, 1971.

Willrich, H., Ver liess König Philip von Makedonien ermorden? *Hermes* 34 (1899) 174ff.

Notes

The Temenid dynasty: Herodotus **5**.22 and **8**.137-9; Thucydides **2**.99.3, **2**.100.2 and **5**.80.2; Diodorus **7**.16.

Philip's wives: Satyrus in Athenaeus, *Deipnosophists* **13**.557b-e; Justin **9**.2.1-3.

The attribution of crimes to Eurydice, mother of Philip: Justin **7**.5.4-8.

Marriage of Philip and Cleopatra: Satyrus as above; Arrian, *Anabasis* **3**.6.5; Justin **9**.5.9, **9**.7.2-6; Plutarch, *Alexander* 9.5-14.

The Pixodarus episode: Plutarch, *Alexander* 10.1-5; Arrian *Anabasis* **3**.6.5.

The assassination of Philip: Diodorus **16**.91-95; Aristotle, *Politics* 1311b2; Justin **9**.6.4-7;

Plutarch, *Alexander* 10.6.

The trial and executions: Diodorus **17**.2.1; Arrian, *Anabasis* 1.25.1-2; Oxyrhynchus Papyri XV, 1978 (discussed by N.G.L. Hammond in *Greek, Roman and Byzantine Studies* 19 (1978), 343ff; Justin **11**.2.1-2 and 5.1; Diodorus **17**.2.3 and 3.2 and 5.1-2.

Suspicions attaching to Alexander Lyncestes: Arrian, *Anabasis* 1.25; Diodorus **17**.32.1-2 and 80.2; Curtius 7.1.5-9 and **8**.8.6; Justin **11**.2.2 and **11**.7.1 and 12.14.1.

Suspicions attaching to Olympias: Justin **9**.7; Satyrus in Athenaeus *Deipnosophists* **13**.557 b-e; Plutarch, *Alexander* 10.6-8; Pausanias **8**.7.7.

Suspicions attaching to Alexander: Justin **9**.7.1-6; Plutarch, *Alexander* 10. 6-8.

PHILIP'S PERSONALITY

Notes

1. Demosthenes **2**.18 and 19.
2. Diodorus **16**.87.
3. Diodorus **16**.2.
4. Isocrates, *Epistulae* **2**.2.
5. Demosthenes **2**.15.

6. Demosthenes **18**.235.
7. Cf. the remarkable work of P. Briant, *Antigone le Borgne*, Paris 1973 which gives an innovative and well based analysis of the assembly of the people in Macedonia.
8. Curtius **8**.6.6.
9. Diodorus **16**.3.1-3.
10. Diodorus **16**.89.2.

11. Theopompus (**Jacoby**, *Fragmente* no. 115, F27).
12. Diodorus **16**.95, 96.
13. Pausanias **8**.7.5.
14. J.G. Droysen, Histoire de l'Hellénisme I, Paris 1883-84, 90.
15. **Glotz**-Cohen III 228.
16. **Cloché** 291-292.

THE ROYAL TOMBS AT AIGAI (VERGINA)

Notes

1. Ph. Papazoglou, *Makedonski Gradovi u Rimsko Doba* (= Les cités macédoniennes à l'époque romaine), Skopje 1957 (with a summary in French).
2. **Hammond**, *Macedonia 1,* 156-158.
3. **Hammond**, *Macedonia 1,* 430ff.
4. This view is accepted in the recent works on Philip published by the historians J.R. Ellis (Philip II and Macedonian Imperialism, London 1976, 35, ct. map 22-23) and G. Cawkwell (Philip of Macedon, London 1978, 28) and by the distinguished archaeologist G. Daux, Aigeai, Site de tombes royales de la Macédonie antique, Comptes Rendus de l'Academie des Inscriptions et Belles Lettres, 1977, 620ff.
5. M. Andronicos, Βεργίνα I. Τό νεκροταφεῖον τῶν τύμβων. Athens, 1969.
6. D. Pandermalis, Ὁ νέος μακεδονικός τάφος τῆς Βεργίνας, Μακεδονικά 12, 1972, 147-182.
7. Ἀρχαιολογικόν Δελτίον 17, 1961-62, Χρονικά, 218 and pl. 262 γ-δ.
8. K.A. Romaios, Ὁ Μακεδονικός τάφος τῆς Βεργίνας. Athens 1951.
9. M. Andronicos, The royal graves at Vergina 1-15 *Athens Annals of Archaeology.* 10, 1977 (1978), 1-72.
10. M. Andronicos, Deux stèles funéraires grecques de Vergina, *Bulletin de Correspondence Hellénique* 79 (1955), 87-101.
11. Plutarch, *Pyrrhus* 26, 6.
12. I expressed these views immediately after the end of the 1976 excavation season in an article in the newspaper "Τό Βῆμα" (3.10.1976) and in *Athens Annals of Archaeology* 9, (1976), 123-129 (Ἀνασκαφή στή Μ. Τούμπα τῆς Βεργίνας).
13. The responsibility for the study and publication of all these funerary monuments has been assumed by Mrs. Chrysoula Saatsoglou-Paliadeli, assistant to the second chair of Archaeology at the University of Thessalonika and my close collaborator in the excavations.
14. M. Andronicos, Ἀνασκαφή στή Μεγάλη Τούμπα τῆς Βεργίνας, (above n. 12), 123ff.
15. M. Andronicos, Ancient Greek Painting and Mosaics in Macedonia, *Balkan Studies* 5, 1964, 301, pl. X.
16. The question goes beyond the theme of the present article and lies outside the bounds of my own field. For an exhaustive treatment of it cf. **Kalléris**, I and II, esp. vol I, 289ff. and vol. II, 461ff.
17. Ph. M. Petsas, Ὁ τάφος τῶν Λευκαδίων, Athens 1966.

All quotations in the text are taken from Lœb editions

MAPS AND ILLUSTRATIONS

The maps and diagrams were drawn by Tonia Kotsoni.

INDEX